# How to Cook Better
## Shaun Hill

Photographs by Jason Lowe

MITCHELL BEAZLEY

To my grandchildren – Oscar, Mathilda, Gaia and Octavia

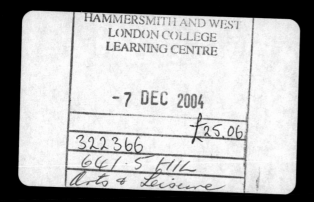
How to Cook Better
by Shaun Hill

First published in Great Britain in 2004 by Mitchell Beazley, an imprint of
Octopus Publishing Group Ltd,  2-4 Heron Quays, London E14 4JP

A CIP catalogue record for this book is available from the British Library.

ISBN 1 84000 774 5

Commissioning editor: Rebecca Spry
Executive art editor: Yasia Williams
Design and art direction: Grade Design Consultants, London
Photography: Jason Lowe
Consultant editor: Hattie Ellis
Production: Sarah Rogers
Index: John Noble

Typeset in Foundry Sans
Printed and bound by Toppan Printing Company in China

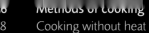
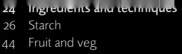

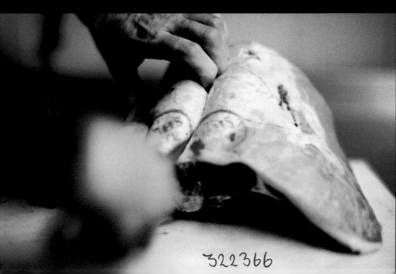

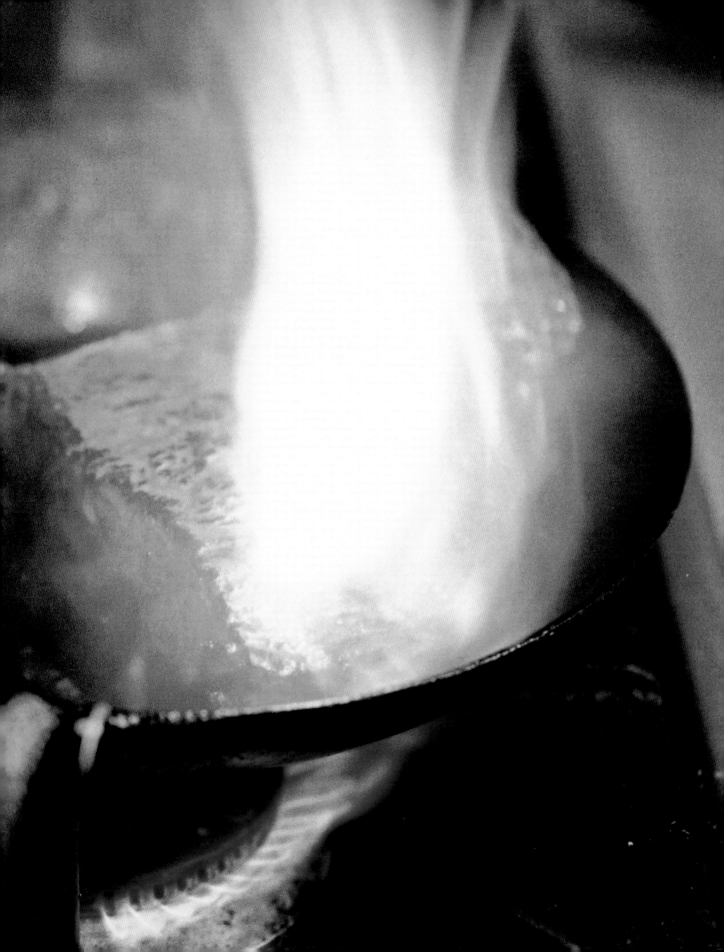

# Introduction

People who do not enjoy eating never make good cooks, and the best introduction to cookery lies in the pleasure of eating and drinking rather than in any acquisition of technical knowledge or recipes. There are skills to be learned though, and these are easier to master once you know why they are needed. This book focuses on the two main and inter-dependent aspects of cooking: the understanding of ingredients and good technical skills. Confidence in these will make you a fine cook, able to handle these and other recipes with ease, but more importantly, capable of adapting and tailoring them to your own needs and taste if need be.

The main thing to understand is the goal of the exercise: how you want the food to taste. This is the part of the equation you must bring to the kitchen in person. I have always found that a little greed is a great advantage in the make-up of any would-be cook or chef. Ambition and hard work alone tend to produce dishes that involve more skill than taste and that are more of an adventure than a pleasure for those at the knife and fork end of the proceedings.

The objective should be simply that your meal tastes good. Anything else should spring from that notion or be secondary to it. Considerations of colour, presentation and suchlike are only important once true flavours have been achieved. Similarly, any conceptions of ethnic authenticity or notions of seasonality should be approached with caution: what appeals and is available to the Delhi household in searing summer heat may not suit Wolverhampton in spring, and the absurdity of chalk-like strawberries at Christmas shouldn't prevent you from buying imported asparagus to accompany your red mullet dish in winter. Use your taste buds as a measure of progress and success and not any perceptions of what's smart.

My background is in the restaurant kitchen, in cooking for a living, but the stimulus to cook came from enjoying food at home and in restaurants. The first surprise when you start cooking as a career is that restaurant meals have less in common with home cooking than you might expect, so not all dishes transfer happily from one to the other.

A chef looks at a dish rather differently from a home-cook because different pressures will be put on him. He will have a whole day's uninterrupted preparation time and the chance to make several last-minute steps at every stage of the meal – nobody expects him to join the table and eat. On the other hand, when cooking at home you aren't daft enough to allow your guests a choice of dishes and you may fairly expect them to sit when the food is ready rather than when they have finished whatever pre-dinner booze they can hold down.

The result is that chefs tend to break dishes into component parts, which may be prepared in advance and pieced together quickly when a dish is ordered. Slow-cooked dishes such as stews and big roasts are difficult in this set-up, so small joints of fish or prime cuts of meat such as fillet or saddle will always be preferred, especially if there is an opportunity to use the extra kitchen time by making top-notch stocks and sauces from trimmings and bones.

Nevertheless, the objectives for home and restaurant cooks are the same: a balanced and pleasurable meal. And the lessons to learn are equally important in both kitchens: good shopping followed by careful preparation and heartfelt cooking. This applies to meals at every level of grandeur. Balance is the key: the right amount of starch to counter the more powerful influences of herbs, spices and chilli; not too much cream and butter or protein.

Most of all, ask yourself whether you would like to eat the meal. If the answer is yes then you will have at least one satisfied diner. With luck – and a little practice – you will have many more. In any case, the cooking should be as much part of the pleasure as the eating. If in any doubt, drink a glass of wine with both.

Essentials

# Timing and preparation

**The order in which you do the jobs involved in making any dish or meal is crucial.** The idea is that all the component parts of, for instance, your main course should be both cooked and at the right temperature simultaneously and preferably finished at about the time expected. Behind this trite observation lie most of the problems involved in producing a complex dinner, especially if it comprises several courses.

For those who cook for a living, timing and preparation skills are every bit as important as any deft handling of pastry or dazzling speed when chopping onions. The secret of a successful restaurant kitchen is that the cooks can serve different meals to a number of people simultaneously, and to do this they must prepare whatever is possible in advance without actually cooking the dish and then gauge how long it will be before each course is needed. Most is common sense.

It is also important for home cooks to plan a meal so that some jobs can be done ahead, or at least so that there is not a panic-inducing series of tasks needed just as the food is to be served. If the meal planned cannot avoid this, then change the plan or enlist help from friends.

There are a few things to take into account when planning the timing of a meal. Those dining start at their most hungry, so if you leave it too long before serving the starter, all the bread, olives or whatever will be gone by the time food arrives and appetites will be dead long before the meal is finished. Gaps between each course need to be progressively longer throughout a meal. And serve your best shots early in the meal – taste-buds are at their sharpest while you are a bit hungry and before the effects of booze and starch take effect.

A main course needn't be bigger than any other course, but it should be the focal point of the meal with the aim of satisfying the stomach rather than stimulating appetite in the way that a first course or dessert might. First courses are often quite acidic and refreshing in a bid to 'open' the appetite, while main courses tend to feature more carbohydrate and the fish or meat of a meal, in order to satisfy the diner.

Don't plan too many last-minute touches. Also, have leeway for the unexpected – for instance, forgotten lemon juice or a blunt carving knife. If you realize that you've forgotten to buy an ingredient, you may need to change your plans at the last minute – sometimes it's simply a matter of replacing the missing ingredient with something else that serves the same function in a dish, but if that's not possible you'll need to replace the dish with something that performs the same function in a meal. A tray of the entire ingredients and equipment needs for a course is a good idea so that it can be checked ahead of time.

Don't trust anyone's advice completely on cooking times. Racks of lamb, for instance, vary in size according to the time of year and breed of animal, so consider the size of the joints and adjust accordingly. Pressing the cooking meat with your finger or the back of a carving fork to judge the cooking progress is a good idea.

# Planning a sample menu

**Take this menu as an example of how to plan ahead.** It's reasonably complex, for it has no cold or previously made starter that can be taken straight from the fridge or ladled from a tureen. All the dishes have complete recipes later in the book: steamed brill with cider sabayon (page 172) followed by rack of lamb with persillade (page 182) served with potato cakes (page 36) and cabbage, leeks and carrots, then Muscat crème caramel (page 142).

### The day before or in the morning:

1   The crème caramels can be made.
2   The racks should arrive. They can be trimmed and brushed with olive oil, then kept in the fridge.
3   Persillade, a herb and fresh breadcrumb stuffing, can be made ready.

### In the morning:

1   Prepare the potato cakes and griddle in a dry pan.
2   Trim the brill and cover in clingfilm.
3   Separate the egg yolks from the whites for the sabayon.
4   Vegetables can be peeled and chopped and covered with water, but not cooked.

### 10 minutes before you eat:

1   The fish can be steamed.
2   The sabayon can be made.
3   The gratin can be put in the oven.
4   The racks can be sealed in a hot pan ready for cooking.

### When you serve the starter:

1   A large pan of water to boil the vegetables can be put on the stove.
2   The racks can be put in the oven.

### After clearing the starter plates:

A first course will take around 20 minutes to half an hour to eat. As the plates clear, you can:

1   Take both lamb and gratin from the oven.
2   Put the vegetables into the boiling water.
3   Fry the potato cakes.
4   Press the persillade stuffing on to the just-cooked racks. Place the racks under a grill to crisp.
5   Add stock to the lamb pan juices for a sauce.
6   Drain the cooked vegetables and season with salt, pepper and a little olive oil.
7   The meal is ready to be plated and served. You can relax knowing that the dessert needs only to be turned out on to a plate.

# Equipment

**Certain bits of equipment are seriously necessary,** but lots aren't. You soon get to realize which are specific to some task you perform once a year and merely clutter the shelves for the rest of the time. This is the hardware that I find essential.

## Knives

**Sharp knives are safer than blunt ones,** as you will need less pressure to cut through whatever you are filleting or carving. There are several basic shapes and sizes of knife, and how many you need depends on the amount you intend using them.

### 1 Boning knife

This is useless for all tasks other than filleting and boning so only worth buying if you intend regular use. There are two types, one where the blade is narrow and pointed to help to round tricky corners, the other with a firmer, wider blade that can cut away fillets of white fish from the central bone as well as lift the outer membrane from loin cuts of meat.

### 2 Couteau d'office

There are two types of knife this size: the one shown, which is used for chopping small vegetables such as shallots, and is basically an extension of the index finger; and a turning knife, which is slightly curved and is used for cutting shapes like batons, allowing you to have all your vegetables the same size.

### 3 Carving knife

A 25cm blade is as long as you will need. Shorter blades and a handle with good grip will give you more control.

### 4 French cook's knife

The chef's most valued and used tool. It is wide at the handle end and tapers to a point. The edge lays flat on the cutting board surface and it can be used to chop or slice more or less anything. A heavier knife will feel intimidating to a novice cook, but reassuring to an experienced one, as the combination of weight and a razor-sharp edge will involve little effort from the user to cut through and chop vegetables or meat.

### 5 Fork

This is essential to keep whatever piece of cooked meat or fish is being carved still while the carving knife does its job. The business of poking bits of steak or fish and turning them over while they cook is secondary, and can be done just as well with a spatula or egg slice. Forks come in two shapes: the long-pronged fork is pretty useless for carving purposes; the other main style, which has a handle with a long metal stem ending in a curved short prong, is my preference, for the upturned prongs will hold down whatever joint you are carving and the prongs can skewer the centre of a chicken or partridge without the slightest difficulty.

### Serrated knife

The traditional bread knife. I prefer a shorter blade for the reasons above, as it gives more control when slicing a fresh loaf and when trimming artichokes and other tough vegetables. This type of knife won't need sharpening.

### Vegetable peeler

Not sure whether this counts as a knife or a piece of small equipment. Look for a peeler that has a good grip. Most are flimsy affairs and will last only a year or two, but are cheap enough to replace as needed

### Steel

Blunt knives are both useless and dangerous – useless because they will squash rather than cut and dangerous because the extra pressure you will need to push them through whatever meat or veg you are cutting means that any deflection will cause an accident.

For chopping and onion see **47**    For filleting fish see **80-1**    For carving meat see **120-21**

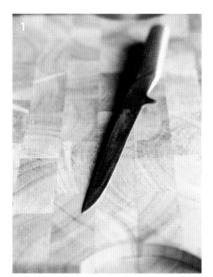

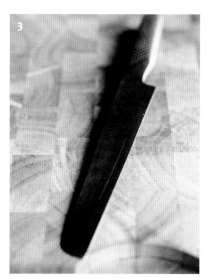

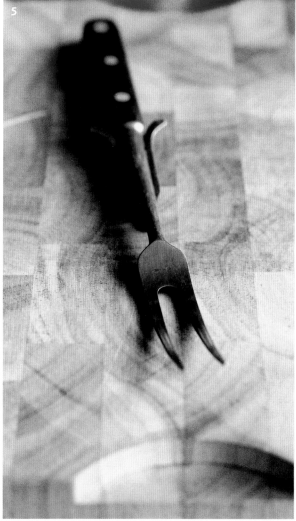

# How to sharpen knives

**Knives that are completely blunt will need to be ground down.** This shouldn't happen, but does, and you will need to ask your butcher to help you out. Butchers will have an electric grinding machine that will cut a blade, and most butchers will happily do this for you – but don't do it too often as you'll end up with a knife that has no blade.

Knives that are quite blunt will need a sharpening stone. You may remember your mother or grandmother sharpening the family carving knife on the stone step to her house, and these pieces of equipment work on the same principle: water and a rough-textured or carborundum stone. Soak the carborundum stone for 10 minutes, then secure it on the table by wedging it on to a damp cloth – you don't want it to move while you are sharpening. Draw the knife towards you across the stone at an angle of around 45 degrees (see opposite, bottom). Alternate the side of the blade edge and repeat the process, drawing the whole blade with considerable pressure across the wet stone each time. You will need to do this seven or eight times before there is noticeable effect on a blunt knife. Clean the blade, then finish the sharpening on a steel.

A steel will hone the blade of a knife that is already quite sharp. If you take care of your knives, you will never need any other method of sharpening. Place the pointed end of the steel firmly against a cutting board or work surface, with a folded kitchen cloth between, then draw the knife downwards toward the board and away from yourself at an angle of 45 degrees, exerting as much pressure as is safe and ensuring that the steel doesn't slip (see opposite, top left and right). Repeat the process with the other side of the blade's edge. You will need to do this seven or eight times and can check the sharpness with your fingertip. It should feel almost electrically charged and be sharp enough to shave with.

For knives see **14**

# Mechanical gadgets

**There are three mechanical gadgets that I find indispensable.** Two of these are the food processor and mixer, which are usually sold as a combination package. The mixing and beating of doughs and the rapid cutting and chopping of a processer will save you a lot of time. The jobs they do could all be done by hand with a spoon, whisk or sharp knife, but the prospect of chopping vast amounts of vegetables or making breadcrumbs by hand could be quite a deterrent in many otherwise straightforward dishes. I even use my processer to chop shallots – but since this kind of machine only works well if a reasonable quantity of food is to be processed, peel and roughly chop around a dozen at a time (leftovers can be brought to the boil in a little white wine and then kept in a small container in the fridge for a week or more for use in sauces or stuffings). The dough hook makes breadmaking possible without having to develop strongman's muscles. And my particular brand has a pasta-rolling attachment, which saves me from using one of those little hurdy-gurdy type machines that clamp on to the table.

When choosing a food processor, your priority should be the quality of the motor. You should partly be guided by price and partly by the reputation of the manufacturer. But spending a lot of money on attachments that you are never going to use is a bad idea.

The other indispensable gadget is a liquidizer. This centrifuges liquid into purée or emulsifies unlikely combinations of stock or wine and oil, things that cannot be done by hand. Domestic liquidizers and blenders are as good as any expensive commercial variety, as neither type will successfully blend more than a third of the jug capacity at a time – I usually buy the cheapest I can find as this is a very basic piece of kit and more money doesn't necessarily equate to better quality. I use the liquidizer for most non-gravy types of sauce, *beurre blanc*, soup, to make herb and olive oil purées for my sauce bases, and to repair emulsified sauces that have split or become flat from hanging around for too long. A warm stock can be thickened with an oil such as olive or sesame as well as, or instead of, butter or cream, giving a lighter, fresher result if you are using this method.

# Kitchen hardware

### Frying pans

The flat-bottomed frying pans are best. I use black steel pans, which are very cheap and durable. They don't look particularly beautiful, but will withstand being heated dry so that a piece of fish or meat can be sealed quickly, whereas an attractive non-stick pan will be ruined after a few weeks of this treatment. When bought, these steel pans are shiny and silver coloured. They need to be seasoned by having oil heated in them a few times and then wiped completely dry before first use – this quickly creates a non-stick patina. They can be washed after use, but need to be wiped dry or they will rust.

### Saucepans

More is better here, for the right shape and size of saucepan can be very useful. Deep saucepans need less water to cover, say, potatoes, than a wide, shallow pan, but a wide pan will safely hold pears or peaches while they poach with no danger of damage, as everything will be kept separate during cooking rather than banging into each other as the liquid boils. Never buy a saucepan that has a plastic handle; these handles smell horrible as they burn – inevitable with small pans over large flames – and cannot be used in the oven. Make sure that there is a tight-fitting lid also unembellished with plastic. I use lots of small pans to cook and heat sauces.

### Woks

I use woks to cook vegetables. They take a while to heat properly, as the narrow base that sits on the heat has to warm the metal as far as the wide brim, but they are easily used for both frying and boiling and are especially handy for tossing vegetables in olive oil or somesuch and salt and pepper after they have had a minute or two of boiling. Like most pans that are used for frying, woks work better when hot. You will need a fraction of the oil to fry with when it is hot and spinning round the wok; much more when it is cool and sluggish.

### Stockpots

All you really need is a large saucepan. Traditionally, stockpots are deep and stovepipe-shaped, so that any bones will be covered by water. Fish stock and chicken stock are easy and cheap to make - the bones are generally free from your friendly local shop, but a request for them will probably provoke astonishment at the supermarket. If you never intend making stock, you needn't waste the cupboard space.

### Steamers

This is a simple pan base with a colander-like top that lets steam into an upper section. You can build quite a strong pressure by boiling the water hard and keeping the lid tightly in place, but in general these steamers are for gentler, slower cooking – steamed puds, fish fillets and the like. Should you need to reheat some stuffing or cooked artichoke, then this will work as well as any microwave. The disadvantage is that it's difficult to keep track of the water level and, if the pan boils dry, there's a nasty cleaning job for later.

### Baking sheets and roasting trays

You can buy *silpat*, non-stick, mats to put on baking sheets if you intend to make biscuits such as *tuiles* or brandy snaps, and you need a very good non-stick surface. Scone trays are handy for Yorkshire puddings and for some types of bread roll. I have a large roasting tray for bones and for the goose at Christmas. Otherwise I try to use the smallest size baking sheet or roasting tray possible, so that whatever piece of fish or meat I'm cooking benefits from the oils and cooking juices in the tray.

### Cutting board

Domestic cutting boards are mostly hopeless. They are generally too lightweight and will move around if anything heavier than a loaf is being sliced. There was a time when wooden boards were frowned upon by the health inspectors, something to do with the grooves and cuts in the wood harbouring germs. But now they are considered kosher once more and I don't have a problem with the heavier wooden chopping boards so long as the wood is thick and hard. Nonetheless, the boards you will see at the commercial kitchen shop will be hardened plastic and come in all sorts of colours, the idea being that cross-contamination will be avoided by using a red board for raw meat and a white one for cooked. You may solve the problem by turning the board over and keeping it well scrubbed between uses. Chopping boards are heavy-duty and need to withstand tougher jobs such as chopping through bones (for domestic uses, ask your butcher to cut the bones to the size you want).

# Health and safety

**Restaurant kitchens get an unannounced visit each year from the Department of the Environment to check on the state of the kitchen and the work practices in operation.** This generally provokes a rush from the kitchen crew to comply with small regulations – for instance, the first-aid kit should be complete, there should be lids on the bins, and nothing should be less than 45cm from the floor. The main aim of these much-unloved visits, however, is to check on careful routines in food handling, refrigeration and food storage rather than to see if the floor needs sweeping.

The fridge shouldn't be overfilled, or the overall temperature will rise above what's safe. Raw stuff must be stored below cooked so that nothing drips down on to food that will not be receiving any further or prolonged cooking. The reason why you can eat street food in Bangkok and not die is because it has just been thoroughly cooked and is still hot; the cooking will have made the meat safe even if it has been stored and handled badly, and you will eat it before it cools enough for bacteria to multiply. The same principle applies at home, where pre-cooked food inadequately reheated poses a more serious risk than lamb chops that are beyond their 'best-by' date.

Cross-contamination is caused by lack of knowledge. The same knife and board used for meat when raw and then for carving and slicing once cooked is a bad idea unless both knife and board have been cleaned thoroughly in the interval. Hand-washing before handling food is a good idea.

Any chicken or cooked egg dish, such as custard, is best cooled as fast as possible. A sink full of cold water will act as an ice-bucket to a container of warm chicken stock, reducing temperatures quickly so that stock that is made at night can still be safely refrigerated before bedtime.

# Health and nutrition

**Those of us who cook for a living in restaurants are in the entertainment business rather than the nutrition and diet trade.** Most of the problems of obesity and bad diet stem from an increasing reliance on convenience foods, which are industrially produced by those who need to hone profit margins rather than feed us in some sort of balanced or nutritious manner, not the occasional visit to your neighborhood trattoria or balti house.

There is an industry burgeoning around people's worries about fat, sugar and salt in their daily diet. In fact, most sodium intake is in disguised form, through flavour enhancers and the like, which are added to ready-made meals, and is unrelated to the amount of table salt sprinkled on your dinner.

Similarly, labels are always more informative about what is omitted than what is included. '90 per cent fat-free' means 10 per cent fat; 'low-fat' doesn't imply low-sugar; 'natural' can mean just about anything, including beetroot juice to colour strawberry ice-cream; and 'fresh' as a culinary term means nothing – do we mean fresh as opposed to stale or fresh in contrast to frozen? Has 'fresh' got subliminal connotations with cool and slightly sharp, as does the French word '*frais*'? Who knows? 'Farm-fresh' eggs means battery eggs; 'free-range' eggs means the chickens get to see daylight but eat the same rubbish as battery birds.

The answer, if you have time, is to avoid ready meals. No meal is quicker than cheese, bread and ham or salami. But it is, of course, easy to preach when you spend all day cooking for a living,

worrying about the provenance of your ingredients and whether the cheeses are in peak condition, quite another to fill hungry mouths on a tight budget after a full day's work.

The aspect of eating that causes the most concern is diet. I'm talking slimming diets here, of course, rather than balanced diets. There's something quite distasteful about expensive self-starvation when common sense tells you all you need to know: if you cut the piece of cake in half you have halved the calories; if you want to eat the lot and still lose weight you have to buy into all sorts of self-deluding diets – the list of diets is endless and the industry that tells people they are fat and offers such solutions is making pots of money. For me, the obvious conclusion from continuing sales of diet books and magazines is that they cannot work or else their readership would be slim and young and beautiful for ever and no longer need to read all about it. Take comfort from the knowledge that it was ever so. In Ancient Rome the great physician Galen prescribed weight-reducing diets for his porky but well-heeled clients, but offered no advice for the malnourished.

# Taste and smell

**Taste and smell work in co-operation with each other.** Together they allow us to detect and then discriminate between possible foods. Here's how it works.

The tongue gives us basic tastes. It's a sledgehammer arrangement with receptors detecting only four basic characteristics: sweet, sour, salty and bitter. Another, called umami, is also thought to be at work, and this is sensitive to savoury tastes that you'd associate with glutamate or Parmesan cheese. There are physicists who think that metallic as a taste may also be separately recognized, and this would be a safety device warning of chemical contamination. But scientists are still unsure whether there are specific receptors to recognize umami and metallic.

Our reactions to these basic tastes are innate, for instance bitterness has associations with poisonous alkaloids and sugar with food and fuel. And the four tastes interact with each other, with each one influencing our perception of another when combined with it. For instance, the relationship between a salad and salad dressing often combines sourness with bitterness to give the dish a refreshing quality.

Temperature affects the tongue's reactions, with muted sensitivity to sweetness and sourness at low temperature, the reverse for saltiness and bitterness. One particularly good tip is that sweet things, such as melon and pineapple, can have their sweetness heightened by salt instead of sugar if that suits you better – handy if you're on a slimming regime, not so good if you're trying to reduce sodium intake.

Smell is altogether more complex and accounts for most of our perceptions of flavour. The aroma of food hits the nose not just on the way to the mouth and gullet, but also through the palate while you are chewing. Your brain has to interpret lots of smells of course, and most have little to do with lunch or dinner, but they give a series of associations, some of which are good and some not. The sweet smell of newly cut grass evokes a sense of summertime just as a damp cellar will conjure up a cool and fungal feel of late autumn, and this holds true whether you are experiencing similar smells in a glass of wine or from a plate of pasta.

The sense of smell has to do its duty as a warning mechanism, hunting aid in most animals, and much much more. The perfume industry uses all sorts of ingredients, musk for instance, that might not instantly strike you as alluring. Small wonder then that our perceptions of good and bad smells affect our mealtime experiences in ways not easy to define.

Taste and smell are chemical senses; we react to the chemical composition of what we are breathing in. Nerve cells in the mouth and nose are stimulated, by traces of chemical in the air and in food, to send signals to the front lobes of the brain, the area where most advanced mental processes take place. Here they are interpreted and evaluated as possible foodstuffs or sources of pleasure or pain. These front lobes work in conjunction with taste buds – clusters of nerve cells on the tongue's surface that send electical impulses separately to different parts of the brain that control feeding behaviour, stimulate salivation and suchlike. We each have around a thousand of these taste-buds to do the job but, interestingly, foetuses and small children have more taste-buds than adults. We lose taste-buds with age, especially once we are past 50. Hopefully a good taste memory covers the loss.

What complicates the matter for the cook is that there is no vocabulary to cover flavour; nothing that defines or pins down specific flavours so that we may all talk about them, or even aim toward them, with any degree of mutual understanding. The wine trade depends on the description of aromas in terms of known and recognizable benchmarks: flower smells or citrus fruit, for instance. But this can soon seem absurd, as tasters juggle with fine differences in flavour. Good Burgundy does in fact smell like jam and pig shit, but the attractive quality to the smell defies the logic of the words and probably has resonances that would entail unravelling all our DNA to explain. Enough to recognize that there is more to it than sweet equalling good and sour bad, and that some associations between flavour and pleasure may be personal and individual.

Nutrition is, of course, little help. Once basic needs are covered and taste preferences come into play, there are diverging opinions across the world. The Mediterranean diet centres on cereal, olive oil and wine, with meat being less important than fish to the animal protein intake. The Ancient Greeks knew how to brew beer – Egyptians had worked that out thousands of years earlier – but held that the consumption of beer and butter were hallmarks of the barbarian races. They may well think the same now. What hope then for our Germanic predilection towards dairy products and a good pint. Luckily it's possible to enjoy both.

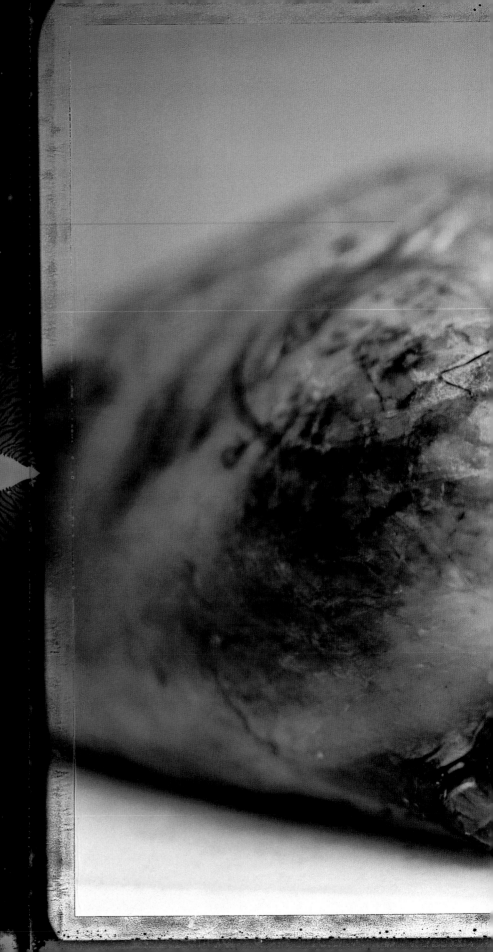

ingredients and techniques

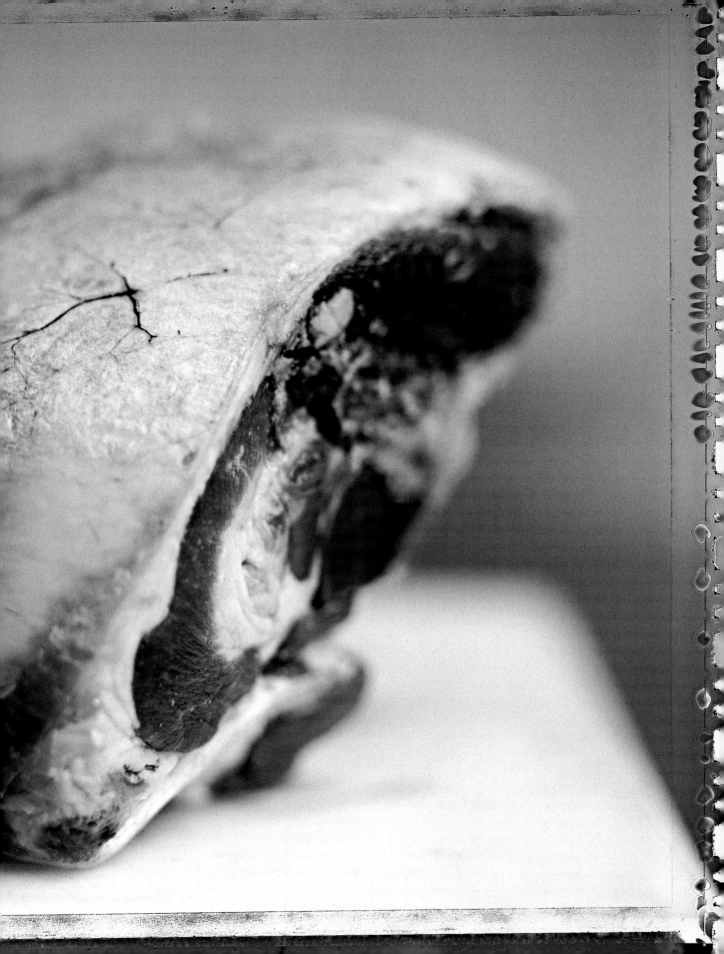

Starch

**Starch gives the satisfaction element to a meal.** The meat or fish may be the focus, but the potato, rice or pasta fills you up. People think of a meal as 'meat and two veg', but really it is meat, veg and starch; and the starch is what stops you feeling hungry.

Starchy foods are relatively cheap and therefore not always treated with the respect they deserve. But cooking them correctly makes all the difference to a meal. This chapter covers the details of how to cook the four most popular starch elements of our diet: pasta, potatoes, rice (in the form of risotto) and bread.

Once eaten, most of the carbohydrates in starchy foods convert quickly into glucose, the body's main fuel, and circulate through the blood to all the body's cells. The body uses carbohydrates first, ahead of fats or protein, so they will always give a quick lift to energy levels. This is why guests coming hungry to the table will reach for the bread basket: your mind automatically connects to what your body wants. Conversely, the dégustation menus of refined French restaurant cooking tend to include very little starch, so that you can eat your way through nine tasting courses without feeling over-full.

When planning a menu, I try to balance the starch element between courses. If I have a starchy starter, such as pasta with chicken livers, lemon zest and garlic, or a herb and saffron risotto, I'll make sure the main course has very little starch – perhaps just a small potato galette, which is more for texture than sustenance.

The starch element varies from country to country according to climate, or even, in some countries, from region to region – pasta or rice across northern Italy, but polenta in the Veneto and pizza from Rome southwards. Interestingly, very few of the examples you would come up with straightaway have any long historic connections. The potatoes of northern Europe came from Peru and only arrived after the discovery of the New World (similarly the tomatoes and sweet peppers you would associate with Mediterranean cooking). We ate quite a bit of cereal in the form of porridge before then; so not everything changes for the worse.

# Pasta

**Good pasta costs very little, so economizing is a dim idea, especially as it will form the bulk of the meal.** If cost is a factor, it is better to use a little less protein in the sauce.

When buying dried pasta, the best tip is that the longer the pasta takes to cook – as stated in the instructions – the better it is likely to be. Fast-cooking pasta is generally a substandard product, and what is the advantage in taking 6 minutes instead of 12?

Fresh pasta is simple to produce (see recipe over), but of course dried pasta is even simpler to use. They are different products, neither superior to each other, but slightly different in the way they handle and in how they keep.

Dried foods continue to dry out with prolonged storage and, while dried pasta has a fairly extended shelf-life, it is not immortal. If you remember it from last year, it may be time to invest in another pack. Fresh pasta must be either used or frozen straight away. Those you can buy at supermarkets with a three weeks sell-by date are a worry; they will have been treated to last so long. Normal dried pasta, whatever the shape, takes 15-20 minutes to cook and is best served slightly underdone, whereas the fresh kind will cook in moments.

When cooking dried pasta, look at the suggested cooking time on the pack and take 5 minutes away from it (they always over-estimate). Lift out a strand of spaghetti or a corkscrew of fusilli and bite it to see whether it's ready: hardish but with no trace of rawness is good, or cook it for longer if that's what you prefer, but slimy and disintegrating is bad.

As regards pasta shapes and sauces, I use thin pasta such as linguine or trenette as an accompaniment to a piece of meat, fish or veg, and the broader, more substantial shapes such as rigatone or fusilli when the pasta is the meal and the sauce subservient to it.

The shape and thickness of pasta you use can affect its taste; the difference between corkscrew-shaped fusilli and super-thin trenette will be greater than that between pasta flavoured by spinach or squid ink. Italians have it that the ribbing on certain types of pasta retains more sauce, and that some shapes are better suited to specific dishes. They have been eating macaroni for a long time so I'm sure they know better than me. The trouble is, of course, finding two Italians who agree on which suits what.

For fresh pasta recipe see **30**

# Fresh pasta

**Generally, fresh pasta has a more fleeting and delicate texture than dried pasta,** and it is better suited to quite subtle treatments – maybe a stock and olive oil based sauce, such as the pecorino, garlic and olive oil sauce (page 231) rather than robust tomato and herb mixes.

**Serves 4**
500g plain flour
4 tbsp olive oil
4 small eggs
a little grated nutmeg
salt and pepper

1   Work all the ingredients into a dough and knead for at least 5 minutes (a mixer with a dough-hook attachment will do this for you, if you have one). What's wanted is a shiny surface to the ball of dough and no stickiness when it is rolled or kneaded. Use a little extra flour if necessary.

2   Wrap the dough in clingfilm and rest it for an hour in the fridge. Unwrap the dough and roll it out until it is a manageable thickness – if you're using a pasta machine, thin enough to fit its widest setting. If you're not using a machine, a rolling pin used with even pressure at each end will produce results just as good.

3   Rest the pasta for half an hour, then roll it through a thinner setting on the machine. You can roll the dough through as many times as you want of course, and it will get thinner and thinner. If you're using a rolling pin, you will probably have to roll the dough four or five times. The defining point is the thickness of pasta wanted, and you roll out the dough until this is reached. This rolling gives scope for fancy footwork. If you are so minded, you can scatter chopped fresh herbs or ground spices along the thin pasta roll and double back the remainder to cover it over before passing this herb and pasta sandwich back through the machine or re-rolling it by hand – the result can be very colourful and fresh tasting, but be sure that you are improving the taste of the finished dish rather than just its colour.

4   Cut the pasta into the shapes you want.

5   Drop the pasta strands into boiling, well-salted water, to which a few drops of olive oil have been added to keep the pasta from sticking.

6   Unless you have made very thick fresh pasta, it will be cooked as soon as the water re-boils. Depending on the thickness of the pasta, you may need to boil it for 2-3 minutes. Drain.

7   Toss in a little olive oil and mix with the sauce of your choice.

## Ingredients

> **If you fancy coloured pasta,** add tomato paste or cooked spinach to the dough before rolling. These are both wet ingredients, so you'll need to reduce the amount of egg accordingly to produce the right consistency; cutting out one egg should do the trick. There are plenty of coloured pastas available and notionally they also have individual flavours – squid ink for black, for instance – but a blindfolded person would have great difficulty distinguishing one from another. Best to be honest with yourself and admit that a dramatic colour is there to liven up the dish's visual appeal.

> **Parmesan, preferably reggiano, or pecorino,** a ewe's milk cheese, is usually served with pasta. But Italians generally never serve cheese with pasta if the recipe contains fish. It's a matter of taste, of course, and you can do what you like.

## Technique

> **Let the pasta rest between rolling.** This lets it shrink back a bit. Don't let the carpets of rolled pasta dough touch each other while resting, or they will stick together.

> **Cooking dried pasta in advance is generally only a mediocre idea,** except as part of a macaroni cheese, cannelloni or some such dish. If you must, or want to keep leftovers in decent condition, then store the pasta free of water, just seasoned and tossed in a little oil to separate the strands.

For pasta with shellfish and saffron sauce see **90-1**   For pecorino, garlic and olive oil sauce see **231**

# Potatoes

**Potatoes come in two broad categories: floury and waxy.** New potatoes are waxy, as they have firm flesh and will not absorb anything like the quantity of liquid during cooking taken in by their floury counterparts. Once the season for new potatoes, spring until summer, is over, close-textured maincrop varieties such as Charlotte and Pink Fir Apple take over the small boiled potato slot. New and waxy spuds take proportionately longer to cook, but are the best for boiling or steaming. Maincrop potatoes are generally floury, but of course some are more so than others: King Edwards for instance are very floury-textured, with most white varieties being similar. Red skinned types, such as Desirée, hold together better during boiling. Floury spuds are the best choice for baking, roasting and frying.

Leave the storage of potatoes to those who know what they are doing. Spuds left in the warm will be covered with sprouts in a week and those left in the light will go green within days. Organic potatoes should, in theory at least, have more taste, but are not automatically superior; they will also be prone to certain problems – discoloured patches and suchlike – because they will not be protected from them by chemical sprays.

The basic potato dishes, mash and chips, are more difficult than people often realize. The techniques that produce them are central to most other potato dishes. It is fine to suggest tricksy variations, using basil and olive oil in mashed potato, or tinkering with the size of the chips so that you may call them *pommes pont neuf* (thick ones) or *allumettes* (thin ones), but the basic skill of careful and sympathetic cooking of the basic mash or chips is what counts,

and any unleashing of creativity on poorly-made specimens of these two dishes will be a waste of time and potato.

Once you have mastered good mashed potato, you can make first-rate hashes and potato cakes or soups thickened with potato. All of these have countless variations that can be as simple or imaginative as you want them to be.

Chips are less flexible to major variation. Cut thick, they will produce more potato flavour; cut thin, they will have more texture, crispness, and the quality of the oil will be more of a factor than the flavour of the spuds.

# Mashed potato

**The amount of butter and milk varies to taste and with each type of potato, and with the degree to which they have been cooked.** I give these quantities as a guideline. The reason why good mash is such a difficult basic item to master is precisely because no recipe works for more than a month, as potatoes on offer move from one variety to another. Similarly, the size of the potato pieces you cut will determine the cooking time.

### Serves 4
1kg Wilja, or other maincrop potatoes
salt and pepper
approx. 25g butter
approx. 25ml full-fat milk

1   Choose potatoes of a similar size, or after peeling, cut them into approximately equal pieces. Otherwise the potatoes will cook unevenly and this has one of two effects. Either the smaller pieces will be overcooked and waterlogged by the time the larger chunks are done. Or, when the small pieces are perfect, there will be some hard lumps from the larger, under-cooked pieces.

2   Add cold salted water until the potatoes are just covered and bring to the boil.

3   Turn the heat down to a gentle simmer and cover with a lid. If the pot is not lidded, any potatoes not entirely covered by water will be hard and underdone when the rest is ready. Also the kitchen will steam up.

4   Test the potatoes after 20 minutes. Obviously the size of the potatoes will have a bearing on cooking time, so lift out a piece and pierce it with a sharp knife. The resistance will show you how cooked it is. If you have any doubt cut the potato in half and eat it. Unlike green veg and red meat, there are no instances where underdone potatoes are an improvement.

5   Once cooked, don't let the potatoes sit in their cooking water or they will absorb some of it. Drain them well and allow the pot to sit on a low heat, or with the lid on, for a few seconds to evaporate any residual moisture. Dry is good.

6   Mash or sieve the potato thoroughly, but with the least amount of stirring and pushing. Over-beaten mash quickly becomes glutinous, like wallpaper paste. Season with salt and pepper.

7   If you are using the mash for potato cakes in some form, maybe as fishcakes or deep-fried croquettes, this is as far as you go. Otherwise, stir in salt, butter and milk until the texture suits you. Finally, beat the potato as hard as you can for a few seconds to fluff up the mash.

### Ingredients

> **Choice of potato:** Floury types of potato, such as King Edward, tend to disintegrate as they cook, giving a watery and even lumpy result. New potatoes are firm-textured and take longer to cook, as are the waxy small spuds – varieties such as Ratte or Charlotte – that substitute for new in the winter. Both can be good. French masterchef, Joel Robuchon, used these varieties to make his famous version of mashed potato just because they were so firm fleshed and could hold much more butter than a standard maincrop potato (he uses about 225g of butter for every 450g potatoes). But there's a limit to how much butter you actually want in mash, so my advice is to buy maincrop varieties that aren't too floury: Wilja and Cosmos are good.

For potatoes see **32**    For potato cakes see **36**    For boiling and steaming vegetables and fruit see **174**

# Chips

**The smell of stale frying oil is able to coat walls and people alike, performing an effective aversion therapy for the appetite.** In this drab thought lies the key to good chips: the oil is as important as the potato. The method for making chips is superficially simple. The potatoes are washed, peeled, cut into batons and then deep-fried.

Any pan in which chips are fried is a chip pan. But some shapes suit the purpose better than others, deep being better than shallow and wide better than narrow. A saucepan used continuously for deep-frying needs to be sturdy but not necessarily heavy like a casserole or stewpan – so no need for cast iron or lids. The most important point to remember is that Archimedes' principle applies, so if you add a large pile of chips to a pan that is too full of hot fat or oil, the hot oil will rise up and over the rim with potentially dangerous consequences. So a large pan is better than a small one.

maincrop potatoes
sunflower or corn oil

1   Once you have peeled and sliced the chips to the thickness you require, wash them briefly. This will help prevent them from sticking together during frying. Dry them on a cloth or kitchen paper before frying.

2   Heat the oil: It should come about half-way up the pan; there are dangers involved if the hot oil is too high in the pan.

3   Chips are best cooked in two stages. First in low-to-moderately hot oil and then, when needed, in moderate-to-hot oil. If you have a thermometer, the temperature you want is somewhere between 180 and 190˚C, for the second, depending on the thickness of your chips. The first cooking should be long enough to change the potato from raw to cooked but not hot enough to produce colour. The second, hotter, frying produces the colour and crispness.

4   If cooking any significant quantity of chips, you should do the amount of chips you want in several batches so that they don't stick together.

5   Thin chips can be cooked in hotter oil than thick ones as the heat hasn't as far to penetrate to produce a crisper finish. However, the more the oil is heated, the shorter will be its shelf-life and, should it burn – start giving off acrid dark smoke – it will be unusable for another frying session.

6   Remove the chips from the pan and drain on kitchen paper.

## Ingredients

> **Choice of potato:** Floury types such as King Edward make marvellous chips (and roast potatoes). New potatoes make poor chips, so maincrop varieties are essential. Good chips, like good mash, are seasonal.

> **Choice of oil:** Avoid oils that are blended solely for prolonged frying. They have a high flash point – they don't burn easily – but neither do they impart much extra to the occasion in the way of flavour. Sunflower or corn oil are fine. I also like groundnut oil, but would avoid using it unless I knew those eating, in case of allergy problems.

## Cooking method

> **Chip pans are a common cause of fires.** The oil will reach high temperatures in moments and catch fire. If this happens, don't touch the pan and certainly don't use any water on the flames for it will turn into a fireball. Switch off the heat and put the thickest blanket or cloth you have over the pan to smother the fire.

For potatoes see **32**    For frying, roasting and grilling vegetables see **194**

# Dauphine potatoes

**These are a quirky mixture of mashed potato and choux pastry and make an interesting accompaniment to anything grilled.** The mash is mixed with a third of its weight of choux paste – that's the pastry you make éclairs with – and then deep-fried in little balls or cork shapes. This mixture is enough for about eight servings. Frankly, it's not worth making any less. Freeze any left-over mixture for another day.

**Serves 4**

**For the mash:**

1kg maincrop potatoes, peeled

3 medium egg yolks

salt, pepper and nutmeg

**For the choux paste:**

165ml water

35g butter

110g plain flour

3 small eggs yolks

1   Make mashed potato as on page 33, but without the final beating in of butter, milk and salt. Stir in the egg yolks. Allow to cool.

2   To make the choux paste, slowly bring the water and butter to the boil; the butter should be melted by the time the water boils. Lift the pan away from direct heat and beat the flour into the liquid with a wooden spoon or spatula. Return the pan to a gentle heat and stir until the mixture comes smoothly and cleanly away from the pan sides. Cool slightly, then beat in the egg yolks, one at a time.

3   Mix the cool mash and choux paste together thoroughly.

4   Mould into ball shapes or, better, wine cork shapes. This is easily done by using a piping bag (no piping tube necessary) and then cutting the line of potato into smallish lengths, say 4cm. Keep the potato corks on non-stick paper until you are ready to cook them.

5   Slide the potatoes into hot ( 175°C ) oil and fry until golden brown – about 4-5 minutes.

**Technique**

> **It's worth making more choux pastry** and using the rest for buns or éclairs.

> **It is obvious when the flour, butter and water mixture is ready** by the transformation into a shiny dough ball.

> **The potato and choux paste mix is delicate to handle so,** once shaped, is best kept in the fridge until you're about to start frying.

For potatoes see **32**   For mashed potato see **33**

# Potato cakes

**These potato cakes are common in Ulster, but little known in the rest of Ireland.** They keep well in an airtight container or biscuit tin and, fried in bacon fat or butter, form an essential part of the cholesterol-rich traditional Ulster breakfast.

Sweetened potato and flour doughs are also used in Austria and middle Europe to make fruit dumplings. The mixture is folded around a ripe, stoned plum, then rolled in sugar and crushed poppy seeds. Very nice too.

**Serves 4**

500g maincrop potato

30g butter

salt

approx. 100g plain flour

1   Make the mashed potato as on page 33, missing out the final stage of beating in the butter, milk and salt.

2   Stir in the butter and leave to cool.

3   Turn the potato on to a floured work surface and incorporate about a third of its volume in plain flour. This should work out at around 100g, but may be a little more.

4   Roll out the dough to a circle of 8mm thickness. Dust with flour and cut into triangles.

5   Griddle the potato bread on a dry pan over a moderate-to-low heat. They will need about 3 minutes on each side.

6   Cool the potato cakes on wire racks and keep until breakfast time, to be fried in butter or bacon fat.

## Ingredients

> **You are aiming for a firm dough,** capable of being rolled out without sticking too badly to the work surface. Different varieties of potato will produce relatively softer or drier mash. Alter the ratio of flour incorporated if the mixture is too slack.

## Technique

> **The mashed potato should be handled as little as possible** before being combined with flour to make the dough.

> **The thicker the potato bread,** the more it will taste of potato; the thinner it is, the more it will be crisp and textured. Do what suits you better.

## Cooking method

> **The potato bread is griddled** – dry cooked on a flat pan – and no fat is used at this stage. A little flour can be sprinkled on the bread as it griddles to give more colour.

For potatoes see **32**    For mashed potatoes see **33**

# Rice: risotto

**A risotto is as time-sensitive as any soufflé.** The difficulty of risotto lies in having it just cooked but still moist or even sloppy, for rice will continue to absorb any hot liquid, overcooking in the process. There are two choices, you can cook the risotto from start to finish and then eat it – this will take 30-40 minutes – or you can conveniently shorten the cycle by part-cooking the risotto in advance.

## Saffron risotto

**This risotto can be made more of an event with the addition of some steamed vegetable – courgette or asparagus perhaps.** Also, it can be made without the saffron and with chopped or liquidized herbs (see roast quail with parsley risotto, page 108) instead.

### Serves 4

1 tbsp olive oil
1 tbsp chopped onion
200g carnaroli rice (or other risotto rice)
salt and pepper
100ml white wine
a large pinch of saffron threads
700ml chicken stock or watery
  vegetable stock
50g butter
50g Parmesan cheese, grated

1  Heat the olive oil in a pan, then sweat the chopped onion for 2-3 minutes.

2  Add the rice and continue to cook gently for another 3-4 minutes. Season the rice with plenty of salt and black pepper.

3  Add the white wine and cook until completely evaporated.

4  Stir in the saffron and 250ml of the stock. Bring to the boil, cover with a lid and leave, away from direct heat, until all the stock has been absorbed. The risotto will be hard and dry but can be kept in the refrigerator for a day or two at this stage.

5  About 10 minutes before you serve the risotto, add the remaining stock and re-boil. Gently simmer until most of the liquid has been absorbed, then stir in the butter and Parmesan.

### Ingredients

> **There are several varieties of rice on the market that claim to be the ideal risotto rice.** Carnaroli is a hybrid of vialone rice, which used to be the connoisseur's preferred choice and still has plenty of fans. Any variety of arborio rice will do the job so long as it has the rugby-ball-shaped grains that absorb lots of stock.

> **Saffron needs contact with hot liquid to release both colour and flavour.** If it is added early this poses no difficulty but if you want to add the saffron later, maybe to have streaks of highly flavoured and deep-yellow rice rather than the homogenous pale colour shown here, you need to heat the saffron threads separately and stir them in at the last moment.

For roast quail with parsley risotto see **108-09**

# Bread

**Making bread is central to becoming a good cook.** A recipe will guide you through the process, but a feel for the changes in dough while it proves and the subtle changes in texture that small alterations in the ratio of olive oil to flour can produce will give a real sense of the essence of cookery – a feeling of creating something personal from your ingredients.

Use good flour. A small increase in the quality of flour will give big improvements in the finished bread. Flour costs relatively little, so it's worth buying the best you can find. I use Doves Farm organic strong white, and their multigrain wholemeal as a base for brown bread. White flour is lighter and can be combined with your choice of brown flour to lighten the texture of the bread. Rye is the darkest and heaviest. I sometimes sprinkle rye flour on to the proved loaves before baking to capture some of the sweet flavour without the heaviness. Don't be afraid to use plenty of salt; bread is tasteless without it. Worries over salt intake in diet are mostly irrelevant in home cookery, as over-salted food is unpleasant to eat. It's the salts which are used in the food processing industry to preserve and enhance food flavour that are the problem because most don't taste salty in the way of kitchen salt and pass unnoticed.

## Soda bread

**The soda in soda bread is bicarbonate of soda.** This is an alkaline substance which, in order to raise the bread, has to combine with something acid, normally cream of tartar. The breads that sport 'soda' in their name are Irish soda breads, known as damper in Australia. Sweetened soda breads are familiar, though called by other names: blueberry muffins are made the same way as this soda bread, for example. Soda bread has no yeast, so there is no need for proving or rising. It is, in fact, a large, savoury scone and surely the simplest introduction to bread-making.

**Makes 1 loaf**
300g wholemeal flour
150g plain white flour
60g oatmeal
2 level tsp bicarbonate of soda
1 level tsp salt
1 tsp cream of tartar
350ml skimmed milk
15g soft butter

1   Preheat the oven to 200°C/Gas mark 6.
2   Mix the first five ingredients together. Separately, mix the cream of tartar into the milk and then mix with the soft butter.
3   Stir the milk mixture into the dry ingredients and mix well.
4   Knead briefly to make sure everything is properly combined, then shape the dough into a round loaf.
5   Use a floured knife to mark a cross on the bread. This makes it easier to break into segments after baking.
6   Bake on a buttered baking dish for 35 minutes.

### Ingredients

> **Traditionally, buttermilk was used in making soda bread.** It is a by-product of butter-making, the almost fatless liquid left when the butter was churned, and can also be found as a cultured dairy product. You don't need to use cream of tartar if you substitute this for skimmed milk, as it's already acid enough.

> **Baking powder** is a mixture of sodium bicarbonate and cream of tartar (tartaric acid). The alkaline and acid elements combine to produce gas, aerating the dough. It loses power once the packet has been opened a while. Similarly, if you are using the components separately as here, throw out any ancient packets.

> **Never increase the ratio of baking powder, sodium bicarbonate or cream of tartar,** in the hope of producing lighter bread. What you get is an unpleasant metallic after-taste and a yellow tinge to the finished loaf.

> **Oils and butter** are added to bread dough to produce a softer crumb (texture).

> **If you prefer a softer crust,** wrap the bread in a cloth when it emerges from the oven.

For olive and shallot bread see **42-3**    For kneading technique see **42-3**

# Corn bread with bacon and thyme

This recipe will produce a pie-shaped bread which is best served in wedges like cake, or it can be baked in individual rolls like muffins with the aid of a Yorkshire pudding tin or mince pie tray. It can also be tailored to suit specific dishes by adding whatever else the occasion demands. You can also use blue cornmeal, which is quite rare and sacred to the Hopi Indians (Native Americans) and is alleged to give a slightly more smoky flavour.

**Makes 1 large loaf**

170g yellow cornmeal

50g wholemeal flour

1 scant tsp salt

1 level tbsp baking powder

1 level tbsp chopped fresh thyme leaves

2 small eggs

325ml skimmed milk

50g unsalted butter

1 level tbsp clear honey

4 rashers smoked streaky bacon,
    cut into dice then grilled

1   Preheat the oven to moderately hot (200°C/Gas mark 6).

2   Sift all the dry ingredients together.

3   Whisk together the eggs and milk.

4   Melt the butter in a 20cm diameter ovenproof frying pan. Make sure the sides are well coated with butter, then pour the excess into the egg and milk mixture.

5   Stir the honey into the liquid (it will sink to the bottom of the bowl if added earlier).

6   Pour the wet ingredients on to the dry and mix the two together. Try to do this quickly and well.

7   Mix in the grilled bacon and pour the resulting batter into the buttered pan. Bake for 30 minutes.

8   Test for doneness by piercing the bread with a sharp knife or toothpick. If it comes out clean, the bread is cooked.

## Ingredients

> **First buy the right ingredients!** Corn and maize are the same thing, though the word corn has been going for centuries to describe almost all types of grain cereal. Cornmeal and cornflour, however, are not the same thing, and if cornflour is substituted for cornmeal the result will be a nasty whitish blancmange. Also be wary of various grades of Italian milled corn, which are intended for cooking as polenta, a sort of yellow porridge. The type you want is yellow cornmeal, preferably American.

> **If you need a gluten-free bread,** for someone with a wheat allergy perhaps, then substitute soya flour for the wholemeal indicated in the recipe.

## Technique

> **The mixture will be slack, more like batter than dough.** This is perfectly OK. In fact, you can add even more liquid, should you want to make what's called spoonbread which, as the name suggests, is soft enough to need tackling with cutlery, and is used in place of rice or potato with main-course fish or meat.

## Cooking method

> **Each oven cooks slightly differently.** Certainly, all cook at different temperatures in different parts – hotter higher and cooler lower down – but it may well be that it can be hotter further back along a shelf, or a little askew in how the heat is distributed. Use cooking times as a guideline rather than gospel.

# Olive and shallot bread

**Black olives should be dark brown rather than black and should be bought stone-in.** Commercial pitted black olives are coloured artificially and are vastly inferior.

### Makes 2 loaves

30g fresh yeast

450ml warm water

2 level tsp fine sea salt

650g unbleached white flour

2 tbsp olive oil, plus extra for frying

150g shallots, chopped

250g black olives, stoned then
    coarsely chopped

grated zest of 1 small orange

a little milk or beaten egg for glazing

1   Dissolve the yeast in a little of the water until it is frothy.

2   Add the salt to the flour, then add the olive oil followed by the dissolved yeast mixture and the rest of the water. Mix into a dough – a food processor with a dough-hook attachment will be fine if you have one. Knead the dough for a few minutes.

3   Cover with a warm plastic wrap and then leave in a warm, draught-free spot to rise, until it doubles in bulk. This should take an hour in a warm kitchen, but may take longer.

4   Heat a little olive oil in a frying pan. Sweat the chopped shallot in the oil until it starts to colour. Leave to cool, then mix with the chopped olives and orange zest.

5   Knock back the dough – this just means kneading it for a few seconds to deflate it – then roll out to a thin oblong. Spread on the olive, shallot and orange zest mixture. Cut in half.

6   Roll the dough into two large cigar-shaped loaves, then leave to rise a second time. This should be a little faster, maybe half an hour. Preheat the oven to 200°C/Gas mark 6.

7   Brush the loaves with milk or beaten egg, then bake for 30 minutes, or until the bread feels hollow when tapped.

## Ingredients

> **Fresh yeast** is vastly superior to dried yeast – the latter was created in a time when fresh yeast was very difficult to come by. It keeps for a good week in the fridge and freezes perfectly. Any baker who bakes on the premises will stock fresh yeast. Failing this, you'll find it at most health-food stores.

> **The best oatmeal** to use is porridge rolled oats, but you can use other grades. Oatmeal softens the texture of the finished bread as well as giving it a specific taste.

> **The water** used in the recipe should be just lukewarm when the yeast is added. Too warm and it will kill the yeast; too cold and it will take ages to work. Err on the side of cool.

## Technique

> **Once the flour, yeast and liquid have been mixed into the dough, it must be kneaded** until it is smooth. The purpose is to stretch the gluten in the flour so that the gas that the yeast produces can be trapped. Some flours absorb more liquid than others, so start off with a soft, slack mixture, reserving a little of the flour, and add more flour as you go. Adding flour is fine, but adding water is difficult. To knead, flatten the dough by pushing it forwards with the palm and heel of your hand, then fold it back towards you with your fingers. This should be done full-force, leaning and pushing against the dough with all your strength.

> **Times for the proving of dough are only a guideline.** The ambient temperature in your kitchen on a July afternoon will be significantly different to that of a February morning and the times taken for dough to rise will vary accordingly. When the volume has doubled in size, the job is done.

> **'Knocking back'** means letting the gas escape from the risen dough. You do this by punching the dough and kneading it once or twice. The dough should then be left to rise once more and then finally baked.

For bread see **40**

# Fruit and veg

**Plants are the basic foodstuffs;** either we eat them or we eat the animals that feed from them. In most parts of the world, vegetables and fruit make up the majority, sometimes the entirety, of our nourishment.

The first plants to be domesticated were grains and legumes – the pea and bean family – and these are still the staples of our diet. The cultivation of fruits and other vegetables, apart from those growing wild and free, came later, and in most people's minds they have always been less central than meat or fish in the mealtime scheme of things.

Vegetables find their way into most parts of a meal. Some vegetables, such as the onion family, are rarely used for anything other than flavouring; in fact most meat-based soups and stocks rely on the inclusion of aromatic vegetables for success.

This chapter explores the effect of traditional storage methods upon vegetables and fruit, the issues to consider when serving vegetables either as a side or main dish, and how to successfully prepare salads and salad dressings.

# Buying vegetables and fruit

**Most fruits and vegetables are still seasonal,** but the boundaries of each ingredient's season are constantly being expanded by modern horticultural methods, and the efficiency of those in the air-freighting business means that produce from the southern hemisphere's summer can be in the northern hemisphere almost as quickly as anything local. The problems with out-of-season fruit and vegetables are less about the time it takes for them to reach the consumer and more about the varieties grown, which are developed for ease of handling rather than for flavour.

And yet we often hear those with only a shadowy grasp of seasonality complaining about out-of-season soft fruit or asparagus in winter. But watch them put lemon into their gin and tonic year-round and take for granted that butcher's meat, which used to be rigidly seasonal as well, should be available and in top condition from January through to December.

The truth is that most things, whether imported or home-grown, have a time when they are in peak condition. Early varieties of apple and pear aren't as concentrated in flavour as those that come later; the late plum, Marjorie Seedling, eats like a ripe peach, but early strawberries are fragrant and fine.

Some vegetables, such as the onion family, store well and can be eaten over a longer period, and some, such as most green vegetables, cannot. More importantly, our food traditions have grown around traditional availability and it would seem just as bizarre to eat Brussels sprouts on a hot summer day as it would to eat fresh apricots in January. The best advice is to use what is in best condition and leave others to worry about the rest.

Finally, organic is good, but not all good things are organic. Your guide should be what tastes the best.

# Storing vegetables and fruit

**Yesterday's solutions to the ebb and flow of vegetables and fruit** gave us jams and marmalade, pickles and sauerkraut, dried peas and beans. Then came the bottling and canning industries, followed by Clarence Birdseye and the frozen food business. Each had successes, which survive the original needs of preserving food from season to season.

Frozen peas are vastly superior, where I live, to anything at the greengrocer's in summer. Peas lose sweetness from the moment they are picked and the specimens available to me fresh will have spent too long in sacks at Birmingham market. Broad beans can also be good when frozen. Broccoli, which chefs know as calabrese, was developed at a research station in Calabria purely for the frozen food industry, and its availability fresh and in good condition is a bonus. The key to the most successful frozen vegetables is that big business can impose discipline upon growers, for instance by specifying which varieties are grown and when they are picked, which may at times be beneficial to the final product. The drawbacks come if freezing is applied to stuff that isn't suited, such as soft fruits or green beans.

Tinned fruit and vegetables are best regarded as separate commodities from fresh, as they are good for different things. I have an affection for tinned petits pois and think the sweet, stewed flavour works well, with the help of a little butter, alongside boiled gammon or roast pigeon. Similarly, I have childhood memories of tinned Bartlett pears (Bartlett are what William pears are called in Australia) as part of sherry trifle that I would still be happy to eat now.

Current solutions, such as irradiating soft fruit to prolong shelf-life and genetically manipulating varieties to protect against disease, are more worrying as they enable careless handling and storage to be less of a problem, and seem to me to have much more advantages for those on the selling side of the arrangement than those on the buying, cooking and eating end.

# Chopping an onion

Peel the onion. It will have an obvious base and top. Halve it from top to base rather than across the middle as you might for onion rings. The onion layers will all emanate from the base and you will need to leave a small section of this base intact in order to control the slicing and chopping, so:

1   Lay the onion half flat-side-down on a chopping board and slice towards the base as thinly as possible.

2   Turn the onion around and cut horizontally into it.

3   for really thinly chopped onion you may do this two or three times. The small section at the base of the onion, which you have left intact, will hold everything together.

Be sure to grasp the onion tightly and then cut down and across the slices until you reach the base. It is important to keep the fingers of the hand that is holding the onion firmly crimped so that there is no chance of slicing your finger as well as the onion, as the blood produced will both wet the onions and frighten the cook.

# Vegetables as side dishes

**Vegetables as side dishes should contribute some quality of texture or taste to the overall dish.** There is an etiquette surrounding the service of side vegetables. At informal meals they line the periphery of the plate or sit in mounds next to the meat, and at more important dinners they are served separately, in dishes at the centre of the table. In the era of grand private houses a third option was in use: silver service. Hotel restaurants took to this in a big way, for it added a touch of theatre to the waiter's task. Once meat was carved and presented on plates, some person wielding a spoon and fork would pile unsuitable vegetables from a silver-plated dish on to the unfortunate chop or partridge. The result often looked like a swill bin, and my preference has always been to use plates that are large enough to cope with all the meal's components and still look appetizing.

In fact, any separation of meat or fish and vegetable until you start eating obscures the point that they are about to become inseparable, sharing both fork and palate. There are a few ground rules that may help. First, don't choose vegetables purely to suit a colour scheme, unless you have passion for carrots, of course. Second, think about the ratio of vegetables to starch and meat; remember that the more spiced or robust the treatment of the vegetable, the less you will need. Third, consider that the starch element will act as comfort factor and the protein will be the main focus of attention, so the vegetable should give another layer of complexity to the overall meal. Some lightly spiced root vegetables will underpin roast venison or some lightly boiled runner beans and mange touts will give freshness and crunch to grilled salmon, while leeks in mustard and Cheddar white sauce will act as foil to boiled gammon in terms of both flavour and texture.

The over-use of vegetable purée during the fad for *nouvelle cuisine* has led to a distaste for this treatment. The mashing and blending of vegetables with interesting texture, such as broccoli or asparagus, was a waste, especially as it was usually done for visual effect to produce a neat array of multi-coloured baby food, an artist's palette around the plate.

Not all vegetables have an interesting texture to lose, of course, and many root vegetables suit the process well. The softening also gives an opportunity for some judicious spicing: sweet vegetables such as carrot, swede and parsnip blend well with nutmeg, cumin or a pinch of curry powder; those with sharper flavours, such as celeriac, can even take a teaspoon of grated horseradish.

# Braised red cabbage

**Braising is always best done in a heavy, lidded saucepan, as a light-weight pan will burn easily.** If your collection of pots doesn't include anything appropriate, the best bet is to buy one. Should temporary poverty or inadequate credit preclude this, you may of course still cook the cabbage dish. Your choice will be to either omit the fried onion, which does most of the discolouring, or resign yourself to a spot of difficult pot-washing later.

**Serves 4**

1 small red cabbage
120ml red wine
120ml orange juice
1 tsp sugar
freshly ground nutmeg, to taste
ground cinnamon, to taste
salt and pepper
1 tbsp vegetable oil
1 onion, sliced

1   Quarter the cabbage and cut out the hard white core. Slice the cabbage into thin strips (a food processor will do the job for you).

2   Mix the wine, orange juice, sugar and spices together, then into the cabbage strips. Season. This can be used straight away, but is better left overnight to marinate.

3   Heat the vegetable oil. Once hot, add the onion and fry until soft but not too coloured, then add the cabbage and its marinade. You shouldn't need any other liquid. Stir well, put on a tightly fitting lid and bring to the boil.

4   Reduce the heat and braise gently for 20 minutes with a lid on. The evaporating wine and juice should steam any cabbage not covered with liquid, provided of course that you have used a tight-fitting lid. It's still a good idea to stir the pan from time to time, in case anything should stick.

## Technique

> **The colour of this dish rubs off** on everything that comes into contact with it. If you prefer not to have blue fingernails and clothes, it's a good idea to handle the cabbage with care or, better still, rubber gloves.

> **Not all orange juice or red wine has the same acidity.** Mix the marinade ingredients together separately and taste the result for its balance of sweet and sour while there is time to make adjustments.

## Cooking method

> **If you have some cabbage left over it will reheat well,** so don't throw away the cooking liquor.

For chopping an onion see **47**   For braising vegetables see **200**

# Spiced root vegetables

**Winter's root vegetables need help if they are to be interesting.** Most are starchy and need butter, oil or cream to be palatable. They do respond well to spices and curry powder, though.

**Serves 4**

400g swede

400g carrots

400g celeriac (celery root)

400g parsnip

2 tbsp olive oil

1 tbsp paprika

1 tsp each of ground cinnamon, ground
   coriander and ground cumin

1 tsp lemon juice

salt and pepper

1   Peel the vegetables and cut them into 2cm dice. Keep them in separate piles.

2   Heat the olive oil in a wok and add the vegetables in the right order, depending on the time they take to cook – the hardest first and softest last, so it will be the swedes first, then after 5 minutes the carrots and celeriac, and then after another 5 minutes the parsnip cubes.

3   Add the spices, then shake the wok. Lower the heat and continue to fry, shaking the wok from time to time, until done. How long this takes depends on the size of the vegetable cubes, but for a 2cm cube will take around 15 minutes.

4   Add the lemon juice and season with salt and pepper.

## Cooking method

> **A wok is ideal** as it holds a large quantity of vegetables frying at the same time.

For frying vegetables see **194**

# Stir-fried spinach

**Recent research claims that Popeye was a touch optimistic about the health- and strength-giving properties of spinach.** So now we can cook it for pleasure rather than because it is particularly good for us.

**Serves 4**
1 tbsp sunflower oil
1kg spinach, washed
½ tsp salt
1 tsp sugar
2 tsp chopped garlic

1 Heat a wok or large pan on a high heat, then add the oil. Add the spinach and salt.
2 Stir-fry for 2 minutes, then add the sugar and garlic.
3 Stir-fry for another 2 minutes, then press out any liquid and serve.

## Ingredients

> **Beware of differences between winter spinach varieties,** such as spinach beet, and the more fragile summer type. Spinach beet is coarse and needs cooking like cabbage.

> **Assess the quality of spinach as if it were salad,** which indeed it can be. If it looks fit to eat raw it will be perfect when cooked. Tough fibrous leaves, any sign of yellowing, or the onset of deterioration through damp are warnings of disappointment around the corner.

> **Spinach needs thorough washing.** The leaves should be dunked in plenty of cold water so that sand and grit lurking on them can be loosened so they sink to the bottom. Don't leave the spinach in the water for too long though. Shake it dry as soon as it is washed and, if it is not for immediate use, store it in the fridge. The best method, if you have room, is to find a plastic bag and poke some holes in the bottom of it, then loosely fill it with washed spinach and suspend it over a bowl or basin – the logic being that residual water that drops from the leaves will escape rather than rot the batch.

## Technique

> **You need a lot of raw spinach to produce modest amounts of cooked,** so be generous. When the spinach is cooked it will retain lots of liquid, which will need to be pressed out with a spoon.

For frying, grilling and roasting vegetables see **194**

# Vegetables as starters or main dishes

**Either of the starters that follow would make a creditable main course if accompanied by a tossed salad and some warm bread.** Otherwise, they will serve as starters or light meals on their own. In either case, the constraints of a subservient role, as side dish, are no longer relevant. The style and strength of seasoning is unaffected by any piece of fish or meat sharing the same plate and the textures of the asparagus, artichoke or whatever can be exploited as they are centre stage.

## Stuffed aubergine

**The most famous stuffed vegetable dishes come from the Eastern Mediterranean and Middle East.** Vine leaves, peppers and courgettes are regular candidates for this treatment, which converts them into more of an event and less of a side dish. In fact, the generous spicing usually makes them unsuitable to be anything other than centre stage.

Aubergine is good for stuffing. This dish is common in various versions across the Middle East, where it's called Imam Bayaldi – the Imam fainted presumably through ecstasy. I have never noticed this effect, and assume that the dish somehow tastes better in desert climes. It can be served warm or cold and, despite what has just been said, will partner roast or grilled lamb at a pinch.

### Serves 4
4 medium-sized aubergines
salt
3 tomatoes
150ml olive oil
1 large onion, chopped
1 tbsp pine kernels
3 cloves garlic, crushed
2 tbsp chopped fresh parsley
1 bay leaf
$\frac{1}{2}$ tsp black pepper
$\frac{1}{2}$ tsp ground cinnamon

### For cooking:
1 tbsp lemon juice
1 tsp sugar

1   Cut the stems from the aubergines, then halve them lengthwise. Scoop out most of the flesh, leaving a little. Sprinkle the skins and flesh with salt and leave for 30 minutes.
2   Preheat the oven to 200°C/Gas mark 6. Skin the tomatoes by pricking the top and bottom with a fork and then dropping them into boiling water, then into cold water, and removing the skins. Deseed them. Cut into rough dice.
3   Heat half the oil, then add the chopped onion and fry. As it starts to colour, add the pine kernels and crushed garlic. Add the chopped parsley, tomatoes, bay leaf, pepper and cinnamon. Season with a little salt.
4   Wash the aubergine skins. Rinse the flesh in a sieve or colander under running water, then squeeze dry and chop. Use the remaining olive oil to fry the flesh for 2-3 minutes, then add this to the onion and tomato mixture.
5   Rinse the skins and then stuff with the filling. Arrange in a roasting dish. Pour in 150ml water, the lemon and sugar. The water should be almost level with the tops of the aubergines. Cover and bake for 45 minutes, or until they are quite soft.

### Technique
> **For this recipe, the aubergines need to be salted for half an hour** before cooking, or they will soak up too much oil, making the finished dish greasy and unappetising.
> **Vegetable stuffings do not automatically have to be put back into the appropriate skins.** Filo will do the job just as well. Nor does it have to involve some chopping and spicing of a vegetable's flesh. Rice is likely to be the main ingredient in a stuffed pepper, and some mixture of pork and breadcrumbs in stuffed cabbage.

For chopping an onion see **47**

# Spiced aubergine fritters

**Deep-frying is a little-used method for vegetables,** and is best known for its role in the Japanese dish tempura, in which vegetables and prawns are coated in a light batter, deep-fried, then served with a spicy dip. This is a more robust batter and the meaty texture of the aubergine works well with the ground spices.

**Serves 4**

1 large aubergine

salt and pepper

a good pinch each of ground cinnamon,
    ground cumin and ground cardamom

1 tsp grated orange zest

sunflower oil, for frying

lemon wedges, to serve

**For the batter:**

4 tbsp self-raising flour

1 tbsp olive oil

1 tbsp water

2 medium egg whites

1   Slice the aubergine into 5mm rounds and season with salt, pepper, spices and orange zest.

2   For the batter, whisk together the flour, oil and water – you want the thickness of porridge. Separately, and with a clean whisk, beat the egg whites until stiff. Fold the whites into the batter.

3   Heat the sunflower oil until hot but not smoking. Coat each slice of aubergine in batter and fry in hot oil until crisp and brown; this takes only a minute.

4   Serve with lemon wedges or as warm component of a salad.

## Ingredients

> **Modern varieties of aubergine don't need pre-salting** to extract the bitterness. 10 minutes contact with the salt and spices will help soften the aubergine, however, and this does no harm.

## Technique

> **The batter will keep for an hour or two** and still be usable, but loses volume during this time. It's best made as near the time it's needed as is practicable.

## Cooking method

> **The initial temperature of the cooking oil is not critical but,** like the thickness of the slices of aubergine, affects cooking time. Hot but not smoking is best.

> **Fry the slices of aubergine a few at a time** in case they stick together in the pan.

For batter technique see **190-91**   For frying, grilling and roasting vegetables see **194**

# Ratatouille

**This Provençal vegetable stew has been a staple of the restaurant repertoire for ever,** often with small variations and additions. The core of the dish is stewed aubergine with peppers, courgettes and tomato and, while I would be happy to add celery or fennel, even mushrooms, to the mix, I would be wary of leaving out any of the four principal players.

The dish can be re-worked in various ways. The principal ingredients can be deep-fried in batter and laid across a garlic and tomato sauce. Alternatively, one of the main vegetables can be promoted to star status and the remainder used as stuffing – say, courgette stuffed with aubergine and pepper or aubergine stuffed with courgette and tomato. Any variation will alter the nature and style of the dish, but the essence remains because these ingredients work well together. I have come across versions that omit the tomato and garlic but I do not prefer them – the stewed vegetables in oil can take on a defeated look.

I tend not to stew the ingredients for as long as usual. I fry the vegetables separately and drain them before combining the lot with the braised tomato for only 5 or 10 minutes. The idea is that the texture will be much better and that each ingredient will stand out rather than meld into the stew.

Ratatouille reheats well and is as good to eat cold as it is warm.

### Serves 4
1 large aubergine
2 medium red peppers, deseeded
3 medium courgettes
2 tbsp olive oil
1 medium onion, chopped
2 large cloves garlic, chopped
100g bottled chopped tomato
salt and pepper
a choice of fresh herbs, chopped

1   Cut the vegetables into whatever sized cubes you fancy. Large dice is fine for a stand-alone lunch dish or to partner roast veal or lamb, but smaller dice would be appropriate as garnish to red mullet or as stuffing for artichoke hearts.

2   Heat half the olive oil. Gently fry the onion and garlic in the hot oil. When soft but not brown, add the chopped tomato and braise for another 10 minutes.

3   Meanwhile, heat a large frying pan or wok and add the rest of the olive oil. Fry the vegetables in turn – aubergines first, then peppers, then courgettes. Drain the vegetables thoroughly and then add to the braising tomato and 1 tbsp water.

4   Put a lid on the saucepan and turn down the heat to the gentlest of simmers. Cook for 5-10 minutes. If the result looks oilier than you had hoped, maybe a little curdled, stir a few drops of water or white wine into the ratatouille. Add the herbs just before you serve.

### Ingredients
> **The quality of the ingredients is, as ever, crucial.** Summer vegetables rather than hothouse imposters are central to the success of this dish. Red peppers tend to be soap-like and flavour-free, so try to search out those that have grown and ripened somewhere appropriately warm.

> **Use bottled chopped tomato rather than fresh** – unless of course you live in Spain or Italy and have plum tomatoes ripening in your garden. The flavour of English tomatoes is delicate rather than robust, and will be lost in prolonged stewing or braising. You could add a little fresh chopped tomato during the final moments of cooking if you want those fresh notes to the stew. It is also good to add fresh herbs such as basil or oregano at the end.

For chopping an onion see **47**   For braising vegetables see **200**

# Salads

**It's difficult to define just what is or isn't a salad.** The image conjured up will be of lettuce leaves mixed with anything from boiled eggs and tomato to avocado pear and chicken. But 'salad' can mean anything from potatoes and mayonnaise to the apple, celery and walnut mixture in Basil Fawlty's Waldorf salad. Salad dressings, with their balance of fresh-tasting lemon or vinegar mixed with the alkaline quality of good oil, are much easier to pin down, and perhaps anything that can be tossed with such a mixture qualifies as salad.

Side salads perform the same function as side vegetables in a meal (see page 48) and tend to be simple affairs of crisp leaves and straightforward dressings of olive oil spiked with lemon or vinegar. More elaborate salad dishes, with a meat or fish component or a strong cheese or nut oil dressing, will stand alone as a starter or light lunch. Either way, they are always intended to be refreshing rather than filling.

Salad is the aspect of cooking and eating that is regularly done least well. You can understand why children have to be bribed to eat their greens once you see a mixture of leaves that don't go together garnished with pieces of unpeeled fruit and, worse, with no decent oil or vinegar dressing, no home-made salad cream or mayonnaise, no salt or seasoning. Yet it's not difficult to make superb salad; it doesn't take years of practice or specialist training, just care with the relative proportions and textures of ingredients.

Salad leaves that are available cover a range from mild and nutty to strong and bitter. A sprig of delicate lamb's lettuce will be lost in a bowlful of radicchio or Belgian endive. Leaves that look alike don't necessarily taste similar – purslane and watercress are as different as strawberries and pears; lettuce varieties will be mild, the chicory family bitter. It's best to work to the tastes and textures rather than the colours and avoid the ready-mixed packs that will major on what's cheapest to include rather than what's most appropriate together.

# Green salad with Roquefort dressing

**All blue cheeses make good dressings.** They do not all taste the same, however, so it isn't a good idea to call them all by the same name. Roquefort is a salty, sheep's milk cheese from south-western France, with a taste that is more austere, less creamy, than, say, dolcelatte or Stilton, both of which make excellent but different dressings

**Serves 4**

selection of green salad leaves, such as frisée, young spinach, purslane, cos and Webb's lettuces

2 slices white bread, for croûtons

1 tbsp olive oil, for frying

2 rashers streaky bacon, cut into strips (optional)

**For the dressing:**

50g Roquefort cheese, crumbled

1 tbsp white wine vinegar

100ml olive oil

black pepper

1 tbsp white wine

1 tbsp chopped fresh chives

1   For the dressing, work the cheese and vinegar together to form a thick purée. Incorporate the oil slowly, stirring continuously. Add a little black pepper, then the wine, to make the dressing more manageable. Finally, stir in the chives.

2   For the salad, wash and dry the lettuce leaves.

3   Cut the bread into cubes. Heat the olive oil and add the bread cubes. Fry until crisp and brown. Drain for a second on kitchen paper. If you are using bacon, grill this at the same time.

4   Toss the leaves in the dressing and scatter on the croûtons and bacon.

**Technique**

> **Roquefort is quite salty, so do not add any extra** – especially if you intend putting hot strips of bacon on the salad.

> **The cheese will produce a thick dressing.** If you want to slacken it so that it is easier to handle, use white wine or water rather than extra vinegar to let it down. Too much vinegar will dramatically alter the overall flavour of the dressing.

For oils and vinegars for dressings see **63**

# Green salad with Stilton quenelles and walnut dressing

**This is an exercise in differing textures as well as tastes.** The point of creaming a little butter into the cheese is to soften its texture so that it almost forms a counterpoint dressing to the walnut oil but without combining completely. Crisp bacon and croûtons are similarly a contrast with the leaves. A salad that is to be more than a side salad needs several points of interest to succeed and this composition can substitute for a cheese course in a formal meal as well as make a serviceable light lunch with some hot rolls.

**Serves 4**
50g unsalted butter
50g Stilton, crumbled
black pepper
grated nutmeg
groundnut or sunflower oil, for frying
4 rashers smoked bacon, cut into strips
white bread cut into cubes, for croûtons
mixture of mostly bitter leaves, such as
  frisée, watercress, cos lettuce, rocket
1 tbsp walnut halves

**For the dressing:**
1 tbsp walnut oil
1 tsp sherry vinegar

1   Use a wooden spoon to mix the soft butter and crumbled cheese together. Season to taste with pepper and nutmeg, then use two spoons dipped in hot water to mould the resulting mixture into quenelles (lozenge shapes).
2   Heat the groundnut or sunflower (definitely not walnut) oil in a pan. Crisp-fry the strips of bacon and cubes of bread separately.
3   Wash and then dry the leaves.
4   For the dressing, whisk together the walnut oil and sherry vinegar, and then toss the leaves. Serve with the walnut halves, croûtons, crisp bacon and Stilton quenelles.

**Ingredients**
> **Use the cheese and butter when soft,** or at least not straight from the fridge

**Technique**
> **Whisk the oil and vinegar together at the last moment** before serving, as there is no emulsion to hold the dressing together.
> **The cheese is salty** so there will be no need to season the leaves further.

For oils and vinegars for dressings see **63**    For basic dressings see **64**

# Celeriac mousse with morel mushrooms, salad and walnut dressing

**Warm salads were all the rage for a year or two.** They give an interesting contrast between hot and cold; sharp vinegar and soothing oil. They don't keep, however, and the effect of the dressing and the warm mousse on the leaves will soon leave you with a sad and limp dish it if hangs around for too long.

### Serves 4

50g dried morel mushrooms

approx. 600g celeriac

salt and pepper

1/2 tsp grated horseradish

2 medium eggs

125ml double cream

butter, for greasing

selection of salad leaves, say 1/3 cos or
little gem, 1/3 endives and 1/3 baby
spinach leaves

sunflower oil, for frying

1 slice white bread, cut into cubes
for croûtons

olive oil, for frying

1 tbsp pine kernels

### For the dressing:

1 tbsp walnut oil

1 tsp sherry vinegar

1  Preheat the oven to 175°C/Gas mark 3.

2  Put the morels in a pan of water and bring to the boil. Drain off the water and cut away any stalks. Take half of what's left and roughly chop to stuff the mousses.

3  Peel the celeriac and cut it into 2cm cubes. Boil in salted water until tender (about 20 minutes), then drain. Blend in a food processor and season with salt, pepper and horseradish. Blend in the eggs and cream, then transfer enough mousse to four buttered ramekin dishes to fill them halfway. Spoon the chopped morel into the centre of each ramekin before adding the remaining mousse.

4  Cover the ramekins with buttered greaseproof paper and place in a roasting tray half-filled with warm water. Bake for 20 minutes; the mousses should be firm to the touch.

5  Wash and then dry the salad leaves. Sprinkle on salt and pepper to taste, then dress them with the walnut oil and vinegar and mix thoroughly. Place a ring of salad on each plate, then turn out the ramekins on to the middles of the plates.

6  Fry the remaining morel mushrooms briefly in sunflower oil, then fry the croûtons in a little olive oil. Spoon over the celeriac mousses with the pine kernels.

## Ingredients

> **Dried morels** are excellent for flavour but, like most dried mushrooms, they have little in the way of interesting texture. They are also supposed to be mildly poisonous unless boiled, so take care to do this.

## Cooking method

> **The milder the temperature at which the mousses are cooked** the better will be their texture, so if you have the time and inclination, an extra 10 minutes at a gentler heat will do nothing but good. In any case, if the mousses get too hot they will soufflé and become stringy.

> **The cooking time for the celeriac will depend on the size** of the pieces you cut. Test the vegetables with a sharp knife to be sure. If they are too well-cooked, the mousse will be sloppy.

For oils and vinegars for dressings see **63**

# Dressings

**Achieving harmony between acid and alkaline is the main objective of salad dressing.** The amount of dressing used is small in proportion to the quantity of vegetables or leaves – much smaller than, say, the ratio of gravy to meat in a roast. The strength of flavouring and seasoning has to take this into account. You can use oil alone to dress a salad, or even vinegar alone if it is aromatic, for instance sherry or balsamic, but you'll need to season the salad with a touch of salt too.

## Oils

**The staple dietary fat of the Mediterranean has been olive oil for thousands of years,** just as our's has been butter and animal fat for most of the time our ancestors shivered through the British winters. Olive oil's popularity here is a recent development, spurred on by a general admiration for the Mediterranean diet on health grounds. Olive oil evidently lowers cholesterol levels as well as tasting good. This only holds true of the oil in its natural state I'm afraid, and it has no advantages in any cooking that involves heat.

Olive oils come in three main styles. First, there's Italian extra virgin, cold-pressed, which is the most expensive, usually coming in sculpted bottles with designer labels. It is annoying that these are so good, for their shameless niche marketing and hefty pricing can give the impression of a purchase from the fashion department rather than the food counter. Tuscan and Ligurian oils have the greatest following, with production centring on the town of Lucca. The oils are thick, alkaline, green and almost peppery. Without a doubt they are the aristocrats of olive oil.

The second style are the fruitier, softer golden yellow oils from southern France, which are also first-rate, and tend to be fruity and powerful. Third are Greek and Spanish olive oils, which are cheaper and have been greasy and dull; they are improving year by year, but still do not reach the heights of the French and Italian products.

Characteristics such as 'fruity' or 'peppery' aside, you are looking for low acidity. 'Extra virgin' mean that the oil must be within 0.2 per cent acidity, in contrast to 1.5 per cent for the standard product. The way to test and compare these products is by dipping small pieces of plain bread into them or smearing a little on the back of your hand for sniffing and tasting like fine wine. Olive oils that can only claim to be refined will taste of little and will generally be a waste of money for salad dressings – money that would be better spent on, say, better groundnut oil.

Of course, just because top-notch olive oils are good doesn't mean that they are good for everything. A mayonnaise made exclusively from olive oil would taste strong but not pleasant – use them sparingly and specifically.

Other oils often used for salad dressings include walnut, hazelnut, almond, sunflower, sesame and groundnut. What you're looking for is a fresh-tasting combination of ingredients. For instance, Oriental salads work well with sesame oil as the ingredients can cope with its strength of flavour.

## Vinegars

**Vinegar is cheap, so you can be generous with quality.** Only use wine vinegars – malt vinegar is made from beer and only good for chips, and unbrewed vinegar is factory rubbish.

Don't waste money on Champagne vinegars and the like; instead buy a good sherry vinegar that tastes of oak and works wonderfully with walnut oil or even by itself. Balsamics are alleged to come from Modena and are soft and sweet, good with strawberries or on their own. They are made on the solera system, famed for its use for sherry, with batches being transferred from aromatic wood barrel to smaller aromatic wood barrels over 20 to 30 years in warm lofts, where a big proportion evaporates as time goes by. In Italy they are rare and expensive, so a certain amount of caution may be in order when they are sold cheaply.

For French dressing see **64**    For mayonnaise see **66**    For salad cream see **68**    For Caesar dressing see **230**

# Basic dressings

**The salad ingredients to be dressed will affect the type of dressing needed.** A salad with lots of bitter endives, or one that has some hot element, can take a powerful oil such as walnut, or a strong vinegar such as sherry, whereas a salad composed of more delicate leaves might be swamped by the same combination.

In order to distribute the seasonings evenly, dressings should be whisked into an emulsion, albeit a temporary one, before use. The alternative is that the first portion of salad gets only oil and the last only salt and vinegar. Also, any salad leaves to be dressed should be first washed and then dried. Residual water will otherwise dilute the dressing beyond recognition.

The tossing of salad does not indicate any acrobatic movement or require dexterity, as in the tossing of pancakes. Just lift the salad leaves and dressing two or three times with two spoons so that the dressing may be evenly distributed. Many salads, especially leaf salads, will droop after more than a few minutes contact with the oil and vinegar. Dress and toss salads at the last moment.

# French dressings

**The classic French dressing vinaigrette calls for mustard as well as salt and pepper.** You can form this into an emulsion by adding the vinegar to the mustard first, turning it into a slack liquid, then slowly incorporating the oil, whisking all the time. The alternative is to measure tried-and-tested quantities and whisk or blend them together just before the salad is to be tossed and served. The resulting mixture will soon separate back into a base of vinegar and seasonings under a pool of oil and will need further whisking before being used again.

Serves 4

1 tsp Dijon mustard
1 tbsp white wine vinegar
3 tbsp olive oil
salt and pepper

1   Stir the mustard and vinegar together.
2   Incorporate the oil, drop by drop, whisking constantly.
3   Season with salt and pepper and whisk again.

Variations
> **French dressing** is an ideal vehicle for chopped fresh herbs. Tarragon, chives, marjoram and parsley work particularly well.
> **A few strands of thyme and some toasted and chopped pine nuts** will convert the dressing into something more substantial that can be used in a salad with roast game or hot chicken livers.
> **The addition of chopped shallot,** in the ratio of 1 tbsp shallot to French dressing, some capers and chopped parsley, will create a dressing to partner warm offal dishes such as brains or sweetbreads.
> **One fat or two small cloves of garlic** can be chopped then crushed to a pulp and added to the mustard at the start of the method with a sprinkling of salt.

Ingredients
> **The main players in a dressing are usually oil and vinegar.** The quality of these two ingredients and the proportion of one to the other are what counts. More expensive is not necessarily better; a mixture of walnut or extra virgin olive oil with mustard and, say, raspberry vinegar will not show off any ingredient to its best.

Technique
> **If the dressing is to be made in any quantity it keeps well.** You may add an egg yolk for every 500ml of dressing to be made – this will not be enough to change the nature of the dressing to mayonnaise, but it will help to hold the emulsion together reasonably permanently. The dressing with this method may seem a little thick, and can be easily adjusted by adding a little white wine or water.

For oils and vinegars for dressings see **63**

# Mayonnaise

As with any dressing, the quality and variety of mayonnaise's constituents – oil and vinegar – will make more difference than any cute variation achieved through adding herbs or gherkins to the finished article. For instance, the substitution of a little walnut oil for some of the groundnut called for in the recipe will change the style of the mayonnaise quite appreciably, as would the use of sherry vinegar rather than the plain white wine variety.

**Serves 4**
3 medium egg yolks
1 tsp Dijon mustard
2 tbsp white wine vinegar or lemon juice
300ml groundnut or sunflower oil
salt and pepper
a dash of Worcestershire sauce

1   Separate the eggs, putting the yolks in a bowl. Add the mustard to the yolks, then whisk in the vinegar or lemon juice.
2   Whisk in the oil – start slowly, adding in droplets, then, as a stable emulsion forms, you may add the oil more quickly.
3   Season the mayonnaise with salt, pepper and a dash of Worcestershire sauce.

## Variations

> **Tartare sauce** is made by adding chopped gherkin, capers and parsley.
> **Cocktail sauce** – the sweetish pink gunk that coats prawn cocktails – is made by adding tomato ketchup and a little extra Worcestershire sauce. Also called Sauce Marie Rose by persons or places wishing to impress.
> **Herb mayonnaise** – liquidized green herbs stirred into the basic mix. Obviously a tarragon purée will instil a different taste to basil or parsley.

## Ingredients

> **Olive oil used alone does not make good mayonnaise,** but it can substitute for half the groundnut or sunflower oil should you wish.

## Technique

> **Curdled mayonnaise** can usually be rectified by whisking in some warm water or vinegar.
> **The ingredients for mayonnaise, especially oil, are affected by temperature.** Cold ingredients emulsify less easily, so try to have all the ingredients at room temperature.
> **Most problems with mayonnaise come from over-thickening the emulsion.** Once you have measured the relative quantities of oil and vinegar, stick to them. Alter the ratio only if you feel the mayonnaise should be more or less sharp. Tap water will thin the mayonnaise without altering the flavour if that is all that's needed.

For oils and vinegars for dressings see **63**    For stocks and sauces see **209**

# Salad cream

**Salad cream is one of the great culinary dressings,** buts its prestige has been lowered by the commercial product that was popular in the post-war era. It's sweeter and more delicate than mayonnaise, but it shouldn't be as sweet as the salad cream you'll remember.

**Serves 4**

2 hard-boiled eggs
1 tsp water
salt and pepper
a pinch of cayenne pepper
1 tsp Dijon mustard (or English if
 you prefer)
1 tsp caster sugar
150ml double cream
juice of 1 lemon

1   Separate the hard-boiled eggs into whites and yolks. Chop the whites and keep to one side to mix into the dressing at the end.
2   Make a paste of the yolks with the water, and some salt, pepper, the cayenne, mustard and sugar.
3   Incorporate the cream by trickling it on to the paste while stirring or whisking continuously.
4   Add the lemon juice. Test the seasonings and add more salt or cayenne if needed.
5   Mix in the chopped egg whites.

### Variations

> **The variations for salad cream are similar to those for mayonnaise.** Herbs or anchovy essence can be added if one or other suits the occasion. You can make the dressing sharper or sweeter by adjusting the amounts of lemon and sugar used.

### Technique

> **Salad cream doesn't keep well,** so only make what is needed.
> **The process of acidulating cream by adding lemon juice stiffens and thickens the cream.** As the relative juiciness of a lemon varies from season to season, add half first, then taste the dressing before adding more in case it isn't necessary.
> **Like any dressing, salad cream is best tossed with the other ingredients of a salad** so that everything can be coated equally, although it does look attractive in a bowl or sauceboat.

# Cheese dressings

**Cheese and lettuces partner each other perfectly.** It is a question of personal preference whether the cheese is blended into the dressing or acts as an ingredient among the leaves.

Blue cheese makes the most distinctive dressing but, again, may be successfully moulded into dumpling shapes with the aid of two spoons and distributed between the salad leaves (see recipe for green salad with Stilton quenelles on page 60 for an example of this).

For oils and vinegars for dressings see **63**

# Fruit

**Few of the fruits available to us now are native.** Apples and pears are European in origin, as are cherries and most soft berry fruits, but the majority of the rest arrived either with the Romans or much later, as a result of world travel for spices and trade. The citrus family was an early import, and originated in the Far East. In fact '*citron*', a not very juicy ancestor of the lemon, was known and imported to Rome and Greece in Classical times, but never really caught on, and it wasn't until the Middle Ages that oranges and lemons were appreciated for the possibilities of their juice as well as of their skin. Grapefruit was an 18th-century hybrid with plenty more – tangelos and the like – to follow.

The main difference between the handling and storage of fruit and that of vegetables is the ripening process. Most vegetables deteriorate after harvesting, becoming starchier and less sweet. Fruit works in reverse: enzymes convert starch back into sugar as they mature and after they are picked. Avocados, for instance, are stored by being left on the tree, where they will never ripen and will only soften once harvested. The only purpose of fruit, unlike any other foodstuff, is to be eaten, and its evolution has been to that end, so it is naturally sweet and approachable and the constraints of the supply chain, which lessens the quality of so much else, regularly work in our favour.

The factors – seasonality, freshness, storage – that affect fruit are similar to those that affect vegetables, and of course the two are bought side-by-side in greengrocers (see page 46).

Fruit's use in our diet is largely unaffected by the cook's art, because it will be eaten in its natural state. The use of fruit as an ingredient in cooked dishes is covered in the pastry and preserving sections of this book, but there is one aspect that is an extension of the ripening process – the poaching or baking whole of fruits such as pears and peaches.

# Pears poached in red wine

**Pears ripen from the inside outwards and are difficult to gauge for readiness to eat.** Some varieties do suit poaching, and this gives an opportunity to add other flavours.

### Serves 4

100g granulated sugar

375ml red wine

2 cinnamon sticks

1 vanilla pod, split

4 large or 8 small William pears

cinnamon, caramel or vanilla ice-cream, to serve

1   In a saucepan that is small enough to ensure the liquid covers the pears, heat the sugar, red wine and spices together slowly so that the sugar melts properly.

2   Peel the pears and put these into the wine syrup. Cover with a lid and poach until done – this normally takes around 20 minutes, but will vary.

3   Leave the pears to cool in the wine syrup and serve with the syrup and an ice-cream that suits the fruit, perhaps cinnamon, caramel or vanilla.

### Ingredients

> **The difference between varieties of pears is significant** and new strains come on to the market regularly. Just when you had grasped the plus and minus points of Conference pears versus Doyenne de Comice, another differently named hybrid of one or the other will appear. Williams are about the best for cooking; they don't disintegrate and have a distinct and fine flavour both cooked and raw.

### Cooking method

> **The cooking times will vary** according to the size of the pears and their ripeness. Fairly hard pears will still be OK to use, but will need longer cooking.

> **The size and shape of pan used to cook the pears is important.** If the pan is too large, the wine will only reach halfway up the pears. You will be lucky to find a saucepan that is exactly right, so use a lid so that steam from the bubbling liquid cooks those parts of the pears not covered, and turn the pears over halfway through cooking so that the flavour of the wine and spices reaches every part of the fruit.

For fruit see **69**    For poaching and steaming vegetables and fruit see **174**

# Chilled summer fruit soup with pistachio and meringues

**Fruit soups are a Middle European favourite.** In Austria and Hungary they serve cherry soup as a starter, the sweetness of the ripe cherries being offset by lemon juice and soured cream. Of course there is no reason why such soups should not serve as puddings, but some texture other than that of the soup itself is called for if the dish is to be a real success. This can be a scattering of soft red fruit on the soup itself or some crisp biscuit accompaniment – macaroons or shortbread perhaps. This recipe takes no chances by offering both. As with standard soups, fruit-based recipes can be made for consumption hot or cold, but not necessarily both, as a warm soup will need less sweetening than one designed to be served chilled.

The meringue recipe will make more than you need to accompany four servings of fruit soup, but it is really not worth the effort to make tiny quantities. Any leftovers will keep for weeks provided they are stored in an airtight tin.

**Serves 4**

150g raspberries
150g strawberries
100ml dry white wine
100ml water
100g caster sugar
1 tbsp lemon juice

**For the meringues:**

4 medium egg whites
125g caster sugar
125g icing sugar
1 tbsp fresh pistachio nuts

**To serve:**

100g alpine strawberries
100g raspberries
1 peach, chopped
100g blueberries

1   Preheat the oven for the meringue to the lowest temperature you can manage – 125°C/Gas mark ½ – the idea being to dry out the meringue as slowly as possible.

2   Whisk the egg whites until they form peaks, then whisk in the caster sugar a little at a time. Keep whisking until the meringue is shiny and smooth – approximately 10 minutes by hand, less by machine. Sift in the icing sugar, folding it into the meringue mixture.

3   Pipe or spoon the meringue on to a baking tray covered with non-stick baking parchment. The objective is to have small biscuits, a mouthful at a time – 2-3cm in diameter would be fine. Put a pistachio on each meringue.

4   Bake in the preheated oven. The cooking time will depend on the size and thickness you have made the meringues, but small ones should be ready in 1½ hours. Test them by checking that they are dry both on top and underneath.

5   Make the soup base by liquidizing the raspberries, strawberries, wine, water, caster sugar and lemon juice. Refrigerate the result.

6   Serve with the remaining fruit scattered on top and the pistachio meringues on the side.

**Ingredients**

> **Pistachios are sold salted as well as fresh, so be careful.** They should be a yellow-green colour and may still be in their skins. The skins are easily removed by dropping the pistachios into boiling water, draining them, then rubbing them in a napkin or kitchen towel.

> **Ripe summer fruit is sweeter than** anything available early or late. If you are making this soup in October rather than August you may need to sweeten it more.

**Technique**

> **Separate each egg white into a small bowl or saucer,** adding the whites to the mixing bowl once you are sure that there is no trace of yolk. The whites will not whisk into peaks if there is the slightest imperfection. Similarly, check the bowl in advance for traces of water or washing-up liquid.

> **Taste the soup after chilling as well as before.** Cooling mutes flavour and sweetness, so be prepared to add a touch more sugar or lemon. Aim for a fresh taste rather than a very sweet one.

For buying fruit see **69**

# Figs with orange and Banyuls sabayon

**Fresh figs are available for most of the year and are at their best in summer and early autumn.** In fact the fig is a bizarre specimen botanically, as it is the seeds that are the fruits, with around 1500 of these individual fruits clustering together to make a single fig. While this is a good fact for the next game of trivial pursuits, it is of little consequence in the kitchen, where cultivated figs have featured for around 5000 years and were particularly popular in Ancient Rome in dried form as a sweetener for meat dishes. Lemons, oranges and spices all blend well with figs' rich flavour. This recipe calls for warm figs and warm sabayon, but could be adapted as a cold dish by chilling the sabayon in its serving dishes and then placing the cooled figs on top. Sabayon and zabaglione are the same thing, the first being a French word and the latter an Italian one, but both refer to egg yolk and booze whisked over heat until you have a smooth ribbon-like consistency. Zabaglione is traditionally whisked with the Sicilian sweet wine marsala. There doesn't seem to be an English word to cover the method, so you can take your pick.

Serves 4

8 figs

75g caster sugar

juice and zest of 1 orange

For the sabayon:

4 egg yolks

125ml Banyuls

65g caster sugar

a pinch of ground cinnamon

a few drops of lemon juice

1   Preheat the oven to 190°C/Gas mark 5. Cut a cross in the top of each fig so that it is opened but not sliced right through. Place in a shallow ovenproof dish and sprinkle with the caster sugar and orange zest and juice. Bake until the figs are soft (about 20 minutes).

2   Meanwhile, heat a saucepan half filled with water so that it is quite warm (around 90°C), but in no danger of boiling. Mix the egg yolks, Banyuls and sugar together in a heatproof mixing bowl (stainless steel is best). Stand the mixing bowl in the hot water and whisk until the sabayon is cooked. This will take 10 minutes of hard whisking and the mixture should have risen to double its size and have the consistency of a light but thick custard. Test the sabayon for flavour and whisk in a pinch of cinnamon and, if needed, a couple of drops of lemon juice.

3   Spoon the sabayon on to warmed plates and place the baked figs on top.

## Ingredients

> **Banyuls is a moderately sweet red wine** from the south-western corner of France, next to Spain.

## Technique

> **Sabayon will become flat if it is kept warm for too long** after it has been made and is impossible to reheat, so make it no more than 10 minutes ahead of time.

> **The object of the whisking while making sabayon is to incorporate as much air as possible** and not just to prevent the egg yolk from sticking to the side of the bowl as it cooks. A lifting motion as you whisk will produce the best result.

For sabayon technique see **172**

# Fish

**There is more variety in fish than meat. The vast range of edible species runs from oily mackerel to dry-fleshed pike,** with 50 types in-between. That's before you consider the octopus and shellfish families, smoked fish such as kippers and grocery items such as preserved anchovies and sardines.

Most fish are still free range, wild creatures that have to be tracked down and caught rather than farmed like a cash crop. So your main consideration at the fishmonger's slab will be what's in peak condition.

Unsurprisingly, fish is expensive. Apart from being an ever-scarcer resource, it doesn't keep, neither improving with age like some meats nor freezing well. The resulting high cost, in comparison to some processed meat produce, has already seen out the fishmonger from most shopping centres. Prices are not purely dictated by supply and demand here, or else fish would be cheaper, but by market prices across Europe. Trawlers that have been fishing off the coast of Spain or Iceland can as easily unload at Rotterdam or Zeebrugge, if that is where their catch will fetch the best price. Similarly, quayside dealers at Brixham can tell you what is being paid for Turbot in Billingsgate in an instant, and the price of sea-bass in Milan a fraction later. Bargains are rare.

This chapter covers the details of how to buy, prepare and cook flat fish, round fish and shellfish, and explains which types of fish suit which cooking methods and what types of sauce best suit fish cooked in a variety of ways.

# Buying fish

**The most sensible approach for the cook is to choose a particular type of fish,** such as white fish or crustacea, and to shop flexibly within that category. With fish dishes that call for anything other than the most plentiful varieties, strict adherence to the species named in a recipe can be frustrating. Even commonplace fish may not represent decent value on the day.

For instance, should the instructions call for herring and your shop has none, you must decide whether you consider that particular fish to be central to the success of the dish or whether an alternative is possible. Of course, if the flavour of herring is essential then only herring will do, but if you're using herring on account of its oily texture and relatively cheap price, then mackerel may fit the bill just as well. Really this is a question of personal preference – usually the fish are interchangeable in a recipe unless you have a particular liking for a certain fish.

Generally, supermarkets are little help when it comes to buying fish. They have not yet come to terms with the specific problems of selling fish; it seems beyond their understanding that neither prices nor supply can be guaranteed and that you must decide on a daily basis what is good value and how long the fish will keep for. At the moment, many supermarkets stick with a limited range of popular fish such as farmed salmon and frozen prawns.

So, if we assume that little or no advice worth having will come from the sales person, then we must rely on the appearance of the fish to decide what's best. There are comments in the 'ingredients' sections of each recipe specific to selecting whatever fish is being used, but in general the advice boils down to searching out fish with firm flesh and sparkling shiny skin and avoiding limp, lifeless or dry-looking specimens.

Fish that has spent too long in the freezer will look tired and defeated, as if it has played on the losing side of a football match. Worse, any fish that have been frozen without first being carefully wrapped will probably be affected by freezer burn; this leaves tell-tale patches of whitened and dry flesh that unhappily translate into a dry, almost inedible texture when cooked. Most fish you buy will probably have been frozen, even if it is advertised as 'fresh'. Shellfish is usually sold either live or frozen, and live is best.

# Storing fish

**The best advice is to buy what fish you need on the day that you need it.** If this isn't practical, there are a few pitfalls to avoid.

First, raw or smoked fish will taint the flavour of sensitive products such as eggs or butter if the ingredients are stored close by in the fridge, so put as much distance between them as possible and wrap the fish well.

Second, always store uncooked fish or meat underneath, rather than above, any foods that are either already cooked or else to be eaten raw – drips from the juices of raw fish or meat in your leftover curry or custard can lead to problems for the stomach, not just the palate. While freezing isn't best advised for fish, it is better to freeze it double-wrapped than to keep it in the fridge for too long (usually more than 24 hours).

Third, the last water a fish should see before cooking is the stream or ocean from which it came. Water dries out the flesh, leaving it less tender. While you are unlikely to leave the fish in a sinkful of water, you may be inclined to pack ice cubes around it, which melt, or leave it in the juices that seep out from it during any prolonged storage in the fridge. Neither is a good idea. If the fish needs rinsing after being gutted or unpacked, pat it dry immediately with some kitchen towel.

The least and shortest contact with water is important, for the same reasons, while preparing and cleaning fish. The only exception would naturally be live creatures such as mussels.

# Cooking fish

**One or two factors affect fish, no matter which cooking method is used.** First, overcooking is the enemy. Even fish that is not technically cooked – marinated fish such as gravad lax or ceviche – will suffer if left for too long in the salt, lime juice, or whatever.

Fish is delicate; clumsy handling and sledgehammer cooking techniques are not appropriate. One of the most celebrated fish dishes, the bouillabaisse of Marseilles, illustrates the problem – there's a dozen different fish overcooking together to produce a wonderful flavour for the soup but little benefit for any of the ingredients.

Any delicate, or low temperature, cooking method will suit fish. But when deciding what to serve with it you must take the cooking method into account. Steamed, poached or baked fish need some sauce if they are not to taste bland, while fried fish can take lemon juice, vinegar, or some sharp relish such as tartare sauce.

Test whether the fish is cooked by pressing your finger gently against the thickest part in order to gauge doneness. If there is the feeling of springiness, the impression of a rubber ball at the centre, then it needs to continue cooking. While developing reliability on such matters, you may wish to test your judgement by cutting into a corner of the fish and comparing the reality of how cooked it is with the impression you had formed by pressing it. With a little practice the two impressions will be identical.

If you are cooking fish on the bone, you will discover that the flesh will part company with the bones only when it is completely done. Should you wish to deliberately undercook a piece of fish (some fish, such as salmon and tuna, is fine at a medium-rare stage), take it off the bone first.

# Changing the texture of fish through preparation

In most recipes, changing the texture of fish through the preparation for cooking isn't a great idea unless it's done for some specific purpose. The effects of the preparation must give you more, in terms of flavour and texture, than you are losing by not serving the fish in its original state. But there are instances where changing the texture is a good idea – when the texture isn't good, where there are too many small bones to contend with (as with pike), or where the fish in a dish are all different sizes and awkward to portion for equal cooking. Fish such as pike are very dry and have no real advantages in their original state, and it's typical of the canny French that they should change the texture of pike for the brilliant pike quenelles of the Loire.

## Whiting and scallop mousseline

Fish mousses that are cooked in a ramekin rather than spooned into quenelles are a little easier to achieve. The mixture will need a touch less egg white to bind it and be less inclined to disintegrate if the proportions aren't absolutely right. This means that fish whose texture doesn't normally lend itself to the treatment can be used. Fish with a pronounced and individual flavour such as scallops can be mixed with drier-fleshed specimens such as whiting or sole – if you're feeling rich – to make a stylish first course or light meal.

### Serves 4

250g whiting fillet
250g white scallop meat
1 medium egg and 2 egg whites
salt and pepper
1 tbsp Irish whiskey or Armagnac
250ml double cream

1  Preheat the oven to 150°C/Gas mark 2.
2  Cut the fish into small dice, then blend in a food processor. Add the egg, then the extra whites one at a time, processing the mixture all the time. Season, then blend in the whiskey. Try to keep all the ingredients as cold as possible.
3  Blend in the cream, then taste for seasoning.
4  Divide the mixture into ramekin dishes and cover each with a circle of oiled greaseproof paper or butter wrapper. Place the ramekins in a roasting tray half filled with warm water and bake for around 20 minutes, until a knife or skewer inserted into the ramekin comes out clean.
5  Serve with a beurre blanc or hollandaise sauce mixed with chopped fresh herbs or infused with saffron.

### Technique

> **Egg whites strengthen the mousseline and cream lightens it.** The balance between these two factors and the firmness of the texture of the fish used is key to the success of the dish.
> **Anything to which cream and egg white are added will become delicate and restrained in flavour.** This can tend toward blandness, so be bold with the salt and pepper.

> **Scallops will absorb water if left to soak,** so it is wise to check the mixture before cooking as any alteration in the fish's texture will affect the ratio of egg white to cream needed to produce a firm, but not rubbery, mousse. Test the mixture by poaching a teaspoonful: If it tends to come apart then more egg white will be needed; if it is too firm a little more cream can be added.

For hollandaise sauce see **226**    For buerre blanc sauce see **228**

# Fish sausage with sorrel and tomato sauce

**All the ingredients must be as cold as possible for the fish mousse.** Remember that prolonged whizzing in a food processor or blender will also heat the mousse, so try to process as little as possible to achieve the right consistency. If necessary, process in two or three stages with a visit to the fridge or above iced water for the mixture between times

### Serves 4
500g fillets of dry-fleshed fish,
    such as pike, turbot, sole or monk
3 large egg whites
150ml double cream
salt and pepper
grated nutmeg
30g butter

### For the sauce:
500g sorrel leaves
50ml white wine
20ml crème fraîche
50g unsalted butter
a few drops of Tabasco
2 tomatoes, skinned, deseeded and diced

1 Cut the fillets of fish into as small pieces as you can manage. Place the fish in a food processor and purée finely. Add the egg whites one at a time, processing them into the mixture individually and making sure they are fully incorporated.

2 Push the mixture through a sieve into a bowl set over iced water. Discard the debris from the sieve and beat half the cream into the purée. Leave the purée to firm up over the iced water for 30 minutes, then whisk in the remaining cream and some salt, nutmeg and pepper.

3 Pipe the mousse into sausages – four large ones or eight small ones, as suits your taste – along strips of clingfilm. Wrap the clingfilm around the mousse and twist the edges so that the sausages look like diminutive Christmas crackers, then refrigerate until quite cold (for at least 30 minutes).

4 Warm a large pan of water – you want a temperature just below simmering – and drop the sausages into it. They will take around 20 minutes to cook and the water should at no time come to the boil; if the water boils, the egg white in the sausages will soufflé up, giving a poor texture to the dish. You can get to this stage in advance, and drop the sausages into iced water to stop them cooking, but you will need to reheat them in the same sort of temperature water before serving.

5 Make the sauce by heating the sorrel in half the unsalted butter and then adding the wine. Boil and then add the crème fraîche and remaining unsalted butter. Whisk until thick, then add a few drops of Tabasco, some salt and the diced tomato.

6 Heat a frying pan with the salted butter. When the butter is foaming, add the warm, unwrapped sausages and let them colour on all sides. Drain on to kitchen paper and serve each on a tablespoon of sorrel and tomato sauce. Depending on the size of your frying pan you may have to do this in two stages.

### Ingredients
> **Sorrel will discolour on contact with heat.** Don't worry; you are using it for its gooseberry-like astringency, not for its colour.

### Technique
> **The amount of egg white you need will vary according to the firmness of the fish.** Egg white strengthens the mousse and cream makes it lighter and more delicate. The firmer the fish, the less egg white you will need. Pike, sole and turbot are densely textured, but salmon will need a touch more. You can test the mixture by poaching a teaspoonful in simmering salted water.

# Flat fish and round fish
## Skinning and filleting a flat fish

If you wish to skin the fish before filleting it, make a cut across the tail, beneath the point at which the flesh ends, in order to sever the skin; do not cut the tail off. Raise a corner of the skin away from the bone, grasp it tightly between the thumb and forefinger, then pull the skin back and away from the flesh; with luck it will come away in one movement. As you pull the skin with your right hand, keep the fish firmly in place by holding the carcass with your left. Repeat on the other side.

To fillet the fish, move your finger along the centre of each side of the fish, from head to tail; the ridge of bone dividing the fish into two fillets per side will feel quite obvious.

1-2 On one side, cut downwards along this line, sliding the knife under the fillets and across to the far side of the fish.

3 The framework of spinal bones at the centre will keep you from penetrating too deeply, so position your knife angled slightly downwards, away from the expensive fish flesh.

4 Work from head to tail, easing the fillets off the bone.

5 Do not worry about taking a long time; concentrate on producing cleanly cut fillets. As with all such operations, practice will crank up your speed.

# Gutting and filleting a round fish

1 To gut the fish, begin by cutting off anything that protrudes from it, such as the fins, but not the head and the tail. If your fish needs scaling, just scrape the knife at right angles to it, from tail to head. You will find that the scales will fly all over the place. Slit the belly and remove the innards. This is not a job for the squeamish, and on large fish such as salmon or bass it will be quite a messy procedure. Use a little salt to dislodge any blood that insists on sticking to the backbone ofthe fish. Rinse in cold water, then dry thoroughly with a napkin or kitchen roll.

2 To fillet the fish, lay it on its side, then cut the skin along the spinal edge.

3 Hold the fish steady with the flat of your hand, then carefully cut away the fillet.

4 Lift out the skeleton of the spinal bone in one piece. Repeat on the other side of the fish.

5 Use tweezers to pull out the line of small bones that run the length of each fillet.

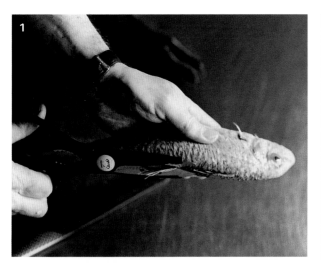

# Papillote of sea-bass with garlic butter

**The most arcane way of using the oven is to cook *en papillote*.** This requires the fish and any other ingredients to be sealed in a foil parcel. The pressure builds up inside the parcel, making it puff up like a balloon, and swiftly cooks the contents. It is a method that appealed to the sense of theatre of swish restaurants in the 1970s because it gives the impression of a successful conjuring trick: when the *papillote* is brought to the table it is pierced and all the trapped aroma of cooked fish and herbs escape.

Serves 4

a little olive oil, for frying, plus extra
   for oiling
2 large cloves garlic
60g unsalted butter, softened
1 shallot, finely chopped
1 tbsp chopped parsley
juice of ½ lemon
4 x 150g sea-bass fillets
salt and pepper

1   Preheat the oven to 200°C/Gas mark 6.
2   Unravel a long sheet of aluminium foil, say 80cm long, and brush the surface of the side facing you lightly with oil – it doesn't matter which side. Fold it back so that the oil side folds in on itself, and you have the top and bottom of your *papillote* ready-joined at one side. Fold back 2cm of each side and press into a well-sealed join. You now have a bag in which to put the fish and flavouring before folding the remaining edge to seal it.
3   Crush the garlic and mix it thoroughly with the butter, shallot, parsley and a few drops of the lemon juice.
4   Season the sea-bass with salt and pepper, and place each piece in an individual *papillote* along with a knob of the garlic butter.
5   Seal the papillote by folding the edges of the opening together in the same way as the sides. Place the *papillote* on an oiled baking tray and bake for 15 minutes. Lift out the tray.
6   Serve the accompanying salad or vegetable, then put the baking tray on to a hot gas or electric ring. Move the tray to and fro a couple of times as the intense heat causes the *papill*ote to puff out. Burst the *papillote* somewhere where the diners can enjoy the aroma.

## Ingredients

> **There are many variations you could use,** but only put ingredients that will cook simultaneously into a *papillote*. Dublin Bay prawns would be fine with salmon or, of course, on their own. Any combination of herbs can substitute for the parsley, though none will have the same impact in any mixture that contains garlic.

## Technique

> **The foil parcel must be buttered or oiled on the inside,** as must the baking tray on which it sits when in the oven, so the bag can easily move around.
> ***Papillotes* are traditionally made in a crescent shape,** but this is ornamental rather than essential; a square will do fine. Be generous with the size, whatever shape you use: there must be room for the hot air and vapour to expand inside.

## Cooking method

> **There is no way of checking the progress of the cooking once the ingredients are wrapped.** Experience will guide you eventually but, in the short term, timing and common sense will help. Usually, the fish is not cooked unless the bag is fully puffed up.
> **Do not worry if the parcel fails to puff up** – unless, of course, there is a leak in one of the sealed edges, in which case a little mending will be in order. If the bag is split, you'll need to start again. Then heat a touch of oil in a roasting tray, put the *papillote* into it and move it back and forth so the *papillote* slides to and fro over the heat and puffs up.

For gutting and filleting fish see **80-1**    For roasting fish see **184**

# John Dory with coriander

**This is a Lebanese dish,** with flavours that typify eastern Mediterranean and North African cooking. The fish is braised and served in its own sauce like stew.

### Serves 4

1.5kg John Dory, filleted

salt and pepper

sunflower oil, for frying

150ml olive oil

4 shallots, finely chopped

8 large cloves garlic, finely chopped

1 tsp ground coriander

1/2 small chilli, deseeded
    and finely chopped

1 tsp ground cumin

juice of 3 lemons

1 bunch fresh coriander, leaves only,
    washed and dried on kitchen paper

1   Salt the fillets, then heat enough sunflower oil to deep-fry them. When the oil is hot, fry the fillets for a minute to seal them and then lift out from the pan.

2   In a separate pan, heat the olive oil. Fry the shallots in the oil until they start to colour, then add the garlic and continue cooking for another minute. Add the ground coriander, chilli and cumin, then pour in the lemon juice and bring to the boil.

3   Add the fish fillets and season with salt and pepper. Simmer for 5 minutes, or until the fish is cooked and the sauce thickened. Add the coriander leaves and serve.

### Ingredients

> **John Dory is about 50 per cent bone and head,** so you can expect around 350-400g of fillet per person from each fish. They are awkward to fillet – they have only one fillet on each side, but they have very sharp bones should your fingers slip. Have the fishmonger do the job for you if possible.

> **The recipe is powerfully flavoured with lemon and garlic,** but can be toned down if this prospect is a worry.

For deepfrying fish see **190**

# Sole fillets in breadcrumbs with tomato béarnaise sauce

**Fresh breadcrumbs suit grilled fish.** You have to think in terms of grilled breadcrumb-based stuffings – gremolata and the like – rather than the tartrazine-coloured crumbs that cover deep-fried specimens. The crumbs stick to the fish because the fillets have been passed through melted butter or a mixture of oils, and these melt away during cooking, moistening the fish in the process.

### Serves 4

3 x 500g Dover sole, filleted

salt and pepper

40g butter, melted but not clarified

1 small white loaf, made into breadcrumbs

### For the tomato béarnaise sauce:

200g butter

1 tbsp white wine vinegar

1 tbsp finely chopped shallot

1 tbsp chopped fresh tarragon

25ml white wine

3 egg yolks

1 tbsp tomato passata

1 tomato, skinned, deseeded
    and diced

1-2 drops of Tabasco

salt and pepper

1 tsp lemon juice

1 Season the fish fillets and then pass them through the melted butter and fresh breadcrumbs.

2 For the sauce, clarify the butter by heating it to boiling point and then allowing the oil to rise to the top, separating it from the salt and other liquid that sinks to the bottom. The oil is the part you use. Heat the vinegar, shallot and tarragon together, then mix with the white wine.

3 Add the egg yolks to the vinegar mixture and whisk over hot water until the mixture thickens. Remove from the direct heat and whisk in the clarified butter. Do this slowly at first, trickling the butter in a drop at a time. Add the tomato passata and the diced fresh tomato at the end, then adjust the balance by adding Tabasco, salt, pepper and lemon juice to taste.

4 The grilling calls for what chefs know as a salamander, an overhead grill – the sort you toast welsh rarebit under rather than a barbecue-style arrangement that you might use to cook steaks. Grill the fish fillets for around 5 minutes on each side and then serve with the tomato béarnaise sauce.

### Ingredients

> **For the crumbs, first cut off and discard the loaf's crust.**
Small dice of the remainder in a food processor will make perfect fresh breadcrumbs in seconds.

### Cooking method

> **All the points for hollandaise sauce apply** (page 226). If the sauce gets too thick or has too much butter, it can be rectified by adding more wine or warm water.

> **If you have a stainless-steel bowl with rounded edges** to make the béarnaise sauce, so much the better. Otherwise use a saucepan suspended in hot water and try not to let too much water escape into the egg mixture.

For skinning and filleting flat fish see **80**     For hollandaise sauce technique see **226**     For grilling and frying fish see **184**

# Hot-smoked monkfish

**You need no special equipment for this: a wok, some kitchen foil and a wire rack or trivet – the sort you might use for steaming – are all that's needed.** The method is in fact very similar to steaming, but with pressure from the hot smoke instead of water cooking the fish and flavouring it at the same time. Smoke taints food. It is the controlled aspect of this that gives interest, just as the smoke from a charcoal grill adds an extra dimension to whatever is being barbecued.

**Serves 4**
4 x 150g monkfish fillet
1 tbsp grapefruit juice
1 tbsp light sesame oil
salt and pepper
2 tbsp granulated sugar
3 tbsp uncooked rice
3 tbsp black China tea

1   Brush the monkfish with the grapefruit juice and sesame oil, then season with salt and pepper
2   Line the bottom of the wok with a folded square of kitchen foil. Put the sugar, rice and tea on to this.
3   Place the fish on a wire rack above the tea mixture, season, then seal with a tight-fitting lid or more foil.
4   Cook on a high heat for 5 minutes. The dry mixture will produce hot smoke to cook the fish.
5   Switch off the heat, but leave the fish undisturbed for another 20 minutes, then lift out the warm smoked monkfish and serve with crisp salads and either a mustard dressing or, if you want to maintain the Oriental feel, a mixture of 60 per cent light sesame oil, 30 per cent soy sauce, and 10 per cent lemon juice.

## Ingredients

> **Monkfish fillets are surrounded by a pale membrane, which will need to be cut away.** Similarly, any remnants of the white bone still attached after filleting will need to be cut away. The membrane will otherwise contract during cooking, pulling and toughening the fish.

> **An unscented tea such as Keemun is preferable** to a smoky one such as Lapsang Souchong, which will lend too strong a flavour.

## Cooking method

> **A large wok is best for you will need some room** for the smoke to circulate, cooking the fish.

For poaching and steaming fish see **170**

# Shellfish

**Molluscs and crustacea are as different from each other as they are from other fish.** Crustacea, such as crabs and lobster, are sweet-tasting and firm-fleshed, whereas molluscs, such as scallops and mussels, can be sweet-tasting and often have an affinity with red meat rather than fish – think of steak and oyster pie. Both tend to toughen when over-cooked, but otherwise they are best considered separately.

## Molluscs

**Two of the most popular molluscs are oysters and scallops.** Oysters have long been associated with braised beef in puddings and stews, and sauces made from them for use with meat are commonplace in the Far East. Scallops are the sweetest molluscs and can be crisp-fried like Dublin Bay prawns.

Cockles and mussels are the cheapest molluscs. They have been gathered on river estuaries for ever, but have still largely been ignored by *haute cuisine* in favour of grander species such as scallop and oyster. This is an absurdity that can be turned to your advantage. Even if the texture isn't apparent in a dish for some reason, these shellfish are plentiful enough to be used for flavour and sauces alone.

Cockles will just need rinsing in a sinkful of cold water before cooking. They will open the second they are cooked and can be removed from the shell most easily then. If you need them raw you must prise them open like miniature oysters. Mussels need more attention. Dutch imports come in scrubbed and clean, but tend to die quickly. Mussels from our own shores will be in better condition, but can be a depressing sight for anyone short of time. Those that aren't rope-farmed may have seaweed and limpets stuck to the shell, huge strands of beard protruding, and the certainty of many changes of water before they are ready for the pot. Persevere; the end product is worth the effort.

## How to prepare mussels

Empty the mussels into a sinkful of cold water. Swirl them around to loosen the worst of the mud and stones, then lift them out one by one into a second sink or bucket containing more water. Discard any stones, those mussels with broken shells and any that have opened. Take a knife and scrape the shells clean and then yank out the beards. A final rinse in clean water completes the job.

The mussels are now ready for cooking. White wine or dry cider and onions or shallots marry perfectly with the mussel's sweetish, fragile flavour. Afterwards you can fiddle around as much or as little as you wish. Those who dislike the texture of mussels or who have over-cooked them will sympathize with an American called William Brad, who felt the same way but enjoyed the flavour – a soup called Billy B, made with mussel stock but containing no actual mussels, was styled in his honour.

Once cooked, mussels are versatile and can be coated in light batter and then fried or, as we used to prepare them at Carrier's restaurant years ago, they can be replaced in the shell and covered with garlic butter before baking as mussels cooked like snails.

For pasta with shellfish and saffron see **90** For mouclade see **92**

# How to prepare scallops

1    Slide a cook's knife into the shell. Cut down along the flat side
      of the to separate the scallop from the shell.

**2-3** Cut out the scallop.

4    Separate the white flesh and coral from the rest of the scallop.
      You can use both, although I only use the white flesh.

5    Lift the membrane from around the side of the scallop.

For scallops with lentil and coriander sauce see **188**    For saffron leek and scallop soup see **212**

# Pasta with shellfish and saffron

**This dish can be as expensive and elaborate as you choose.** The work will be the same whether you pile in clams and langoustine or stick with cockles and mussels, and in truth so will the flavour as it is these last, comparatively cheap and humble, ingredients that will impart most to the finished dish. But the more types of shellfish you add, the more interesting the textures of the dish will be, and the selection here is a guideline only. The sauce that coats the pasta derives from the cooking liquors of the ingredients and you may use dried pasta if you don't feel like making fresh. Don't put Parmesan on the pasta.

**Serves 4**

pasta (one batch recipe, page 30)

For the shellfish sauce:

500g mussels, cleaned and prepared
500g cockles, cleaned and prepared
100ml white wine
2 shallots, finely chopped
2 large cloves garlic, finely chopped
1 small chilli, deseeded and finely chopped
8 langoustines
4 clams
8 shell-on prawns
1 large pinch saffron
1 tsp anchovy essence
1 tbsp crème fraîche
4 tbsp olive oil
1 tbsp lemon juice
salt and pepper

1   Place the cleaned mussels and cockles in a pan and pour on the white wine, shallots, garlic and chilli. Cover with a lid and bring to the boil. Add the other shellfish, replace the lid, reboil, then simmer for 2 minutes. When the mollusc shells open the fish are cooked.

2   Discard about half the shells – there's a limit to how many you want cluttering the plate – and any cockles or mussels that have failed to open. Decant the cooking liquor into a saucepan. Bring this to the boil with the saffron, anchovy essence and crème fraiche, then blend in a liquidizer along with the olive oil, lemon and seasoning.

3   Put the sauce back in the pan with the cooked shellfish.

4   Boil the pasta in salted boiling water. Fresh pasta will be cooked the moment the water re-boils; dried pasta takes longer and it's best to follow whatever instructions are on the packet.

5   Toss the pasta in the sauce and serve.

## Ingredients

> It is essential that the cockles and mussels should be live rather than ready-cooked, as the juices they produce while cooking are the core of the dish. It is less crucial, though preferable, that the langoustines or prawns should be raw. If you can only find cooked specimens, then add them later to the dish so that they heat through but don't really cook further. Lightly cooked crustacea are sweet but over-cooked are dry and tasteless.

> Most mussels are sold cleaned, with shiny black rather than barnacle-encrusted shells. These save a long cleaning job but the battering of machine-cleaning reduces their shelf-life, so buy near the time you need them. Cockles and mussels need a final wash in cold water in any case as they are likely to be gritty. Pull out any beards that protrude from the shells at this point too.

## Technique

> This is a messy dish to eat, with so much fish still in the shell. Paper napkins are a good idea, even finger bowls with warm lemon water to help get through the meal without serious dry-cleaning bills.

> The sauce will be quite thin, and is best scooped up with clam or mussel shells or negotiated with a spoon.

For how to prepare mussels see **88**

# Mouclade

**This is a spicy treatment of mussels,** using saffron and curry spices such as cumin and coriander. The sweetish flavour of mussels works well with these soft spices and the result you are after is more korma than vindaloo.

**Serves 4**

2kg mussels, scrubbed and prepared
300ml dry white wine
60g butter
100g shallots, finely chopped
1 clove garlic, crushed
1 tsp curry paste
1 pinch saffron threads
35g plain flour
200ml crème fraîche
1 tbsp chopped fresh parsley
salt and pepper

1   Bring the mussels to the boil in the white wine – use a lidded pan so that the steam from the boiling liquid cooks the mussels that are not submerged. As soon as the shells open the mussels are ready, so have a sieve or colander set in a bowl or container handy and drain the mussels (reserve the cooking liquor, as it will form the base of the sauce). If mussels will still have straggly hair known as the beard, this needs to be tugged out. You may also take off the lips around the rim of each mussel if you wish. Discard most of the shells and leave only a handful for decorative purposes. Discard any mussels whose shells have not opened.

2   Melt the butter in a separate pan and sweat the shallots and crushed garlic until cooked but not coloured. Stir in the curry paste and saffron, then cook for a few seconds more before adding the flour. The flour too has to cook for a few moments, and will come cleanly away from the base of the pan when ready.

3   Stir in a third of the mussel stock and bring to the boil. Stir hard until this makes a smooth paste, then stir in the remaining stock and repeat the process. Add the crème fraîche and parsley. Season to taste.

4   Mix the hot sauce and mussels together to serve.

### Ingredients

> **Mussels available in the shops are almost always rope-grown in clean water and are quite safe to eat.** Wild mussels gathered at the beach need more care – you must be certain that the sea water is clean before considering eating these as they tend to absorb any pollutants in the water and have been responsible for some nasty poisonings.

> **Curry powders and pastes vary in strength and depth of flavour.** I opt for pastes, not because they are better but because they retain their vibrancy of flavour for longer once opened. Old dried curry powder tastes of little. Of course, you could roast your own spice mixture and use that but, unless you have it ready-prepared, the extra work will transform this from being a simple dish to a long drawn-out one.

### Technique

> **All curry spices need to fry for a second before any liquid is added,** so the order in which you add the ingredients is important. Late-sprinkled curry powder or paste will always taste uncooked.

For how to prepare mussels see **88**

# Crustaceans

**The members of this family that concern us are mainly lobsters, crabs and prawns.** They yield sweet meat and are available all year round. Lobsters and crabs are more plentiful and consequently less expensive in the summer, and are caught in specially-designed and baited traps, known as pots. Once caught, they are kept in tanks until someone buys them. As they are sold live there is no problem with deterioration.

However, the reason they are sold live is because once dead they deteriorate quickly. So on offer will be three choices: live, frozen or ready-cooked. Live is best, ready-cooked least good, as the chances are the crustacean will have been cooked for long enough to be safe for a few days but too long to give peak texture and flavour. Short cooking times are essential: 8-10 minutes' simmering should be more than adequate for a 700g lobster and for a similar-sized crab. Shrimps and prawns are best cooked in the minimum of water and will tell you when they are ready by changing colour from blue-brown to pink.

Gender matters. A hen crab will yield proportionately more meat than a cock crab and a hen lobster has a wider tail as well as the intensely-flavoured coral running along its body. The coral will colour as well as flavour sauces or soups made from lobster. To complicate matters, there are those who claim the meat from cock crabs and lobsters is superior. So you pays your money and takes your choice.

The fish sold as langoustines have had several incarnations under different names. They were hugely popular 30 to 40 years ago as 'scampi', their Italian name, and before that as Dublin Bay prawns and Norway lobster. Langoustines don't change colour during cooking but otherwise all the advice about short cooking times still applies.

# Langoustine tartare

**The simplest way to ensure that your langoustine is not overcooked must be to eat it raw.** This dish makes a first-rate starter, especially if something roast or fried is to follow. Of course it's ferociously expensive so perhaps just for a special occasion.

Serves 4

12 langoustine tails, out of their shells
1 tbsp lime juice
1 tsp soy sauce
 a few drops of Tabasco
4 tsp crème fraîche
4 tsp caviar

1  Finely chop the langoustine.
2  Just before serving, stir in the lime juice, soy sauce and Tabasco. Do this a touch at a time until you reach the degree of spiciness that suits you.
3  Spoon the langoustine mixture on to chilled plates, then top with a teaspoon of crème fraîche and caviar.

Ingredients

> **Keep the langoustine refrigerated as much as possible.** It has better texture chilled. The shells can be removed simply with a pair of scissors.

> **Caviar comes in various styles depending on which type of sturgeon it came from.** Beluga are the largest and Sevruga the smallest. None are cheap, but I prefer Oscietra caviar which is, relatively speaking, middle of the range. Caviar destined for the American market will be markedly saltier than that for European consumption, something to do with food regulations there.

> **My preference is for hot, crisp potato galettes as an accompaniment.** These are easily made by bringing a large potato to the boil and then letting it cool in the water. Peel and grate the potato, then shallow-fry it in hot sunflower oil until crisp.

Cooking method

> **Only add the lime juice and seasonings when you are about to serve the dish.** These can 'cook' the fish within as little as 30 minutes, changing its texture for the worse.

# Poultry and game birds

**Over the last 50 years, chicken has shifted from the status of a celebratory treat to that of a standard and routine component in everyday meals,** being now cheap(ish) and permanently available. In the process it has become increasingly bland, needing some masking or special treatment in order to be of interest. Sadly this is a side-effect of the breeding and production methods that have made it so inexpensive.

The same intensive rearing techniques have perniciously spread to most other poultry production. While all this may make sound commercial sense, it now represents a real menace to anyone who cares about the food we eat. And no system that calls for a cocktail of growth-enhancers and hormones to be pumped into de-beaked animals living in murky conditions can instil confidence in the long-term safety of poultry as food.

The answer is to take care over the shopping. Good-quality poultry, decently reared and fed, is not much more expensive than bog-standard rubbish. The flavour is also immeasurably superior, and it can be simply roasted as there is no unpleasant flavour that needs masking. A moment's scrutiny of the label, or questioning of the shopkeeper, will let you eat better and feel better. It's always wise to buy meat from a butcher who you know and trust – that way you can find out something about how the animal was reared. Organic is good, but it can be expensive, and not all good meat is organic.

The power of the discerning consumer is enormous. Witness the packaging and marketing efforts of those with something to hide – illustrations of animals skipping around fields are often seen on packaging, and terms such as 'farm-fresh' or 'free-range' may not say quite as much about animal welfare as you think.

Millions of tons of worryingly cheap chicken is imported from unlikely countries such as Brazil. If it is not labelled on chicken sold in the butcher's shop, then it is certainly arriving at the dinner tables in some other guise – as an ingredient in ready-meals, for instance. Do not be put off. Real poultry is still a treat.

Game birds are generally wild creatures, and even those reared by gamekeepers will be bred for their hunting qualities rather than for any special succulence on the dining table. Their culinary and gastronomic aspects are secondary to their status as trophies to somebody with a shotgun. Those who shoot are the ones paying the most money, not those doing the cooking and eating – a bizarre arrangement, but one that works to our advantage.

This chapter considers what to think about when buying poultry or game, how to prepare the birds and how best to cook and serve them.

# Preparing and serving poultry and game birds

**Raw poultry and game birds should be handled with care.** Do not cut up raw chicken or duck on the same board or work surface on which you intend to cut up anything cooked or foodstuffs such as salad that are going to be eaten raw. The dangers of cross-contamination are higher with poultry than with most other meats.

Ideally, keep separate cutting boards for cooked and raw food. Alternatively, use one side of the board for each purpose on a permanent basis. Otherwise you should scrub well between uses. The same goes for any knife you use.

The best methods for jointing or carving cooked poultry or game birds are dealt with on an individual basis for each type of bird in its section. Basically, chicken, small game birds, and Aylesbury duck are jointed into segments, whereas Barbary ducks and large birds are carved into slices. In all cases, it will be a neater and easier operation if the wish-bone is removed from the bird before cooking.

The process for removing the wishbone is the same, whatever bird you are preparing. The pictures (right) show removing the wishbone from a partridge, still with the head on.

1 Lay the bird on its back, still with the head on.
2 Cut the head off near the body and lift up the flap of skin around the neck.
3 Use a sharp knife to ease back the skin as you pull it away from you.
4 When the breast meat appears, run your finger along the arch of the neck cavity and locate the wishbone.
5 Cut the wishbone out with either a knife or scissors.

# Storing and cooking poultry and game birds

**Most poultry and game birds tend to be dry** – notable exceptions are quail and some good chicken. Keep the birds covered or brush with a little oil to prevent any further drying in your fridge. As with all meat, store in the bottom of the fridge where possible, lest raw juices drip on to cooked food, dairy produce, or any other food that isn't going to be cooked before it is eaten.

Ideally, poultry should be kept in the fridge and used on the day of purchase – although it may keep for longer in the fridge, depending on the size of the bird and how well wrapped it is. If you don't plan to cook the meat on the day of purchase, it is better to buy fresh poultry and then freeze it than to buy a frozen bird.

When roasting poultry, the right-sized roasting tray will prevent your oven from suffering during cooking: too large a tray and fat spatters over the oven wall; too small and the juices drip over the side and down to the oven floor. When braising or boiling poultry, the right-sized pot will ensure that any stock or liquid produced will be in the quantity and strength needed, whereas a vast pot used for poaching will need gallons of water and will produce weak stock.

For roasting, a trivet or small metal rack is useful for keeping the bird above the roasting tray surface and to let the hot air circulate more evenly. Aylesbury ducks and geese produce quite a lot of fat as they cook making a trivet especially useful.

Cooking times can vary with the size of your oven. Just as a large turkey will fill a small oven, reducing the temperature in the short term fairly considerably, a small bird such as a woodcock or quail will make little impact on the heat levels and will start cooking straight away. Take the recovery time of the oven temperature into account when planning how long to cook a bird for. There's more specific information about cooking times and temperatures in the sections on individual birds.

For hanging and plucking game birds see **112**   For roasting and braising game birds see **113**

# Roast turkey

**The handling and carving of turkey** is slightly different from that of other poultry because of the turkey's size.

There is little point in cooking turkey in any way other than whole and roast. The flavour is slightly different to, but not necessarily superior to, good chicken and the point has always been the bird's size. It makes an imposing centre-piece to an important meal and can be carved ceremoniously in front of those dining. Making nuggets and pies from the meat is perfectly acceptable as a means of rehashing left overs, but a strange use of the bird otherwise.

### Before roasting:
Take out the wishbone (pages 96-7).

Putting stuffing into the main cavity of the bird isn't a good idea. The heat will not be sufficient to cook it properly until the turkey itself is over-cooked. If you are cooking a stuffing, you should either pack it in under the neck skin before it is replaced, or wrap it in greased kitchen foil to cook in the roasting tray alongside the bird.

Smear plenty of butter over the turkey – 250g for a medium-sized bird would be about right – and roast it in a moderate oven (170°C/Gas mark 3). A 5.4kg turkey will take about 3 hours.

### During roasting:
Baste large joints four or five times during cooking to stop them from drying out.

The bird is cooked when you put a skewer into the base of the thigh and it runs clear.

### After roasting:
Let the bird rest for 15-20 minutes for the meat to settle and the gravy to be prepared (see page 217 for chicken gravy instructions).

Carve one side at a time. Take the leg off and divide it into thigh and drumstick. On a small-to-medium bird, there may be volunteers to eat one of these whole. Otherwise, carve down the length of each to cut the meat into strips. Take the breast right off the carcass by cutting along and down the ridge of the breastbone. Lay the breast flat on a cutting board and then carve into even slices. It's much easier to carve the meat if you don't carve it on the bone.

# Roast goose

**Goose is the alternative candidate for major celebratory meals,** especially at Christmas. It is still a completely seasonal meat and is available from late September until January only. Geese will not withstand intensive rearing and are consequently always free-range and always expensive relative to turkey.

A 6kg goose will feed six people but provide no leftovers in the way a similar weight turkey might. The ratio of bone to meat is far greater in goose and the amount of fat generated much higher. This fat, though, is a superb ingredient, the best there is for roasting potatoes or greasing some skinny pheasant you might want to eat in January.

### Before roasting:
Cover the drumsticks with foil so that they are protected from burning during the roasting process. Prick the neck and tail-end all over to help release fat while cooking Place the bird, breast-down, on a large roasting tray, then roast at 170°C/Gas mark 3 for 2½ hours.

### During roasting:
Halfway through cooking, turn the bird breast-upwards so that it crisps properly and pour off the accumulated goose fat. Some of this can be used to roast potatoes and the rest kept for another day, along with whatever fat renders down during the remaining cooking time.

### After roasting:
To carve the goose, cut away the legs and divide each into thigh and drumstick. The thighs can be further divided into halves either side of the bone. Carve away each breast from the bone and lay them flat on a cutting board. Carve lengthways into long slices.

For roasting, frying and grilling poultry see **180-81**

# Chicken

**Roast chicken calls for top-quality poultry.** There's no hiding place with interesting herb or spicing treatments if the bird's substandard. So buy well. Chickens that have been dismantled and sold separately as breasts or legs are rarely top-quality either, so it's best if you have the freezer space to buy the bird whole and use whatever bits aren't needed some other time. You are also left with chicken bones for stock this way.

## Chicken escalope with tarragon and leeks

**Escalopes are slices from white meat.** Usually they are flattened out with a cutlet bat, partly as a tenderising measure and partly so there will be an even thickness of meat that will cook uniformly.

Chicken legs make a more flavourful version than breasts, but are more fiddly as the legs will need boning as well as flattening.

Crisp breadcrumb-coated escalopes will be left soggy by most sauces and are best served with salad or pasta or, as in this recipe, a vegetable accompaniment that doubles as a sauce and gives a contrasting soft texture to the meat.

### Serves 4
4 chicken breasts, boneless

salt and pepper

8 tarragon leaves

2 eggs, beaten

a small white loaf, preferably 1-2
    days old, made into crumbs

25g unsalted butter

10g plain flour

150ml milk

grated nutmeg

1 tsp Dijon mustard

a dash of Worcestershire sauce

1kg leeks, washed and thinly sliced

1 tbsp chopped fresh tarragon

sunflower oil, for frying

1   Flatten the chicken slightly by wrapping it in two layers of clingfilm and then hitting it a few times with a hard object – the objective is to tenderise it and to achieve an even thickness all the way through. Remove the clingfilm and season the chicken with salt and pepper. Place 2 tarragon leaves on each escalope and then dip in beaten egg followed by fresh breadcrumbs.

2   Melt the butter on a medium heat and stir in the flour. Let this cook for a few seconds. Stir in the milk in two stages; lumps may form if the milk is not stirred in properly as you go. Bring this to the boil and season with salt, nutmeg and pepper, then add the mustard and Worcestershire sauce.

3   Drop the leeks into boiling water. When the water re-boils, strain and add them to the sauce with the chopped tarragon.

4   Heat the oil, then fry the escalopes on a high heat, turning the heat down part-way through cooking to make sure they cook in the middle – they should take about 4 minutes on each side, depending on their thickness. When they are cooked through, serve them alongside the creamed leek and tarragon.

### Technique

> **Fresh breadcrumbs are easily made** and keep well in a fridge for a week or more. Cut away the crusts from a white loaf, then cut the bread into cubes. Food process until you have breadcrumbs.

> **Use a plastic food bag to ease the flattening of the meat.** The plastic clings to the meat and the escalopes flatten quickly. The meat need not be very thinly batted out; if it is too thin you will taste only the fried crumbs. But the thickness should be even.

> **Leeks can have soil and grit trapped in their layers.** Cut the leeks into strips, then wash them by dunking the strips into a big bowl of water, then lifting them from the bowl into another container. The grit will sink to the bottom of the water.

For roasting, frying and grilling poultry see **180-81**

# Roast chicken with stuffings

**Roast chicken gives a crisp skin and finish** whereas pot-roast chicken – done with a lidded pot – will be more moist but have less texture. The best accompaniment to this dish is the chicken's own gravy (see page 217), and this may be jazzed up with mustard, a herb such as tarragon or parsley, or some dried wild mushrooms should the occasion warrant. Stuffings lend interest to the dish if gravy is the accompanying liquid of choice and don't seem to worry less adventurous diners in the way that any sauce might.

**Serves 4**

1.75kg chicken
2 tbsp olive oil
15g butter
salt and pepper
1 lemon, sliced

**For the chestnut stuffing:**

25g butter
1 shallot, finely chopped
400g sausage meat
100g fresh breadcrumbs
2 apples, peeled, cored and diced
2 pears, peeled, cored and diced
1 small tin unsweetened whole
   chestnuts, chopped

**For the watercress and apricot stuffing:**

100g dried apricots
100g shelled hazelnuts
1 bunch watercress
300g fresh breadcrumbs

1   Heat the oven to 220°C/Gas mark 7.

2   Remove the chicken's wishbone (see pages 96-7), then paint the bird with olive oil and butter. Season, then place the lemon in the cavity and pour 100ml water in the roasting tray with the bird.

3   Roast for 15 minutes, then add any potatoes for roasting to the roasting tray, lower the temperature to 190°C/Gas mark 5 and continue roasting for another 50 minutes.

4   Meanwhile, make the stuffings. For the chestnut stuffing, heat the butter and then sweat the chopped shallot before adding all the other ingredients. Season well with salt and pepper, then roll into a thin sausage shape in some buttered kitchen foil.

5   For the watercress and apricot stuffing, boil the apricots in a saucepan of water for a few minutes to soften. Drain and roughly chop them, then chop the hazelnuts and watercress. Add to the breadcrumbs, then process these ingredients together for a few seconds. When the chicken is half-way though cooking and you are basting and turning it (see stage 6), take 3 good tbsp of the hot buttery cooking juices and add these to the stuffing mix. Stir it thoroughly and then roll into a thin sausage shape in buttered kitchen foil.

6   When the chicken has been in the oven for 30 minutes in total, turn it over so that the thighs and legs cook evenly too. Baste with pan juices and add any stuffings.

7   When the cooking time is up, check the chicken is cooked, then take it from the oven and leave to rest for 10 minutes.

8   Carve the chicken into breasts and legs, then divide each breast in two and each leg into thigh and drumstick. Pour any juices that escape the bird during dismantling back into the roasting tray to help the gravy along.

9   Serve slices or pieces of chicken with stuffing and gravy and, if wished, with the roast potatoes and/or some fresh asparagus.

**Ingredients**

> **The lemon helps moisten** the meat as well as perfuming the gravy. It can be omitted if this doesn't suit.

**Cooking method**

> **Test for doneness** by piercing the thigh of the chicken, then watching the juices that escape. If they run clear the bird is done; any trace of blood, it needs more time.

For roasting, frying and grilling poultry see **180-81**

# Paprika chicken

**This chicken dish produces its own stock.** When I cooked this dish in a Hungarian restaurant I worked in 30 years ago, it had to produce enough sauce to cover all the pork and most of the veal dishes as well. Like goulash, the dish was served with an accompanying marinated cucumber salad to cut through any creaminess in the sauce.

**Serves 4**

sunflower oil or lard, for frying

1 onion, chopped

1 small stick celery, chopped

1 leek, chopped

1 red pepper, deseeded and chopped

2 cloves garlic, finely chopped

1 tbsp paprika

½ small chilli, deseeded and finely chopped

1 tbsp tomato passata

salt

1.5kg chicken

2 tbsp soured cream

1 tbsp plain flour

1 tsp white wine vinegar

1   Use a heavy-based pot with a tight-fitting lid. Heat the pot, add the fat and then fry the vegetables and garlic until they start to colour. Add the paprika, then the chilli and passata.

2   Pour on 500ml water and season with salt. Bring to the boil, then add the chicken.

3   Cover with a tight-fitting lid and lower the heat so that the bird simmers gently. After 40 minutes it should be perfectly cooked. Lift out the chicken.

4   Whisk the soured cream and flour together, then whisk this into the cooking liquor. Let it re-boil and thicken, then blend in a liquidizer. The balance of the sauce will need adjusting with a few drops of vinegar.

5   To serve, break up the chicken into eight joints: two drumsticks, two legs, two breasts and two thighs and serve two joints per person.

### Ingredients

> **The condition of the paprika is important.** Once opened, a packet of the spice will quickly lose strength. There are four grades of paprika in Hungary and these range in hotness from the mild rose paprika upwards. Mostly you will not have this choice and will be offered a mild all-purpose variety. Half a small chilli or some Tabasco will put things right.

### Technique

> **Paprika must fry for a few seconds before any liquid is added** but it mustn't burn. The best method is to take the pot away from direct heat and then add it. Added any other way, the paprika will always taste uncooked.

> **Don't be too liberal with salt** in the cooking water, for it will form the finished sauce afterwards

> **Take care when lifting the bird from the cooking liquor,** as the central cavity will be full of stock.

For chopping an onion see **47**    For poaching and steaming poultry see **166**

# Duck

**The duck most seen in our butchers' shops is the Aylesbury duck variety descended from the Chinese Peking duck,** a strain that has been bred for the table for around 2000 years. It is rich and fatty, with moist, tender flesh and a thick skin that turns sweet and crisp when cooked. For roasting, this is the best type.

It is not the only one on offer though. Some varieties, such as mallard and the French Barbary and Challans ducks, need to be tackled in a completely different way, more like steak in terms of texture and to some extent flavour. Ditto new British breeds of duck, such as the Gressingham, which is in some ways similar – or at least closer, being a hybrid between a wild duck and a French Barbary type duck – to the wild species.

# Barbary ducks

**You will regularly find only the breasts (*magrets*) on sale.** Should you buy the duck whole, you will have to treat the legs separately as they take much longer to cook. Barbary ducks are meatier than Aylesbury ducks but, with less fat covering, tend to be dry. Unusually, you may even have to add extra fat or oil during cooking, especially when using breasts from large ducks.

Like steaks, these duck breasts should be cooked under done. This isn't an affectation for smart-arses who like everything semi-raw. Meat from the Barbary duck is dark and close-textured, like its wild relatives, and will be dull and dry if cooked beyond the pink stage. Bearing in mind this tendency toward dryness and toughness, the carving and service of these ducks is as important as the cooking of them. This is how to handle them.

Heat a dry-roasting tray or frying pan to hot, then place the breasts, skin-down, searing the skin until it colours. Don't turn the duck over. The skin will be inedible if it is not cooked through completely, and you need to soften the membrane underneath which separates flesh from skin.

Place the tray, with the duck breasts still skin-side-down, in a moderately hot oven – say 180°C/Gas mark 4 – until the breasts are cooked but still bloody. The time varies with the size and thickness of the duck breasts, but you should be OK if you plan on 30 minutes, plus or minus 5.

Lift out the breasts and allow them to settle for a further 5 minutes, in the same way as you would rest beef or lamb (see page 118) so that the under-done parts set pink. If the meat is carved straightaway, most blood and cooking juices will seep out, losing both colour and flavour from the meat.

Carve the meat into thin strips. Tough, or even tough-ish, meat needs carving into thinner slices – the tougher the meat, the thinner the slices should be. It is the same principle as that of slicing salami and does not imply any inferiority, just practicality. Try cutting salami or Parma ham as thickly as standard boiled ham and you will find it is like shoe leather. By the same token, a rare piece of duck breast will be perfect if it is cut into thinnish strips, but inedible if left intact and attempted solely with a knife and fork.

How you carve the duck – across the breast, at a bias down the breast as with smoked salmon, or along the length of the breast – is a question of preference. My preference is to hold the meat steady with the back of a roasting fork and then slice the breast lengthwise into long thin strips. If the meat is a touch too rare, reassemble the breast so that the flesh is once more protected by skin and flash it through a hot oven or under a grill.

Barbary duckling can also be poached in stock. It will still be best cooked under-done, and can be served in the cooking liquor much in the same way as *pot au feu* or *boeuf à la ficelle*.

# Aylesbury ducks

**Aylesbury ducks don't suffer from being well-cooked,** so you may have both legs and breasts perfect from the same oven simultaneously. Salt and pepper are all that are required for roasting them.

You may like to prick the skin all over with a fork to let extra fat escape during cooking, and you may wish to lift the bird above the fat that accumulates in the roasting pan by placing it on a trivet. Neither process is essential. A 1.5kg duckling will take about 1½ hours to cook at 190°C/Gas mark 5.

There is scope for brushing honey and spices over the duck either before it goes in the oven or as it is cooking. It is not an arrangement that appeals to me, as I prefer to look forward to the sweetness inherent in the duck without any such embellishment.

# Accompaniments for duck

**Sauces containing some sharpish fruit or aromatic herbs and spices lend contrast to the fattiness of the meat.** Any stuffing or sauce that suits pork will generally suit duck. Stuffings designed to partner turkey or chicken will not necessarily go so well with duck, as they are partly intended to moisten dryish meat, which is not a problem here.

## Blackcurrant sauce

Blackcurrants give a powerful and sharp foil to the richness of roast duck or goose and are fine with well-flavoured game birds such as partridge – much better than the hideous sweet concoctions involving oranges and cherries that were wished on roast duck in days of yore. The aim is to lend a balance to the gravy. So start the sauce, as gravy, in the usual way by deglazing the roasting tray, this time with a glass of red wine as well as a little stock or water, then add 1 tbsp crème de cassis and 1 tbsp fresh or frozen blackcurrants. Boil the result and thicken it with 1 tsp of arrowroot dissolved in 1 tbsp water. Crème de cassis is an alcoholic syrup made from blackcurrants, most famous mixed with cold white wine as a Kir. It is quite sweet, which will help offset the sharpness of the blackcurrants.

## Duck liver and apple stuffing

Fry a chopped medium-sized onion and 2 cloves of crushed garlic until they start to colour. Add the duck's liver and a peeled and diced eating apple and fry until the liver has coloured on all sides. Season with pepper, salt and nutmeg (a tablespoon of Calvados could also be added) and blend in a food processor or liquidizer. Thicken with a tablespoonful of fresh breadcrumbs.

# Poaching and steaming duck

**Poaching and steaming are methods rarely used on Aylesbury duck,** but an exception is the Welsh recipe for salted duck from Lady Llanover's eccentric book *The First Principles of Good Cookery*, first published in 1867. My friend Franco Taruschio uncovered and then revived this dish to great effect at The Walnut Tree near Abergavenny when it was his restaurant. He served it cold with pickled damsons, as a first course or light lunch.

The method calls for a whole duck on which the breasts only are rubbed with coarse salt, in the ratio of 40g salt to each pair of breasts, every day for three days. The duck is then washed off and gently poached for around 1½ hours. By this time it is completely cooked but still tender.

There is a Chinese method for cooking duck that combines steaming or poaching with frying. Basically, this is the secret of the dish Peking duck, and can be tackled thus. Take out the wishbone, which forms an arch around the bird's neck (see pages 96-7). Without it, the bird will be easier to carve once steamed.

Season the duck with salt and pepper, then wrap in kitchen foil. Steam or poach, covered in water, in a lidded pan for 1½ hours and then leave to cool.

Unwrap the bird and dismantle into legs and breasts by cutting off the legs and then the breast and slicing. Heat a wok or frying pan with 1cm depth of groundnut oil and then fry each piece separately until it is crisp. If you crowd the pan the duck will tend to be soggy. Serve with salads or a well-spiced purée of root vegetables.

For boiling and steaming poultry see **166**

# Poached duck with duck liver sauce

**Interesting as a method, and most enjoyable to eat,** is Aylesbury duck poached and then served with a sauce made from its liver. I spotted this recipe in Elizabeth David's *French Provincial Cooking* about 35 years ago and have never seen it served anywhere or cooked by anyone other than myself.

When I was head chef at the London Capital Hotel in 1980, Mrs David was an occasional customer – she liked the consommé there – and I requested that we put her dish on the menu. After some discussion, it was decided to ask her along to eat a version and voice an opinion. However, on the day of the trial I was given the day off (a rare treat), and another chef was brought in to cook the dish. I don't know what happened, but nothing remotely similar ever appeared on the menu again.

In her original version it is called '*caneton à la serviette*', or 'duckling cooked in a napkin'. In fact, although an old napkin or length of cheesecloth would make handling the duck easier, it is by no means essential to the arrangement.

You will need a pan large enough to hold the duck to make this properly. If you have no such pot and don't want to invest in one until you know that you are going to like the dish, then separate the duck into the crown, both breasts still joined and on the bone and the two legs similarly still together (see page 114 for description of how to do this).

Elizabeth David made a rice pilaff as an accompaniment, using liquor from the poaching duck. You could just as easily boil new potatoes in with the duck and they too would benefit from the stock.

### Serves 4
1 x 2.5kg duck, including giblets
1 small onion, chopped
1 large carrot, chopped
50g unsalted butter
1 shallot, chopped
200ml red wine
salt and pepper
grated nutmeg
a few drops of lemon juice

1    Put the duck in a saucepan just big enough to hold it and cover with water. Add the giblets (except the liver), and the onion and carrot as aromatics for the stock. Bring to the boil, cover and simmer for 80 minutes.

2    20 minutes before the duck is ready, add the liver and poach this too.

3    When the duck and liver are ready, remove from the pan. Heat a large knob of the butter and then sweat the chopped shallot. Add the red wine and the same volume again of the duck and liver cooking liquor. Let the sauce reduce a little.

4    Blend this mixture with the cooked liver, remaining butter and a few drops of lemon juice in a liquidizer. Season to taste with salt, pepper and nutmeg.

5    Cut the poached duck into breasts and legs, then divide each into two. Serve with potatoes or rice, some poaching liquor and the duck liver sauce, accompanied by bitter salad leaves.

### Technique
> **Try to find a pot that covers the bird fairly tightly** and without much room to spare. This way you will need less water and as a consequence end up with a more concentrated cooking liquor.

> **Let the duck simmer gently rather than boil fiercely.** The stock will never rise above 100°C so it won't cook any faster if it moves to a rolling boil, but it will damage the texture of the meat.

> **Test the duck for doneness** by skewering the thighs and watching to see if it runs clear.

### Cooking method
> **When taking stock from the pan,** dip your ladle as deep as possible to take clear stock rather than fat from the surface.

For chopping an onion see **47**    For duck see **103-04**    For poaching and steaming duck see **105**    For poaching and steaming poultry see **166**

# Squab pigeon

Squab is the word used by restaurants to denote pigeons that are bred solely for the table. In fact, it is an American term that refers to any pigeon, wild or otherwise, but has been pressed into use to differentiate between ingredients, particularly when the specially-reared pigeons cost three times as much as the wild ones.

These corn-fed pigeons aren't widely available but have a specific and fine flavour that is a particular treat during the summer, when game birds such as partridge – to which pigeon is similar – are out of season. The flavour of these pigeons is distinct but delicate, so there is limited point in the use of big spice mixtures to mask it. Use your skill and imagination on the accompaniments. Pulses will partner pigeon well and absorb all the pan juices in their cooking.

## Squab pigeon with braised haricots and white wine

Squab pigeons take a surprisingly long time to cook – 40 minutes for a relatively small bird – but the legs will be ready at the same time as the breast. Remember to take out the wishbones (see page 96-7).

Serves 4

100g haricots tarbais
4 large squab pigeons
a little olive oil, for cooking
2 tbsp finely chopped celery
4 rashers smoked streaky bacon, chopped
2 tbsp finely chopped carrot
4 shallots, finely chopped
100ml chicken stock
50ml white wine
1 small Savoy cabbage, cut into strips

1   Soak the haricots for at least 2 hours, and preferably overnight.
2   Boil the soaked beans until tender – this should take 20 minutes, but may take longer if you are using other types of dried white haricot bean.
3   Brush the pigeons with olive oil, then seal in a hot dry pan. Brush once more with olive oil, then transfer to a roasting tray and roast at 200°C/Gas mark 6 for 35 minutes.
4   Meanwhile, heat some olive oil, then fry the celery, bacon, carrot and shallot until just coloured, then add the stock and white wine. Bring to the boil, then add the cooked haricots and allow this to continue cooking and slowly reduce.
5   Bring a saucepan of salted water to the boil and cook the cabbage strips for 2 minutes. Drain, then add to the beans. Pour in any juices from the pigeon, then serve.

Ingredients
> **Haricots tarbais are a particularly tender variety.** You can use whatever you find but may need to soak the beans for longer.

For braising poultry and game see **204**

# Quail

Quails take a long time to cook, but obviously bigger birds take longer than smaller ones.
They are rare among poultry in that the legs will cook at the same speed as the breast. The British
quail industry seems to have shrunk and I can only find French specimens. These are first-rate,
but often come with head on and guts in, which means extra work.

## Roast quail with parsley risotto

**This makes a substantial first course, before a lighter fish main course maybe, or a good
lunch with salad leaves.** The heart of the dish is the risotto, which is finished differently from
the standard saffron job, and gives a fresher taste – like hedge trimmings but nicer. The roast
quail is a good foil to the rice, but could be replaced with other poultry if quail is hard to find.

Serves 4

4 fresh quails

salt and pepper

a little olive oil

For the risotto:

1 tbsp olive oil

1 tbsp chopped shallot or onion

150g risotto rice (carnaroli, vialone
     or arborio)

75ml white wine

500ml chicken stock or water

25g Parmesan cheese, grated

For the parsley purée:

200g parsley, washed

200ml olive oil

a little lemon zest

a small clove garlic, crushed

1   Preheat the oven to 200°C/Gas mark 6.

2   Make the parsley purée by blending the parsley with the olive
    oil, lemon zest, black pepper and crushed garlic. It should be
    completely smooth and a dark, rich green colour.

3   For the risotto, heat the olive oil, then sweat the shallot before
    adding the rice. Season. Gently cook this for a few minutes –
    you don't want the rice to colour. Add the wine and reduce
    right down before pouring in a third of the stock.

4   Re-boil, cover and leave until the rice absorbs all the liquid. Pour
    in the remaining stock and bring to the boil. Simmer very gently
    for a further 10 minutes – the whole operation from raw will take
    around 35 minutes, until the rice grains are just cooked but still
    a little firm. If the stock dries out, add more water.

5   Take the pan from the heat and stir in the Parmesan followed by
    2 tbsp parsley purée. The risotto will turn bright green, but this
    will soften to something more appetizing by contact with the
    heat for 1-2 minutes. It would turn khaki eventually, if left for
    an hour. You want it to taste fresh and herbal, so quite a strong
    colour is the aim so that you know the herb is still vibrant.

6   Season the quails and brush with a little olive oil. Heat a dry-
    frying pan until it is quite hot and then colour the quails on each
    side. Transfer to a roasting tray and roast until done (for around
    20 minutes). Rest the quails before carving into legs and breasts.

7   Lay each quail beside a pile of risotto and pour on cooking juices.

Ingredients

> **Flat parsley has a stronger taste than curled,** but either will do.
  You can blend most of the stalks as well as the leaves so long as
  they are well washed.

Technique

> **The parsley purée is easier to make in a larger quantity** –
  you need to throttle the liquidizer to make it work for smallish
  amounts. The purée keeps for a week in the fridge or for ages
  in the freezer, and can be used to flavour sauces and stuffings.

For roasting, frying and grilling poultry see **180-81**

# Game birds

**Autumn and winter are prime seasons for game birds.** Like the soccer season, though, the first game comes at the height of summer, when wild salmon and home-grown soft fruit are still in the shops. The 12th August sees the beginning of the grouse season, and the following schedule the rest. Do not forget that there is an end to each bird's season, as well as a beginning, and that the quality of the older birds may well be very different toward the back end of the season – these birds are delicate when young and stronger when old, so birds you buy late in the season are like to be tougher. Only young game birds are roasted; braising is best for anything else.

| | |
|---|---|
| Grouse: | 12th August to 10th December |
| Partridge: | 1st September to 1st February |
| Pheasant: | 1st October to 1st February |
| Snipe: | 12th August to 31st January |
| Wild duck (mallard, widgeon, teal): | 1st September to 31st January |
| Woodcock: | 1st October to 31st January |
| Wood pigeon: | Have no closed season but are best in the autumn, when they're feeding on better stuff. |

Beware defrosted game birds from the previous year. At the start of each season the birds tend to be scarce and pricey. Defrosted birds will generally be oven-ready and, like anything defrosted, have tell-tale puddles of liquid in their packaging.

For hanging and plucking game birds see **112**    For preparing, serving and storing poultry and game see **96**

# Hanging and plucking game

**You can buy game straight from the supplier, but this isn't always to be recommended,** as the supplier may not know how to store and handle the game as well as a butcher would. Game requires hanging in order to improve its flavour and tenderness, and generally hanging is a business for butchers.

Modern techniques are shortening the length of time for which a bird needs to be hung – which is advantageous for the butcher, as it cuts down on the time the bird needs to be kept in his shop. Most birds should be hung for about a week, but there's no easy way to tell how long they have been hung for. Again, the best advice is to buy from a butcher you know and trust and ask him how long he's kept the bird for.

One of the less desirable aspects of fresh game, when it arrives in feather, is the need for it to be plucked and drawn. My advice is to carry out this task with both bird and hands firmly within a clean plastic rubbish bag; otherwise the feathers get everywhere. Start plucking the breast and neck by tugging the feathers away from the base of the neck and towards the head. You do not have to pluck the head, so tuck it away some place you will be safe from its staring eyes. Try not to tear the skin as you pluck.

Turn the bird breast-side-down and cut off the head. Slit the neck skin and lift out its neck. Put your fingers just inside the neck cavity and remove the crop. Draw the bird by making a small cut in the skin at the tail end and then pulling out the intestines. Move your fingers along the tope of the breastbone, loosening anything in the way, until you reach the neck, then draw out the remaining entrails. Wash your hands. Then wash and dry the bird.

The feet may be cut off with a sharp knife and any remaining feathers singed from the carcass over a naked gas flame. Or, of course, you can buy the bird ready to cook.

When considering how best to tackle game birds, remember that grouse, wild duck, woodcock and snipe and other dark-fleshed game birds are robust in flavour and suit stock-based, gravy-type, accompaniments. They are totally unsuited to creamy sauces. Partridge, pheasant and the like are more amenable to this sort of thing.

For preparing and storing game see **96**   For game bird seasons see **110**

# Roasting game birds

**You should not need to marinate young game birds in order to make them tender;** they should be sufficiently hung for their own flavour to have fully developed. Once plucked and drawn, there is no value in keeping them for any further length of time, but brush the birds with oil to prevent them from drying out if you do not intend cooking them straightaway.

The degree to which the birds are cooked is partly a matter of taste and partly of convention. Red meat grouse, wild duck and woodcock can be served under-done, and in my view are best that way. Partridge and pheasant, however, will be better if cooked through, although a few flecks of pinkness will be an acceptable price to pay for the meat not drying out through over-cooking.

All the birds can be roasted whole. Smear the breast meat with generous amounts of butter and baste the bird eight to ten times during cooking. Lay the bird on its sides, turning it over at least once while it roasts. The legs need more cooking than the breasts and benefit from being where the heat is more intense. A little squeeze of the breast will tell you whether the bird is cooked: if it feels like there is a hard rubber ball inside, the meat is under-cooked. Alternatively, pierce the meat with a sharp knife; if the juices run clear then it is cooked.

## Cooking times

> **Woodcock and snipe:** take between 15 and 20 minutes in a hot oven 200°C/Gas mark 6 and are supposed to be cooked intact, i.e. not drawn. The brains are a delicacy and the head should be left on during cooking, perhaps wrapped in kitchen foil to prevent charring. Split the head before serving. It all sounds and looks a touch barbaric but tastes distinctively good.

> **Wild duck:** roasted at 200°C/Gas mark 6, comparatively larger types, such as mallard, will take around 45 minutes. Small duck, such as widgeon and teal, take less time; 35 minutes for widgeon, 20 for teal.

> **Partridge:** these come in two varieties: the English grey partridge and the French red-legged. The grey costs more and tastes better. The red-legged are often bred for the table rather than for shooting, and tend to taste indistinguishable from baby chicken. Allow 30 minutes at 200°C/Gas mark 6 for the former and slightly less for the latter.

> **Pheasant:** these are now quite cheap compared to other game birds. Watch out for the tail-end of their season, when they are very susceptible to being tough and dry and should only be braised. Roast your pheasant according to its size, which also varies quite significantly, at 200°C/Gas mark 6 – 45 minutes is a good guideline.

> **Wood pigeons:** these are rarely considered as game and are traditionally stewed in pies and the like. The breasts are excellent roasted rare. Allow 10 minutes at 200°C/Gas mark 6 and forget the legs, which will still be inedible at this point.

# Braising game birds

**Older game birds should be braised.** If you have the energy, you can also braise the legs of any game bird you intend roasting. This can be done in advance and has two advantages: you can pleasurably eat the entire bird and the braising process provides a sauce for the entire dish.

Game birds, and for that matter all poultry, have an optimum cooking time beyond which the meat dries out and forms shreds. Forget any advice directed at more fatty braised dishes such as oxtail stews or lamb curries, which implies that the longer or more often a braised dish is cooked, the better it will be.

Brown the birds gently in butter at the start of the braising process. The meat is delicate and would suffer from more fierce frying. Then add liquid – water, stock, or wine – and a lid. The tougher the bird, the more liquid you should add. Old pheasant or wood pigeon should be more or less covered with stock, wine or whatever liquid you are using; partridge will normally need less, the steam produced by the braising being sufficient for successful cooking.

Autumnal vegetables such as celery and cabbage are excellent partners in this type of braised dish. Bacon or salt pork also work well, as do most pulses. If you think seasonally, you won't go far wrong.

For braising poultry and game see **204**    For roasting, frying and grilling poultry and game see **180-81**

# Roast pheasant breasts with braised legs in soft spices

**This dish encapsulates the advantages of braising and roasting.** The legs are gently poached until tender, while the breasts are roasted quickly just before serving. The soft spices are nutmeg, cinnamon, coriander seed and, to a lesser extent, ginger. As there is no heat from chillies, the dish will taste a touch unbalanced unless a few drops of lemon juice or a dash of vinegar are added.

**Serves 4**

2 pheasants
50g butter
50g brown lentils, soaked for at least 1 hour
1 medium-sized onion, finely chopped
1 stick celery, finely chopped
1 clove garlic, crushed
1 tbsp ground coriander
1 tbsp ground cumin
1 tsp ground ginger
500ml chicken stock of water
salt
4 shelled cooked chestnuts, chopped
1 tsp ground cinnamon
1 tsp grated nutmeg
juice of 1/2 lemon
1 tbsp plain yoghurt

1   Prepare the pheasants by separating each into the crown, both breasts still joined and on the bone, and two legs. As when dismantling chicken, cut away the skin from the legs and press them back until the ball joints snap free to break them off.

2   Melt 30g of the butter and brown the pheasant legs gently in it.

3   Meanwhile, put the drained lentils in a pan with plenty of water and bring to the boil.

4   Lift the legs from the pan and put to one side. Fry the onion and celery in the same pan for 3 minutes. Add the garlic, coriander, cumin and ginger and continue to fry for a few seconds.

5   Add the stock and lentils, then return the legs to the pot.

6   Season with salt and, as soon as the stock boils, turn down the heat and cover with a lid. Simmer for an hour.

7   Meanwhile, preheat the oven to 200°C/Gas mark 6. 20 minutes before serving, brush the pheasant breasts with the remaining butter and brown in a pan. Transfer to the hot oven and roast until just done. A little squeeze of the breast will tell you whether the bird is cooked: if it feels like there is a hard rubber ball inside, the meat is under-cooked. Alternatively, pierce the meat with a sharp knife; if the juices run clear then it is cooked.

8   Add the chopped chestnuts, cinnamon, nutmeg, lemon juice and yoghurt to the pheasant legs and lentils. Lift the legs from the pot. If the other ingredients need adjusting, perhaps a little more yoghurt, salt or lemon juice, this is the time to do it. Then spoon the lentil and spice mixture on to the pheasant legs and breasts and serve.

## Ingredients

> **I always use brown lentils,** as they have a better texture than either green or split. If you can't get hold of brown lentils, Puy are the best alternative.

> **Vacuum-packed cooked chestnuts are good,** or you could roast your own.

## Technique

> **The spices that are used for their taste,** such as coriander seed and cumin, will need frying for a few seconds as part of the cooking process. Those which are meant to give an aroma to the finished dish, such as cinnamon, are added towards the end in the same way as garam masala in Indian cookery.

For roasting, frying and grilling poultry and game see **180-81**    For roasting game birds see **113**

# Wild duck with passion fruit

**Generally I am not a fan of fruit-and-meat combinations.** The passion fruit here, however, is quite sharp, cutting through the richness of the dark meat and providing a contrast to the pan juices that come from the braised legs. The recipe calls for mallards, which are the most common wild duck on offer. A mallard makes a generous portion for one person or a scanty portion for two persons, so judge your quantities on the size of the meal and the size of your diners.

**Serves 4**

4 mallards
a little sunflower oil, for frying
1 shallot, chopped
1 small stick celery, chopped
1 carrot, chopped
1 tbsp plain flour
25ml red wine
500ml water or stock

**For the sauce:**

4 passion fruits
2 tbsp granulated sugar
100ml orange juice
1 tsp arrowroot

1  Preheat the oven to 175°C/Gas mark 3. Cut the legs from the ducks. Heat a little oil in a heavy pot, then fry the legs, skin-side down, with the shallot, celery and carrot, until brown. Sprinkle flour over the legs and let this cook for a few seconds before adding the red wine and just enough water to cover the meat. Bring to the boil and then cover with a tight-fitting lid. Cook in the oven for about 2 hours; the meat should be completely tender.

2  Cut out the wishbone from each duck (see pages 96-7). Heat a pan and then sear the skin on each duck so that it is dark brown. Transfer the birds to a roasting tray and roast until pink. My practice is to place the braising legs on the lower shelf of the oven and add the tray containing the seared crowns to the top shelf about 25 minutes before you plan to serve the dish.

3  Scoop out the passion-fruit pulp and bring this to the boil with the sugar and orange juice. Moisten the arrowroot in 1 tbsp of water and stir until dissolved. Whisk this into the fruit juice and bring back to the boil. Sieve into a small pan and reheat when needed. Test the sauce for balance and add more sugar if needed.

4  Pour off the cooking liquor from the legs and skim away the fat, which will be about a quarter of its volume. Strain the liquor into a saucepan and re-boil.

5  Cut the breasts from the carcasses. Should they be too rare, put them back on the roasting tray and cook for 1-2 minutes more – they will cook quickly once off the bone and must be at least pink and preferably rare if they are not to be tough and dry. Carve the breasts into three or four slices lengthways. Meat that tends to be chewy should be carved as thinly as possible.

6  Place two braised duck legs on each plate, then drape the slices of breast on top. Moisten with 1 tbsp of the reduced cooking liquor and a spoon a little passion fruit sauce to the side. Serve with mash and Savoy cabbage or a tossed salad of winter endives.

**Ingredients**

> **The wild duck family come in differing sizes,** but generally with a similar shape and flavour. Teal are smallest, widgeon make a good single portion but are not common, then mallards.

> **Ripe passion fruit have very wrinkly and sunken skin,** so avoid anything that looks smooth and fresh.

**Technique**

> **Passion fruit is bitter and the sweetness of orange juice varies,** so use your judgement when adding sugar. You want a fairly tart sauce.

> **Arrowroot acts like jelly in hot liquid** and doesn't give the mucous-like texture that cornflour can. It loses strength if cooked for too long.

For roasting and braising game birds see **113**    For mashed potatoes see **33**

**Meat forms the focal point of any meal in which it features.** It's also expensive, so a little respect is called for.

When cooking, try to think of meat by joint rather than by animal. There are more similarities in the cooking of prime cuts of beef or lamb, a chop or steak perhaps, than there are between cooking different cuts from the same animal, for instance oxtail and beef fillet. Since you are likely to use particular cuts for particular cooking techniques, there's more connection between successfully braising a similar cut of venison or pork than between stewing two different cuts from the same animal.

What's important is to use each cut of meat in the way that suits it best. A fillet steak cooked well-done is a waste of money, for your steak will be dry as its juices will have been lost in the cooking. Equally, diced brisket or silverside that has not been braised for long enough to be completely tender is a waste of time and effort.

When cooking prime cuts of red meat, an understanding of timing and touch are instrumental for success, and this gets easier with practice. However, there are a few indicators that you will find useful – and you'll find those in this chapter. When stewing and braising the tougher cuts there is more leeway, and 5 minutes' more or less cooking is unlikely to be crucial to the success or failure of the dish; small differences in timing will matter less than the temperature at which the meat is cooked, whether the pot has a tightly-fitting lid, and how much liquid is produced by the meat during cooking compared to how much is added.

This chapter considers the issues surrounding buying and then storing meat, seam butchery, which cuts of meat are suitable for which cooking methods, and carving.

# Buying raw meat

I wouldn't want to cast a shadow over the pleasure of cooking and eating top-quality meat, but the meat industry has some unpleasant aspects: intensive rearing of pigs, growth-enhancing hormones, antibiotics, and other chemicals stuffed into cattle. Those responsible for nasty systems of meat production are reacting to market pressures toward a cheaper and more plentiful supply, but if a better and safer product is demanded, perhaps the market will have to respond. The answer is to pay a little more, maybe eat a little less, and certainly take more care. The Chinese thinker Lin Yutang said if a chicken is killed and then not properly cooked then that chicken has died in vain. So think on. Each section in this chapter contains information about the specific issues involved in buying different types of meat.

# Storing raw meat

If rule number one is to buy good meat, then rule number two must be to look after it properly during the interval between purchase and cooking. A day in the fridge means clingfilm over the meat; more than a day means you should lightly brush the meat's surfaces with vegetable oil – this will protect it in much the same way as a marinade, but without affecting the flavour. The smaller a cut of meat, the quicker it will deteriorate, so rib joint of beef for roasting, or the Christmas turkey, should be OK if kept in the fridge for a week, but chops or mince won't be. You should buy small cuts of meat as near as possible to when you plan to cook them. The most likely problem with chops or steak is dryness; cut surfaces start to dry out almost immediately and no amount of care in cooking or expense with good oil and butter will prevent the finished dish from being substandard once this has happened.

A butcher will have a large cold-room kept at a temperature geared solely to the needs of storing raw meat and can keep things in decent condition for much longer than any domestic arrangement, where meat such as cutlets and steaks will be affected by the flavour and smell of other types of food kept close by, and vice versa, giving a dull fridgy taste. Well-hung meat should be hung at butchers and abattoirs, not by consumers with limited time and a small fridge.

In commercial kitchens there are regulations about the storage of raw and cooked meat if they are to share the same fridge. Raw meat must be stored below anything that is cooked in case there are drips or spillages from the raw meat on to food that is not due any further cooking before being eaten, cooked meat or salads for instance.

The idea is that the heat involved in cookery will kill off anything unpleasant so you can be relatively carefree, on safety grounds at least, with most meat until it is cooked and thereafter you are in more murky waters. Most problems are caused by poor storage and inadequate reheating of previously cooked food, giving bacteria time to multiply and not giving enough heat to kill them off, or by cross-contamination – using the same knife and cutting board for both cooked and raw meat without giving them a thorough cleaning in-between.

# Resting meat

Here's a laid-back sounding topic for the busy cook, but sadly it only refers to the final part of the cooking process before carving. While the heat is pushing through the outer layers of meat, the core will still be cool and raw. If you want the meat to be pink or rare you must, of course, shorten the cooking time, but you must also rest the meat for a few minutes – longer for large joints – so that the residual heat on the outer part of the chop or joint can travel slowly to the centre, warming and part-cooking as it goes.

For a rack of lamb 5 minutes should be enough; for a leg of lamb 15 minutes is about right – the objective is to rest the meat for long enough to cook it through without it starting to cool.

Resting is also an opportunity for you to collect any meat juices that are escaping on to the pan, so pour off the fat or oil straight away and allow the cooking liquors to gather, ready to be made into gravy or added to whatever sauce you are making.

# Carving meat

**The point of carving is simple:** the meat should be cut into slices that can fit neatly, possibly even elegantly, on to a plate. Do not be disheartened if you lack the dexterity of a Japanese sushi chef or the poise of an experienced waiter. Remember that the object is to leave the bone (if there is one) clear of meat, and that the rest is merely a matter of aesthetics.

The simplest joints are boneless ones, which are no more difficult to carve than a loaf of bread is to slice. However, the grain of the meat (the way that the lines of meat on a joint run) can be mixed up by the rolling process, and the resulting meat may be tougher in patches than you expect. At the other end of the scale, the most awkward joints are shoulder joints, as the blade bone faces both outwards and upwards simultaneously. The trick is to carve down and then outwards on each side of the bone – you'll never get the neat, even slices you'd get from a leg joint, but the compensation is that the meat is both sweeter and cheaper. Don't be tempted to ask the butcher to bone and roll the joint, as it unravels once carved and doesn't cook easily, and the bits of fat on the outside can end up in the middle and have the texture of blobs of snot.

Whatever you're carving, a sharp knife and a long-pronged fork are essential. A carving board that has a dip or groove in which juices can collect is nice, but not critical.

This is how it's done. First allow the meat to rest for a few minutes when it comes out of the oven. This allows some of the juices to settle and lets any residual heat travelling through the meat to slowly set any under-cooked parts at the centre – important when carving joints of red meat that you want to keep pink in the middle. Have some kitchen paper handy to mop up fat and cooking juices that escape during slicing, or your kitchen will look like a battleground.

Hold the joint firm with the fork. Its job is to act as a vice, keeping the meat secure while you wield the sharp knife. Slice downwards and across the grain of the meat. The thickness of the slices is partly a matter of preference and partly of practicality. Generally, the tougher the meat, the thinner it should be carved – think of Parma ham cut thick and you'll get the picture – so it would be thicker slices for roast sirloin than roast topside. However, the thinner the slices, the quicker they lose heat, so plan your carving and dishing up accordingly.

Loin or rib joints are fairly straightforward. If the meat has been chined (the chine bone is the backbone) then the butcher will have loosened or removed the spine when the meat was raw, so it may be cut away after cooking, leaving only the ribs. These are easily carved away leaving a piece of boneless meat to slice.

With leg joints, hold the shank, or bone end, firmly with a carving fork – prong inverted is best, with the base of the fork pressing down on the top of the meat, so that you hold it securely while not actually stabbing the meat – leaving the meatier side uppermost. Cut a small wedge down to the bone from where the meat begins and then carve slices until you reach the thicker end of the joint. Turn the meat over and repeat the process. You can vary the size of the slices by altering the angle at which you carve.

With pork you need to lift off the crackling, which will be brittle, before carving.

For knives see **14**   For resting meat see **118**

# Lamb

**Look for fine-textured meat, which is lean and not too dark in colour.** The age of a lamb can vary from a few months to a year – hoggets – and this doesn't necessarily affect quality, just handling and cooking time. As the lamb ages, its flavour develops, coming closer to mutton as it approaches its first birthday. The joints will be correspondingly larger and the leg of lamb that fed five or six people in May will comfortably serve seven or eight in November. It will also be denser in texture and take a little longer to cook. As with beef, lamb needs to be properly hung before cooking or it will be tough, regardless of quality or price. This is the job of the abbatoir and butcher, and if your dinner is chewier than expected, you may point the finger of guilt at them for skimping on this aspect of their job.

The price of lamb rockets in late spring. Curiously, this happens while the meat is likely to be at its least appealing, just before the end of old-season lamb and then at the beginning of the new season. There may be several factors at work, but one of the most influential is supply and demand. Lamb is associated, ritually and religiously, with springtime. A leg of lamb on Easter Sunday has the same significance as turkey at Christmas, only with a much longer pedigree of tradition – albeit one connected with the Middle East climate, where lamb comes into season earlier thanks to the warmer weather, rather than our own.

The lamb on offer will usually come in just two varieties: English or New Zealand. For most of the year, English will be superior as it has less chilling and freezing involved before reaching you. Less commonly, you will find meat from small upland varieties such as Shetland or Orkney lamb. These give much smaller joints, with dark, almost gamey meat. Sheep aren't fed the hormones and growth enhancers that blight other livestock, and they graze ground that is regularly unfit for much else, so they don't suffer the problems of intensive farming. The result is that lamb is usually a safe and decently reared meat source.

Halal and kosher lamb differ from the usual only in slaughter method. Both Muslim and Jewish dietary laws demand that the lambs are fully aware before slaughter and that they are bled afterwards. It doesn't bear too much thought really but, in truth, nor does any of the slaughtering aspect of meat production.

And it will be no worse for the beasts than the long road journeys to markets and abattoirs dictated by our own bureaucrats and general agricultural incompetence.

All parts of the lamb are good for roasting and grilling. The most tender cuts are at the rear end of the animal: the legs, saddle and best ends. The forequarter is cheaper and a bit fattier, but good nonetheless, and my preference will always be for roast shoulder rather than leg, as the meat is paler and more delicate, just a little more difficult to carve. Boiled leg of lamb is a version for today of the traditional boiled leg of mutton, but no worse for that.

A nastier throwback from the days of mutton rather than lamb is the use of redcurrant jelly and mint sauce. This made perfect sense to cut through the strong, fatty flesh of a mutton chop but is absurd with a delicate lamb cutlet. Commercial mint sauce is a nasty confection of dried mint, cheap vinegar and green colouring and I must say that it seems extraordinary that people ask for this after they have asked that there be no garlic or sauce with their meal, as they don't like their food mucked about with.

Lamb gravy and sauce will be thinner than that from beef or veal because the bones are not so gelatinous. A commercial kitchen overcomes this by combining veal stock with that from the lamb but it makes sense to make a paste of plain flour and softened unsalted butter and whisk this into the sauce or gravy if you need a little help with thickening.

# Seam butchery

**Seam butchery involves separating the joint into muscles rather than just removing bone,** usually for a mini roast or braising meat. It's not difficult and, in the case of a leg of lamb or veal, it will produce the same sort of sub-joints that qualify as silverside, topside and the like, as when the same process is applied to a leg of beef.

1   Carefully cut away the skin from a leg of lamb, then the muscle pattern will be obvious. This picture shows silverside and topside.

2   You can separate most muscles with the fingers, using a sharp knife to cut away those parts attached to the bone.

3   The resulting joints can be trimmed and diced and will cook evenly without any pieces of fat or sinew lurking on the inside.

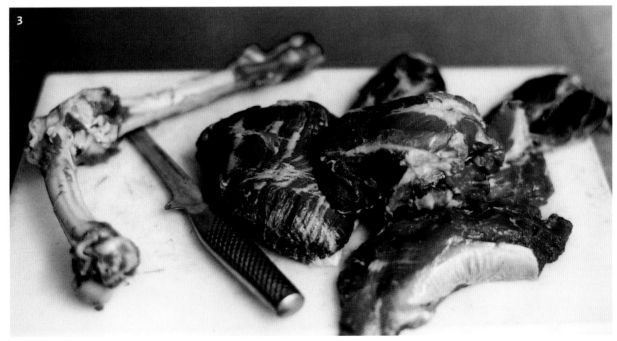

For knives see **14**

# Spring lamb stew

**This dish wastes nothing of the fragrance and subtlety of new-season lamb.** Herbs such as rosemary, marjoram, thyme and parsley, along with garlic and olive oil, seem to partner the meat perfectly. Most alleged stews of lamb are really no such thing, and famous dishes such as Irish stew or Lancashire hotpot are really an exercise in poaching lamb and then revelling in the distinctive taste of the cooking liquor it produces.

Serves 4

2 tbsp olive oil

salt and pepper

700g boned lamb, diced into 5cm cubes

1 medium onion, chopped

2 cloves garlic, chopped

1 tbsp tomato passata

1 level tbsp plain flour

200ml white wine

4 small carrots, chopped

4 small leeks, washed and cut
    into 5cm lengths

8 asparagus spears, cut into 5cm lengths

4 small courgettes, cut into 5cm lengths

100g shelled peas

1 tbsp chopped fresh parsley

1 tbsp chopped fresh basil

1  Heat the oil in a heavy-bottomed pan, then season and fry the lamb, onion and garlic together. After 5 minutes, add the passata.

2  Add the flour and let this cook for a few moments. Pour on the wine and stir while bringing to the boil. Turn the heat down to a gentle simmer and cover with a lid. Cook until tender (about 50 minutes).

3  In a separate pot, bring some unsalted water to the boil. Add and cook the vegetables in the order of cooking time – carrots first, then leeks, then asparagus, then courgettes and peas. Drain, reserving a little cooking water.

4  When the lamb is ready, add the vegetables to it and use some of the water to adjust the consistency of the stew – it will tend to become dry as it cooks. Lastly, and away from direct heat, add the chopped herbs.

5  Stir together and serve with Jersey Royal new potatoes.

## Ingredients

> **Shoulder and neck fillet will be good for this dish,** but so too will leg of lamb, provided you use seam butchery techniques to arrive at your lamb cubes (see page 123).

> **The dish can include whatever vegetables are coming into season,** as it is a celebration of late spring/early summer. The choice and variety will affect the finished dish and, although this is nominally a stew, most spring vegetables are green and tender so will not benefit from being cooked for as long as the meat. The trick is to add them later so that each will be at its best simultaneously. The herbs are added at the very last minute for the same reason.

> **Don't use any ingredients that are too powerful,** such as tomato purée or heavy red wine, and don't put in too much in the way of herbs and seasonings or else the flavours of the meat and vegetables will be over-powered and the point of the dish lost.

For chopping an onion see **47**    For lamb see **122**    For seam butchery see **123**

# Beef

**There is very little to help you when shopping for meat,** and this is never truer than when buying beef. The only breed that merits a separate mention is Aberdeen Angus, as clear guidelines are given for its rearing. Yet there are many breeds that suit rearing for meat rather than milk – Welsh Black and Hereford cattle are good on the Welsh borders where I live, and Devon Reds provided fine meat in the West Country when I lived there.

The problem is that the quality of the meat is influenced by much more than just the breed – factors such as what the animal is fed on, its experiences at the abbatoir, butchery and hanging skills are also important, but are more difficult to define as part of the beef's background. In the past, the reputation of a butcher's shop would be your guarantee and bona fide, but with the dominance of supermarkets in recent years, individual and personally-run shops are comparatively rare.

To make matters more complicated, there are differing schools of butchery. The French will cut away beef skirt from the attached sirloin and sell it separately as '*onglet*', skirt steak. In mediocre butcher's shops and supermarkets, forequarter joints – the chewier cuts – will regularly be jumbled up and sold in cubes under the heading of 'braising' or 'stewing' steak.

Most joints cook at differing speeds and need to be handled and cooked accordingly. The hindquarters – the fillet and sirloin – are the most tender and are good for roasting. After that, the topside is the softest, followed by the rump, then the wing ribs and finally fore ribs. If you have the time, there is real benefit in buying meat and then mincing or dicing it yourself.

# Sauerbraten

**This is a deeply unappetising name for a good dish.** The beef is marinated in red wine and vinegar before being braised and the result is actually quite refreshing, like a nicely pickled gherkin in flavour, and almost summery.

This treatment of less fatty joints such as silverside or topside is popular in southern Germany and in Austria. I'm not sure what the technical name for a brother's mother-in-law might be, but my brother – a long-time resident of Basel in Switzerland – offers this recipe, which his mother-in-law Heidi makes as a party piece. I have eaten her version of it and it is excellent. The braised meat is also good cold.

### Serves 6
1.5kg silverside
butter, for frying
2 onions, chopped
150ml red wine
salt and pepper
250ml double cream

### For the marinade:
250ml water
1 tbsp salt
3 onions, finely chopped
200ml red wine
50ml red wine vinegar
1 tbsp fresh coriander, chopped
1 tbsp fresh marjoram, chopped

1   Bring the marinade ingredients to the boil, simmer for 10 minutes, then leave to cool.
2   Place the whole joint in a deep dish and pour over the cooled marinade. If the beef is not completely covered you will need to turn it regularly. Cover, refrigerate and marinate for three days.
3   Preheat the oven to 190°C/Gas mark 5. Take the meat from the marinade and wipe dry. Heat a little butter, then fry the onions before adding the meat to brown on all sides. Strain the marinade on to the meat, along with the red wine, salt and pepper to taste. Transfer to a casserole or lidded pot and braise until tender – about 3 hours.
4   Remove the meat from the pot and place on a serving platter.
5   Add the cream to the cooking liquor, heat through briefly, then strain this over the meat.

### Technique
> **Some recipes give a much greater ratio of vinegar to wine.** This will produce a much sharper dish. It doesn't suit me, but it might appeal to you.

### Cooking method
> **The longer the beef is marinated for,** the more pronounced the pickle flavour will be.

# Pork

**All the strictures about avoiding fatty specimens that apply to so much meat are irrelevant here.** Pork fat is superb, and animals that have only a light covering will be tasteless and dry. In fact most pork was inedible for years in this country, as businessmen with gross profit margins and government subsidies to think about rather than dinner were persuaded that the public would not eat meat with fat attached and proceeded to develop breeds that complied. The result was rubbish. So if you don't like pork, that's probably why. If you want pork but don't want fat, cut it off, either before or after cooking. The eye of meat that remains will still be moist and flavourful.

Look for pork from rare breeds. I use meat from Berkshires, but would be happy with that from Tamworths, Middle Whites or Gloucester Old Spot. They all taste similar and have a good layer of fat. Also, the type of producer rearing these old breeds will tend to feed them, and look after them, properly. As with beef, the hindquarters are the most tender.

Pork is best cooked well-done. Historically this has been necessary to kill off parasitic worms that can attack pigs and remain in the flesh. But even without this reason, the meat is still best cooked right through as its texture under-done is unpleasant.

This doesn't mean that you have to cook it to death of course; the removal of all traces of blood and any opaqueness in the meat is enough.

Pork is the only meat – poultry from the duck family excluded – that partners fruit successfully. The richness works well with almost any acidic accompaniment: apples, prunes or whatever you fancy. Pork can also take on spices that would destroy lamb, so ginger, cardamom and the whole range of Chinese spices and pickles will just lift and highlight the character of the meat.

# Minced pork meatballs with marjoram and garlic

**Minced meat is always a dubious option,** for there is little doubt that all the least desirable bits of meat will have been used in its making. The best option is to buy rare breed pork and mince it yourself or, if you have the gravitas to intimidate your butcher, buy the meat and have him grind it in front of you. With minced beef and lamb you may be persuaded to serve the results underdone, but with pork the decisions are easy – cook it right through. I like the sweetness of best-quality pork fat, so I use belly for this recipe; otherwise 500g cut from the shoulder will be fine.

### Serves 4

1 shallot, finely chopped
500g minced pork
2 cloves garlic, finely copped
1 tbsp marjoram, chopped
salt and pepper
sunflower oil or lard, for frying

### For the sauce:

100g smoked streaky bacon, finely diced
50g haricot beans, tinned or soaked
    overnight then boiled until tender
1 shallot, finely chopped
1 chilli, deseeded and chopped
1 tsp paprika
4 tbsp chopped tomato
25ml chicken stock or water
salt

1. Combine the shallot, minced pork, garlic and marjoram until well mixed. Season with a little salt and plenty of black pepper.
2. Divide the mixture into 12 small golf ball-shaped meatballs, then press each into a patty shape, like a small potato cake or burger.
3. Heat a frying pan, then add some sunflower oil or lard. When the oil is hot, cook the patties until brown on each side, then lower the heat and cover with a lid. Cook for 6-7 minutes more, until the patties are completely done.
4. In a separate saucepan, heat some sunflower oil and fry the bacon, haricots and shallot. When they are cooked but before they turn brown, add the chopped chilli and then the paprika and chopped tomato. Let this cook gently for 5 minutes before adding a little stock or water.
5. Combine the pork patties and the sauce and serve.

### Ingredients

> **Commercial chopped tomatoes will give a better result** for this dish than fresh home-grown tomatoes, painstakingly peeled and chopped. The tomatoes used in jars and tins tend to be fuller-flavoured Mediterranean types that will hold up well against the other ingredients. Also, you are looking for cooked tomato flavours here rather than the freshness of the nearly raw. I use tomatoes from a jar in preference to tinned.

> **Marjoram can be awkward to find,** so you may substitute it for its more glamorous cousin oregano if necessary.

### Technique

> **Cook the patties in batches** so that they have some chance of browning on each side. This browning improves the flavour and helps the meatballs hold together.

> **The paprika should fry for a few seconds** to release its flavour before the tomato is added.

# Crisp belly pork with mustard and a herb dressing

Belly of pork is cheap and, like most cheap cuts, needs more work to shine gastronomically. The meat is, however, always moist and tender and its combination of fat and meat in alternating strips means that it bastes itself while cooking and that large amounts of the fat will have melted away by the time it is cooked.

This dish is a series of contrasts: hot crisp meat against cool salad leaves, and a sweet and sharp dressing that cuts through the richness of the meat as well as coating the salad leaves.

**Serves 4**

700g boneless belly pork

1 medium onion, chopped

1 carrot, sliced

1 stick celery, sliced

1 tbsp Dijon mustard

150g fresh breadcrumbs

selection of salad leaves, such as rocket,
    corn salad, frisée and watercress

1 tbsp caperberries

1 tbsp sunflower oil, if frying

**For the dressing:**

1 tsp white wine vinegar

1 tsp white wine

1 tsp caster sugar

3 tbsp olive oil

salt and pepper

1 tbsp chopped fresh parsley and chives

1   Preheat the oven to 200°C/Gas mark 6.

2   Roast the belly pork with the vegetables. This should take just over an hour. Discard the vegetables.

3   While the pork is still warm, cut it into strips and coat with mustard and then fresh breadcrumbs.

4   Mix together the salad leaves.

5   Whisk together the dressing ingredients until they form a temporary emulsion. This distributes the seasoning evenly and lets you know if the proportions are OK.

6   Arrange the salad leaves on the plates. Re-whisk the dressing if necessary, and dress the leaves. Spinkle some caperberries over the top.

7   If frying the meat, heat the sunflower oil. Grill or fry the pork until it is crisp and hot, then arrange on top of the dressed salad.

## Ingredients

> **Check there are no bits of gristle** left in the pork by the butcher.

> **The pork will dry out if left in the fridge for too long.** Wrapped properly, it will be fine for four to five days; unwrapped and even 24 hours is too long.

> **Fresh breadcrumbs** are best when they are made from a loaf that is one to two days old.

> **You can swap the wine vinegar** in the dressing for raspberry vinegar or any other fruit vinegar and the dish will be equally fine.

## Technique

> **The dressing should be refreshing** and the point of the sugar is to maintain the balance.

## Cooking method

> **Should the pork be too fatty when cooked**, cut some off rather than hope that the oven heat will make it disappear.

> **It's difficult to over-cook** this user-friendly cut of pork.

> **The pork can be cooked well ahead** of time.

For chopping an onion see **47**   For pork see **128**

# Veal

**Veal is not popular.** Anaemic Dutch veal with little flavour and the lack of a veal-eating tradition doesn't help. You can now buy good home-reared veal, though, and the meat is worth seeking out – not for veal escalopes particularly, for they are not very exciting.

Braised veal dishes are, however, a different story and Hungarian *gulyas* or Italian *osso bucco* well made are among the best dishes anywhere. The braising chapter will show you how.

Buy veal that is pale but not white. The meat will render up lots of liquor as it cooks so don't worry about stocks and sauces. The joints are similar to those for beef, but infuriatingly have different names – topside is known as cushion of veal – so ask the butcher where each joint originates.

# Offal

**This is the most interesting part of the animal.** Muscle joints vary according to the amount of work they do, with hard-working areas such as the front legs having more sinew and taking longer to cook than, say, the back legs – watch an animal getting up from the ground and you'll see what I mean – or an inside joint such as the fillet that does no work at all. The meat will always have a similar taste and texture wherever it comes from, keeping an overall lamb, beef or pork flavour. Offal, however, is usually tender, but varies enormously in flavour. The flavour of calf's kidneys will be closer to lamb's or pig's kidneys than it will to veal loin. The same holds true for liver, brains and sweetbreads.

There are two schools of thought about which animal provides the best offal, but the shortlist will always be the same: it's between lamb and veal. Ox liver is coarse and pig's liver only marginally better. You can eat either or both – and you can eat pork offal – in the same kind of dishes as you would use veal or lamb offal. Ox kidney needs a lot of slow-cooking and gives a powerful flavour; you'll remember it well from steak and kidney puddings and pies, and it's not everyone's preference.

Veal has unfortunate associations with unpleasant husbandry methods and isn't popular with many people, which is a pity as good veal, decently reared and fed, is now available and the offal especially is very fine.

For veal stock and demi-glace see **218**

# Calf's sweetbreads with sorrel and shallots

**Sweetbread is a catch-all word used by butchers to cover lots of different glands and parts.** This is a nuisance to shoppers, for you are likely to be offered testicles and whatever as sweetbreads when what should be on display are two similar pieces of offal known as throatbreads and heartbreads. The one you want is the fist-shaped heartbread – the thymus gland. Butchers often do not charge more for these vastly superior delicacies than would be charged for the stringier throatbreads, which are long and narrow but otherwise similar in colour and texture.

### Serves 4

700g veal heartbreads
1 tsp wine vinegar
salt and pepper
olive oil, for frying
2 shallots, finely chopped
20ml white wine
60g unsalted butter
1 bunch sorrel, cut into strips

1   Wash the sweetbreads in several changes of cold water. They will be covered in a white membrane and also possibly by clusters of deeply unappetizing-looking tubes. Cut most of this away and leave only enough of the outer membrane to hold the meat together.

2   Put into a saucepan with the wine vinegar, some black pepper and just enough water to cover. Lay a circle of greaseproof paper, or the wrapper from a butter pack, across the top. This is to ensure that any parts of the meat that rise above the water level will still cook but that the liquid will not come to as sharp a boil as it would if covered with a lid – a matter of temperature control, for you want all the cooking to be gentle.

3   Bring the sweetbreads to the boil and then lower the heat to a gentle simmer for 3-5 minutes, depending on the size and shape of the meat. Turn off the heat and let the sweetbreads cool in their own cooking liquor. They should be set and firm but still soft. When they are cool, trim away any membrane you missed before and cut the meat into thickish slices.

4   Brush the slices with olive oil, then fry in a heated pan until brown on each side. I like to finish the cooking in the oven for a few minutes at 200°C/Gas mark 6, but this is only absolutely necessary if you have cut particularly thick slices. Thicker slices have more flavour, and so are ideal for people who really enjoy the flavour of sweetbreads.

5   For the sauce, heat the shallots and white wine. Whisk in the butter piece by piece – as if you were making a *beurre blanc*. Stir in the sorrel and simmer for a few moments; the sorrel will melt into the sauce.

6   Spoon the sauce on to warmed plates and lay a slice of crisp cooked sweetbread on top.

### Ingredients

> **Sweetbreads suit sharp and slightly acidic sauces,** such as hot salad dressings or watercress sauce. Sorrel has a flavour like unsweetened gooseberry and fits the bill nicely.

### Cooking method

> **Don't be too disappointed if your sorrel loses its brilliant chlorophyl-green** and becomes a less thrilling khaki as soon as it meets the heat, as this is normal.

For buerre blanc see **228**

# Calf's liver with Armagnac-marinated sultanas and black pepper

**Sweet flavours go best with liver.** The traditional accompaniment to *foie gras* is sweet brioche bread, and in Finland they make a bizarre-sounding but very acceptable pudding, *maksalaatikko*, from lamb's liver minced with rice and treacle then all baked together.

**Serves 4**

25g sultanas

25ml Armagnac

25ml Madeira

1kg calf's liver, sliced

salt and pepper

a little sunflower oil, for frying

45g unsalted butter

1 Put the sultanas in a pan with the Armagnac and Madeira, warm, then leave to soak for at least an hour.

2 Season the slices of liver with some salt and coarsely ground black pepper. Heat a little sunflower oil with 20g of the butter in a hot pan. When the butter foams, but before it browns, fry the slices of liver quickly for 1-2 minutes on each side, depending on the thickness of the slices. The aim is to caramelize each side quickly. You may need to do this in two batches. If you prefer liver pink, take the slices from the pan as soon as they have browned; if you prefer it well done, lower the heat and cook for a further few minutes.

3 Remove all the liver from the pan and then pour in the sultanas and marinating liquid. They will plump up in the heat. Turn off the heat and stir in the remaining butter to thicken the pan juices and booze. Pour this over the liver and serve with mashed potato perhaps, and some spinach or salad.

## Ingredients

> **The darker the liver, the stronger the flavour.** If your preference is for a more subtle liver flavour, soak the slices in milk or a mixture of milk and cold water for a couple of hours. This will draw out the blood and leave you with a more anaemic-looking but gentler liver. Drain and dry the liver slices before use.

## Technique

> **The thicker the slices, the more liver flavour there will be.** Thin slices give a higher ratio of crisp surface to soft interior, thick slices the reverse, and it is that soft interior that has the most distinctive liver taste. So your choice depends on what you want – crisp texture with delicate liver notes or big liver taste.

For mashed potatoes see **33**    For offfal see **132**

# Lamb's kidneys and black pudding with mustard sauce

**The flavour of kidney marries well with mustard.** Lamb's kidneys are particularly easy to prepare. There is a small white piece of gristle visible to one side. Split the kidneys, leaving the halves joined at this bit of gristle. If it doesn't bother you to have the kidneys split completely then you can halve them lengthways and cut out the gristle at the core altogether.

**Serves 4**

sunflower oil, for cooking
45g unsalted butter
salt and pepper
12 lamb's kidneys
1 tsp plain flour
1 tbsp chopped shallot
1 tbsp wholegrain mustard
25ml Madeira
2 tbsp chopped parsley
100g black pudding, sliced

1 Heat a little oil and 20g of the butter in a pan, then season and fry the kidneys on each side in a hot pan. Sprinkle the flour over the kidneys and let this cook for a few moments, stirring.

2 Add the shallot and mustard, then pour on the Madeira. Place a lid over the pan and let the kidneys cook on a low heat for 5 minutes.

3 Stir in the remaining butter to thicken the cooking liquor and then add the parsley.

4 In a separate hot pan, fry the slices of black pudding in a little oil – when it's hot in the middle it's cooked – and lift these on to the kidney and sauce.

## Ingredients

> **Black pudding comes in various guises.** My preference is for the French varieties, which are smooth and may even have a little apple or brandy added, rather than the British specimens, which often have big lumps of fat spread throughout.

## Technique

> **If the central gristle has been left in, the kidneys** will tend to curl back into their original shape while cooking. You can prevent this by threading a toothpick across either side of the centre. Remember to take the toothpick out before serving.

> **There is an outer membrane on any kidney which needs removing.** This is most easily done with your fingertips once the kidney has been split.

For offal see **132**

**The appeal of sweet things is universal.** Harold McGee, in his book *On Food and Cooking* surmises that this may be connected with early man's diet of ripe fruit while he was leaping about in the trees, and calls the simple carbohydrates known as sugar, 'the standard currency of chemically-stored energy'. Good stuff. I'm sure he's right.

However, the sugar we use now is a relative latecomer to the sweetness store-cupboard. Honey was the main sweetener for thousands of years. Table sugar derived from canes only appeared on the western European scene from Asia in medieval times and, even then, it was expensive and its use largely medicinal. The Romans used grape juice, but unfortunately boiled it down to syrup in lead pans. The effects of lead poisoning are believed to have given the sadistic Emperor, Caligula, a good portion of his psychosis and are unlikely to have had much benefit for the lesser members of the population either.

Sugar cane plantations in the West Indies during the 18th century were the engines of mass-production and consumption and gave us the product we know today, until a combination of distaste for the slavery on which the industry was based and developments in refining sugar beet back in Europe changed the pattern of manufacture once again. Sugar had moved from expensive luxury to an everyday ingredient.

Now sugar is over-used and has become one of the villains in the mealtime story, substituted often by dubious chemical alternatives. There is no problem if it is used in moderation and, just as with that other villain salt, it is in manufactured foodstuff that the really large amounts can be unwittingly eaten.

There is an association between sugar and some spices. Cinnamon, nutmeg and vanilla, for instance, seem to sit as easily with sweet stuff as savoury. But it is with bitter tastes that sugar really becomes important, balancing the power of ingredients such as chocolate or liquorice or, more prosaically, the bitter quinine in tonic water. Many ingredients that you buy, such as chocolate, will have been blended with sugar already, and it will be with the balancing of savoury concoctions such as salad dressings or some soups and sauces that the judicious use of a little sugar can help.

# The role of sweetness in a meal

**Pudding, the end of the meal, is associated with sweetness and sugar, as are between-meal snacks of cakes and biscuits to go with coffee and tea.** The reasoning for this varies from dessert being a reward for good children who have eaten up all the boring meat and starch in the main course, to theories about the difficulty of following a palate coated with sugary tastes with anything much else. Neither bears much scrutiny. Most *apéritifs* are sweet, and those that are not, such as gin and tonic, have little credit gastronomically after numbing both brain and palate in advance of any food. The gourmet French will tuck into port ahead of their first-course soup and will be delighted to knock back a glass of Sauternes with their foie gras shortly afterwards.

The reality probably lies in appetite. It would be a miserly dinner if you were still hungry after the main course, and the allure of something sweet will attract when little else will appeal. A change of pace in temperature or texture, with the likes of ice-cream or some confection of fruit and custard, will also tempt the jaded to another mouthful.

There is a restaurant in Barcelona that only serves desserts. It was interesting that the meal, after five courses of well-judged fruit and confectionery, none of it overly sweet, still felt unsatisfying and incomplete. While there is an immediate attraction to sweet things, there is a more satisfying element to the tastes we perceive as savoury and a good meal balances the two, irrespective of where they are slotted in.

For custard see **140**   For ice-cream see **144**   For pastry see **146**   For chocolate see **153**

# Cooking with sugar

Sugar comes in several guises:

**Brown sugars:** have some of the molasses – dark syrup residue formed in the production of sugar – left in and these have a degree of caramel in their flavour. They come as soft sugars, called muscovado, or in hard crystals, called demerara.

**White sugar:** this is the sugar you will use the most – has all the molasses and impurities refined out. It's pretty much a sweetener and nothing else. It does, however, come in varying crystal sizes ready for differing uses. For reasons unknown, there is a significant difference in price between these grades of white sugar.

Granulated sugar has medium-sized crystals and forms syrup particularly easily when mixed with any liquid – thus it is good for making caramel as well as sweetening your cup of tea.

Caster sugar is formed into smaller crystals. I have read that the name derives from its suitability for use in a sugar caster – shaker – though perversely in America this grade of sugar is called 'granulated'. Perhaps the sugar shakers there had bigger holes. This size of crystal blends most easily with fats and flour in bakery.

Icing sugar is powdered and useful for icing and for dusting over any burnt or unsightly bits of a baked tart – the pastry cook's equivalent of chopped parsley.

**Sugar syrups:** those available in the UK are treacle, dark and deep-flavoured, and golden syrup, which is lighter. Syrup is more versatile than treacle and is used in a lot of biscuits. You can buy glucose for use in advanced, decorative sugar work – it's added to the boiling syrup to make it more pliable and less prone to crystallization. Americans use corn syrups rather than sugar syrups. Corn syrups are extracted from maize and work well, but I have never seen them on sale here, so assume they add nothing more than the cane-sugar-derived syrups we have.

**Stock syrup:** this is a pastry cook's store-cupboard item. It comprises a pound of granulated sugar brought to the boil with a pint of water. I have no idea of any metric equivalent that has superseded this basic formula. It can be used in the making of sorbets and ice-cream as well as sweet sauces. Outside the heat of the kitchen, it is handy mixed with Tequila, lime juice and salt for making margueritas.

# Custard

**Custards needn't be sweet – the basic mixture for quiche is a savoury custard – but the combination of eggs and milk cooked together can come in various textures.** It can be made as a sauce or set into something more imposing, or at least more solid.

French cookery divides custard sauces into *crème anglaise* (thin custard) and *crème patissiere* (thick custard). *Crème anglaise* is made by whisking together four egg yolks with 2oz (55g) caster sugar. A pint (565ml) of milk is boiled, then whisked on to the egg and sugar mixture, then the custard is slowly stirred over a low heat until it thickens slightly but removed from the heat before it boils. You may want a flavoured custard, in which case you add vanilla, cinnamon, coffee, chocolate or whatever suits to the milk before heating it. Then the custard can be sieved into a jar and cooled for use another time and poured around whatever is the central feature of the dish, perhaps a steamed pudding, some baked apples or a tart.

*Crème patissière* is easier to handle and is made like this: six egg yolks are whisked together with 6oz (170g) caster sugar until they whiten, then 3oz (85g) plain flour is stirred in. A pint (565ml) of milk is boiled, then whisked into the egg, sugar and flour mixture off the heat. This is then returned to the saucepan and heat and stirred until it comes to the boil. This gives a thick custard that is good for trifles and suchlike, and that will set solid once cooled. Part of the flour can be substituted by cornflour for a silkier result.

Whole eggs set with milk or cream will be the basis for all the *crème brûlée* and baked custard recipes you ever see. The essential point is to take care over temperatures with any custard that is thickened without the help of flour. Patience is the key: slow-cooking at a moderate-to-low temperature, so that the egg doesn't over-cook, scrambling into something unsightly to look at and useless for binding together the other ingredients.

For ice-cream see **144**

# Muscat crème caramel with prunes in Armagnac

This recipe falls into two parts: the *crème caramel* and the marinated prunes. Each would be fine without the other, but the combination makes a dish better than the sum of its component parts. It's essentially a re-working of prunes and custard of course, and can be made into a re-working of pineapple and custard by cooking pieces of pineapple in a light caramel instead of the prunes, or banana and custard by turning slices of banana in darker caramel as a substitute.

### Serves 4

**For the crème caramels:**

90g granulated sugar

190ml Muscat or other sweet white wine

275ml double cream

75ml milk

2 eggs plus 4 yolks

175g vanilla sugar

**For the marinated prunes:**

2 Earl Grey tea bags

60g caster sugar

1 cinnamon stick

100g pitted prunes

150ml Armagnac

1   You prepare the prunes first. Make 500ml tea with the Earl Grey tea bags. Let it brew for a few minutes, then fish out the tea bags. Pour the tea into a saucepan along with the caster sugar, cinnamon and prunes. Bring this to the boil, then lower the heat so the prunes simmer gently for 5 minutes. Let them cool, then add the Armagnac. Keep the prunes and cooking liquor in a lidded jar until you are ready to serve the dish.

2   Preheat the oven to 150°C/Gas mark 2. You will need four dariole moulds – the traditional containers for making crème caramel – or six ramekin dishes. Heat the granulated sugar with 3 tbsp water. Keep an eye on the sugar as it caramelizes and take the pan away from direct heat as it nears the colour you want – dark brown. Pour some caramel into each mould or ramekin.

3   Heat the wine and cream/milk in separate saucepans. Whisk together the eggs, yolks and vanilla sugar. When the wine and cream come to the boil, remove from the heat. Whisk first the hot wine and then the hot cream into the egg and sugar mixture. Pour some of this custard on to the caramel in each mould or ramekin. Place the moulds in a steep-sided roasting tray and carefully fill with warm water until about halfway up the moulds. Cover loosely with kitchen foil, then bake in the middle of the preheated oven for around 45 minutes.

4   Let the *crème caramels* cool and refrigerate overnight. To serve them, run the tip of a hot knife around each and turn it out. Heap a good spoonful of the marinated prunes around each.

### Caramel technique

> **The water added to the sugar serves to make it a syrup,** and the idea is that the sugar will cook and colour more evenly in this state. In fact, the sugar will not start to cook properly until all the water has evaporated, but by this time the sugar will be at the same temperature throughout.

> **The transformation of sugar into caramel is straightforward, but needs care** as caramelizing sugar is sticky and very hot. Once the sugar turns a light brown, take the pan from the direct heat and let it colour more slowly. Sugar gets progressively less sweet as it colours, and will turn bitter beyond the stage of dark brown.

### Custard technique

> **The cooking time is a guideline,** for it will vary slightly depending on the reliability of your oven thermostat and the shape of the cooking mould or ramekin. To test for doneness, lift the foil, which is there to prevent the custard browning on the top, and shake one of the moulds gently; the custard should be just set.

For custard see **140**

# Ice-cream

**Custard's most popular incarnation is as ice-cream.** Ice-cream is churned in the same way as sorbet and the best method is to use an ice-cream-making machine. These can be fairly cheap attachments to an existing deep-freeze – there are modest Italian machines that make a litre of ice-cream and are aimed at the domestic market (this is what I use), or all-singing, all-dancing machines that take up a large chunk of your kitchen space and weigh as much as the car, which are really for commercial production only. Lastly, and proportionately the most expensive, are the Paco jet machines that make a couple of portions in an instant, so that your ice-cream is always just-made; they can also produce ice-creams from unlikely ingredients, so most savoury ice-creams in cutting-edge restaurants have been made possible by this gadget. I am agnostic on the merits of these ice-creams and find most have novelty value only. This is much more pleasurable...

## Chocolate chip ice-cream

**This is a good exercise in basic ice-cream-making.** You can leave out the chocolate and add cinnamon or caramel to the custard if you prefer. The chocolate makes the ice-cream more of an event however, and will make a serviceable dessert with a couple of shortbread or brandy snap biscuits. I have always used this formula, which is in imperial measures rather than metric.

Serves 10

1 pint milk

1 pint double cream

1 vanilla pod, split in 2 lengthwise

7 egg yolks

8oz caster sugar

6oz chocolate couverture, grated
   or chopped

1   Bring the milk and cream to the boil together with the vanilla pod. Whisk together the egg yolks and sugar until they turn pale.

2   Whisk the milk and cream mixture on to the egg and sugar mixture, than return the result to a low heat.

3   Stir until the custard thickens, then pour into a bowl to cool. When cool, take out the vanilla pod. Run the blade of a sharp knife along the cut edges of each side to scrape out the vanilla beans, then put these back into the custard. Discard the pod.

4   Slowly melt the chocolate. The best way to do this is to put it in a bowl and stand the bowl over warm water, stirring occasionally.

5   Churn in an ice-cream-making machine. As the ice-cream thickens, trickle in the melted chocolate.

### Ingredients

> **Chocolate couverture is cooking chocolate.** It is usually vastly superior to that found in standard choccie bars, and will show the percentage of cocoa solids to sugar on the packet. This can be as high as 70%, with Green and Black offering a very fine product.

### Technique

> **Custards in any guise, even frozen as ice-cream, are an ideal breeding-medium for bacteria.** Commercial ice-creams contain chemicals to stabilize and sanitize them. So eat your ice-cream over a few days rather than keep it for weeks. Also, commercial deep-freezes for ice-cream are usually kept at a higher temperature than is ideal for your domestic deep-freeze, so your ice-cream will become very hard. Store it in batches in several small containers.

> **Chocolate couverture needs to be melted slowly** or it will form white streaks. Leave the grated or chopped chocolate in a bowl over warm water and stir occasionally for the best results.

### Cooking method

> **The custard must never boil.** The consistency changes as it heats, and will visibly alter from raw milk and egg to custard.

For custard see **140**    For chocolate see **153**

# Iced walnut and honey parfait

*'Parfait'* **is a silly word that means 'perfect' in French, and can mean just about anything on a restaurant menu.** It normally implies something smooth-textured – chicken liver parfait as an example – and in frozen pud terms means something that has been set in the freezer rather than churned. But we have no better word at the moment.

**Serves 10**

75g granulated sugar

100g shelled walnuts, chopped

4 egg yolks

75g caster sugar

50g honey

200ml milk

1 vanilla pod, split in 2 lengthwise

2 tbsp lime or lemon juice

300ml double cream

1   Melt the sugar and bring to the boil. When the colour starts to change into caramel, add the chopped walnuts and cook for a further few minutes. Pour on to an oiled baking sheet to cool, then break up into smallish pieces.

2   Whisk the egg yolks and sugar together until pale, then add the honey.

3   Bring the milk and vanilla pod to the boil, then whisk this on to the egg mixture. Stir over a low heat until the custard thickens – do not allow it to boil. Pour into a jug or bowl to cool. When the custard is cool, fish out the vanilla pod. Run the blade of a sharp knife along the cut edges of each side to scrape out the vanilla beans, then put these back into the custard. Discard the pod.

4   When the custard is completely cold, stir in the lime juice, then whisk the cream and add this and the chopped walnut brittle to the custard. Mix well and spoon into a 1 litre rectangular mould. Freeze.

**Technique**

> **Let the caramelized walnuts become cool** and brittle before breaking them up.

> **Wait until the custard is cold** before mixing in the whipped cream.

> **Honey is easier to handle** if warmed slightly.

# Pastry

**Unlike bread doughs, pastry doughs need the least possible gluten development from the flour used.** This is because the more developed the gluten is, the more it helps the dough to hold in air, and you don't want too much air in pastry dough. So, the reverse procedures produce the finest results: minimal handling so that the gluten is not pulled and stretched, plenty of fat content and a softer flour.

The main purpose of pastry is to act as a base or container for some filling and this filling will be the star of the show. It does, however, give form and shape to a dish, and an opportunity to bring together differing textures of fruits, nuts and custard, into a reassuringly familiar and easily handled format.

There are lots of methods and variations in the ratio of flour to fat, but two styles predominate for their versatility: short pastry and puff pastry. Once you have the measure of these two, tarts and pies of all types will be easy.

## Short and sweet pastry

**Sweet pastry is a variation of short pastry.** For savoury tarts you need only omit the sugar and for suet crust you need to both omit the sugar and substitute chopped suet for butter. The 'short' in 'short pastry' derives from shortening – butter or lard – and not the time taken to make it. This is a particularly rich version, using lots of butter. It adds to the overall pleasure in taste as well as texture of the finished dish, but is more awkward to handle than a recipe that uses less butter.

2 egg yolks
225g unsalted butter, cool rather than cold
1 tbsp caster sugar
350g plain flour

1   Beat the egg yolks, butter and sugar together, then stir in the flour.
2   Knead just once or twice to make sure that the ingredients are evenly distributed, then cover with a butter wrapper or clingfilm and refrigerate for at least an hour, or until needed.

### Technique

> **There are two major styles of combining the ingredients.** Traditionally, the butter is cut into the flour until it has the texture of fresh breadcrumbs and then the dough is completed by the addition of a few drops of water or beaten egg. My prefererance is to beat all the ingredients except the flour and then incorporate this right at the end. This is for two reasons: firstly it enables you to cream the sugar into the butter and secondly there is less opportunity for the gluten in the flour to become over-stretched. To achieve this you will need cool rather than cold butter, which is difficult to beat.

> **Rest the pastry each time it is handled** – an hour in the fridge is fine – otherwise it will tend to shrink during cooking, leaving you with reduced sides to your tart.

> **Don't worry if your pastry refuses to roll out** into a neat unbroken sheet. You can piece it together like a jigsaw in the tart case if need be. Just remember to rest it in the fridge afterwards.

> **Pastry keeps in the fridge** for a few days and it freezes well.

### Cooking method

> **Most tarts are baked blind,** i.e. before the filling is added. This gives a crisper finish to the tart base as well as ensuring that it is actually cooked. Some people like to fill a foil case with dried beans or some such ingredient and place this in the tart case to help prevent the pastry from rising during baking. I don't subscribe to this idea. The beans prevent the base from cooking and crisping nicely, and this is the whole point of baking blind in the first place. Halfway through cooking, take a clean cloth and press any blistering patches of pastry back into place.

For puff pastry see **151**

For rhubarb and meringue tart see **146**   For plum and almond tart see **148**

# Rhubarb meringue tart

**Rhubarb is at its best well before any of the earliest varieties of soft fruit and represents one of the few genuine winter treats at the pudding stage.** And it's winter we are talking about: forced rhubarb, not the outdoor variety that reaches the shelves in spring and summer, which is coarse and bitter. Forced rhubarb is toothpaste-pink and comparatively fragile in flavour. Traditionally it is grown in Yorkshire but the enterprising Dutch now offer thicker, though not superior, rhubarb at around the same time.

## Serves 4

½ quantity of sweet pastry (see page 146)

1kg rhubarb, cut into 3cm lengths

3 egg yolks

120g demerara sugar

a pinch of salt

2 tbsp plain flour

3 egg whites

3 tbsp caster sugar

1  Preheat the oven to 200°C/Gas mark 6.

2  Line a 26cm pastry case – preferably with a detachable base – with sweet pastry and bake blind.

3  The rhubarb goes in next. Then mix together the egg yolks, demerara sugar, salt and flour and spread this over the fruit (or more technically the veg).

4  Bake in the preheated oven for 10 minutes; this will start the rhubarb cooking.

5  Meanwhile, whisk the egg whites until stiff. As they stiffen, trickle in the caster sugar.

6  Take the tart from the oven and spread the meringue on top.

7  Reduce the heat to 180°C/Gas mark 4 and return the tart to the oven. Bake for a further 25 minutes.

## Technique

> **Egg whites must be completely free of imperfections** – including yolk – if they are to be successfully whisked. The bowl used must be dry and clean also. Don't add the sugar too early; the whites should already form peaks before you start.

For buying vegetables and fruit see **46**   For storing vegetables and fruit see **47**   For sweet pastry see **146**

# Plum and almond tart

**This is a decent example of a cooked tart.** Other stone fruits, such as cherries and apricot, would substitute perfectly for plums. Soft summer fruits such as strawberries and raspberries are better suited to assembled tarts – just arranged on top of a cooked base and some fruit purée or *crème patissière* – for they will not be improved by further cooking.

**Serves 4**

½ quantity of sweet pastry (see page 146)
50g ground almonds
50g unsalted butter, softened
50g icing sugar
2 tbsp caster sugar
1 tbsp double cream
1 egg
1 tsp Amaretto
500g plums
1 tsp semolina

1  Preheat the oven to 190°C/Gas mark 5.

2  Line a 26cm pastry case, preferably with a detachable base, with sweet pastry.

3  Bake the tart in the preheated oven until crisp. Reckon on 15 minutes for this, but take a look after 10.

4  Whisk together the almonds, butter, sugars, cream, egg and Amaretto.

5  Stone the plums and arrange across the base of the cooked tart case. Dust with semolina.

6  Spoon over the almond mixture and then bake for 40 minutes. The mixture will puff out a little and turn brown.

**Ingredients**

> **Most varieties of plum will be fine in this tart** – from early Prolific to the late Marjorie's Seedling – but my preference is for the good all-purpose variety, Victoria.

> **Amaretto is a sweet** *digestif* made from apricot kernels and tastes similar to almond.

# Puff pastry

**There are times of the year when it is difficult to make puff pastry – hot humid days are the worst.** Otherwise the results from home-made puff pastry are completely different from the shop-bought product, which uses strong flour and pastry margarine rather than soft flour and butter. It is possible, in the restaurant trade, to buy well-made puff pastry, but it is far too expensive to be available at your local supermarket. This may change, but meanwhile the time and effort involved in making this is well spent.

450g unsalted butter
500g plain flour
1½ tsp salt
25ml white wine vinegar
200ml cold water

1  Melt 50g of the butter.

2  Place the flour and salt in a large bowl. Mix in the melted butter, vinegar and water to make a dough.

3  Roll this into a cross – just like the St George one on the English flag. To do this, cut a cross shape out of a ball of dough, pull out the dough and roll.

4  Between two sheets of clingfilm, roll the block of butter into a square that fits neatly into the centre of the pastry cross.

5  Remove the butter from the clingfilm and place in the centre of the pastry cross. Fold over the flaps of your pastry cross to enclose the butter and make a pastry parcel.

6  You will then need to make four 'book' turns, with at least an hour-long interval between each for the pastry to rest. A 'book' turn is done like this: roll out the pastry parcel into a long strip like a stair carpet. Fold each end back to the middle, like an open book, then close the newly formed 'book' into a new pastry parcel. Keep the fold to the right.

### Technique

> **Cool butter is good.** Butter is disastrous if it starts to melt and hard labour to roll out if rock hard. Use fairly cold butter to start with, but take the dough out of the fridge 10 minutes before each rolling so that it is easier to handle.

> **Puff pastry keeps in the fridge** for a few days and it freezes well.

For short and sweet pastry see **146**

# Pear and puff pastry tart with caramel sauce

**Puff pastry should be crisp, not soggy, so err on the side of cooked rather than raw.** Pears partner caramel well but the variety of pear is important: William and Comice pears are ideal; hard varieties such as conference are less good.

### Serves 4

¼ quantity of puff pastry

2 Comice or William pears, peeled, cored
   and cut in half lengthways

25g unsalted butter

1 tbsp caster sugar

icing sugar for dusting

### For the sauce:

250g granulated sugar

175g unsalted butter

150ml double cream

1   Preheat the oven to 200°C/Gas mark 6.

2   Roll out the pastry thinly, cut into four flat discs about 12cm round and prick all over with a fork.

3   Cut the pear halves into slices the thickness of a £1 coin, and spread across each disc. Dot with butter and sprinkle with caster sugar.

4   Place on a baking sheet and bake in the preheated oven until the pastry is crisp, about 15 minutes.

5   Make the sauce by heating the sugar until it caramelizes. Stir in the butter and cream and bring to the boil.

6   Pour the sauce around the crisp pear tarts.

### Technique

> **Take care when making caramel,** especially when adding cream or some other liquid, as it has a tendency to splutter. Let the caramel cool for a few seconds before adding anything to it.

> **These tarts freeze well** and can be made in advance and kept in the freezer until needed.

> **The sauce also keeps well,** but will set solid in the fridge so needs gentle reheating.

For buying fruit and veg see **46**   For storing fruit and veg see **47**   For puff pastry see **151**

# Chocolate

**Bitter chocolate is used as a savoury ingredient in Spanish and South American dishes.** I am not a fan of this and, what's worse, have tasted unpleasant versions of venison stew and braised hare to which sweet chocolate has been added by enthusiastic but misguided cooks. Chocolate manufactured with judicious amounts of sugar – that is not too much – and with the cocoa butter content intact rather than replaced by greasy substitutes, is one of the great pudding ingredients.

Chocolate has affinities with many spices, with nuts and some fruits. Cardamom, cinnamon and vanilla will add a layer of complexity to chocolate mousse or truffles, while in no way detracting from the essential chocolate flavour of the prime ingredient. Almonds, walnuts and hazelnuts will act as counterpoints in terms of texture as well as taste, and the success of chocolate and nut combinations is evidenced by the commercial choccie bars that rely on this mixture.

Fruit is more controversial, and there are plenty who dislike the combination of chocolate and fruit, whatever fruit or grade of chocolate is used. I agree where soft fruits such as strawberries and raspberries are concerned, but some fruits work well with chocolate, for instance oranges – especially the peel – bananas and even passion fruit. Cherries are good with chocolate too, and are the classic partner in Black Forest gâteau, which has become a cliché dish, its status not helped by the commercial versions on offer. But, as with many other over-used and much-imitated dishes, the central idea is good. Chocolate, booze-soaked cherries and cream make for a nice cake.

## Chocolate truffles

**There is jargon for chocolate work.** A mixture of melted chocolate and cream is called 'ganache'. This can be a cake-filling, but is usually cooled and used mixed with rum or Cointreau as chocolate truffles. Truffles are the perfect accompaniment to a final coffee in a long meal. They can be flavoured with any spice or liqueur you want and are just fine without any extra flavouring.

### Serves 4

600g couverture chocolate, grated or
   broken into pieces
200ml double cream
50ml rum
300g unsalted butter, softened

### To coat:

250g couverture chocolate, melted
300g cocoa powder

1   Melt the chocolate. The best way to do this is to put it in a bowl and stand the bowl in warm water, stirring occasionally.
2   Boil the cream, then let it cool. Mix the cream, melted chocolate and rum, or whatever you are using as flavouring, together.
3   In a large bowl, whisk the softened butter and then pour in the chocolate cream mixture. Refrigerate until ready to use.
4   Make a small production line with the ganache – chocolate mix – the melted couvertures and the cocoa powder.
5   Make small balls of ganache with a parisienne cutter or some such tool. If you don't have a cutter, just cut the ganache into whatever shape takes your fancy.
6   Use a toothpick to spear each ball, then dip into the melted couverture, then roll in cocoa powder. Store in the fridge.

### Technique

> **Chocolate couverture needs to be melted slowly** or it will form white streaks. Leave the grated or chopped chocolate in a bowl over warm water and stir occasionally for the best results.

> **The boiling of the cream is largely for health reasons,** to sterilize the cream. It keeps better and more safely this way.

> **The variations on this are endless.** Almost any sweet booze or spice can be added, as could sultanas that have been soaked in rum or chopped nuts.

# Chocolate cake

This chocolate cake can be partnered by a fresh cherry compote – just bring cherries to the boil with granulated sugar and a few drops of lemon juice – to achieve a decent re-working of the idea in pudding form. Alternatively, you could just make a pot of coffee and eat it as cake. Cream is optional but the cake will be better for a dollop of crème fraîche, should your dietary regime allow.

225g plain chocolate, grated or broken
   into pieces
100g unsalted butter
4 eggs
225g icing sugar
a few drops of vanilla essence
2 tbsp cornflour

1   Preheat the oven to 190°C/Gas mark 5.
2   Melt the chocolate and butter together. The best way to do this is to put the chocolate and butter in a bowl and stand the bowl in warm water, stirring occasionally.
3   Whisk the egg whites until stiff. Be sure to use a clean bowl and whisk.
4   Separately, whisk the yolks, icing sugar and vanilla essence together, then add the cornflour. Whisk until the colour of the mixture lightens perceptibly.
5   Add the melted chocolate and butter to the egg yolks.
6   Next add the whisked egg white, folding it in a third at a time.
7   Line a 18cm cake tin with parchment paper and pour in the cake batter.
8   Bake in the preheated oven until done – for around 30-40 minutes.

## Ingredients

> Vanilla extract or a natural essence from Madagascar are fine. Anything else isn't.

## Cooking method

> The recipe calls for the chocolate to be melted. This must be done gently and slowly. The chocolate can be grated so that it melts faster if time is important.
> There may be a tendency for the cake to sag in the middle if not completely cooked through, as there is very little flour – no wheat flour at all. This is not a huge problem if it happens as there will be no flour to taste raw and uncooked in the finished dish. At worst it will be gooey and fondant. In fact, better under-cooked than over-cooked.

For chocolate see **153**    For chocolate chip ice-cream **144**

# Methods of cooking

**Heat is not the only method of altering food so that it becomes easier or safer to digest.** There are plenty of processes that use enzymes and bacteria instead – cheese-making being the most obvious – or some form of drying and salting, as with hams and bacon, or pickling. The rationale has usually been preservation, extending shelf-life if you like, rather than enhancing flavour or texture. Salt draws out moisture, and the drier a piece of fish or meat becomes the less bacteria of any kind are able to multiply. Acid reduces the PH level to the point where bacteria can't multiply.

As the need for such traditional preservation diminishes, these methods are used purely for reasons of taste and texture. We like the taste of ham, we like the acidity of pickles, and there is even a market for sauerkraut, which is salted and then fermented.

The same applies on a smaller scale to any salad or vegetable that is tossed in dressing. The combination of acid, salt and oil will start to 'cook' whatever you have dressed, and fragile-textured leaves such as lettuce will wilt, just as green vegetables such as beans or asparagus will yellow, after a comparatively short time.

At its simplest, you may carve salmon into slices, brush these with lime juice, a light sprinkling of salt and some ground black pepper and serve immediately. The fish will taste fresh and vibrant. If you leave the same slices for 20 minutes before serving, the texture and appearance will have changed to that of cooked fish and the distinctive salmon flavour will have lost its battle with the lime juice. As with the dressed salad leaves, timing is crucial.

The processes of salting and pickling without pre-cooking doesn't suit fruit and vegetables. Most delicate-textured plants are best eaten raw. Vegetables used to be pickled as a means of prolonging shelf-life but unless they were pre-cooked (as in the canning industry), they had to be kept in brine before pickling in order to draw out excess moisture. This affected the flavour for the worse and the idea has not survived the arrival of deep-freezing. Similarly, fruit is boiled in vinegar and syrup before pickling and of course in plenty of sugar before transforming into jam.

Cooking by microwave doesn't really come into this category, though it appears to generate heat without applying any to whatever is being cooked. It involves electromagnetic radiation to make the water molecules in any foodstuff vibrate, heating up rapidly in the process – kinetic energy. It has no effect on the surrounding air and concentrates all its effect on whatever is being cooked, so is at least efficient in its use of energy. It is handy for heating up anything pre-cooked, maybe a warm tart or steamed sponge pudding, but has several disadvantages if used to replace conventional cooking methods. The speed at which it works gives greater loss of moisture and, as a consequence, drier meat or fish.

# Dressing and marinating

Marinating has two main functions: **to give a flavour (although this is not essential) and to break down tough tissues.** For steak tartare, the meat should be enhanced by the dressing rather than completely masked by it, and so the dish is in the dressing for a very short time before being eaten. For the soy-marinated fish, the longer the fish is pressed with the salt and marinade, the stronger the Oriental spicing will come through and the denser and more smoked-salmon-like will be the texture; three days suits me and will give a reasonably subtle feel to the fish.

## Steak tartare

**The origins of this dish are claimed to be Cossack and involve horse-meat tenderised under the saddles of warrior types.** I am sceptical about this, having listened to many wily-headed waiters weaving tales to make a dish seem more exotic than the reality would suggest. For sure, this was one of the staple brasserie dishes for many years and can be made as spicy as you want. My preference is for a milder end result, as I would begrudge spending large sums on the top-quality fillet steak needed to produce the dish only to have it taste of Worcestershire sauce and Tabasco.

**Serves 4**

600g fillet steak

3 egg yolks

1 tsp Dijon mustard

1 tsp wine vinegar

4 anchovy fillets

1 tbsp finely chopped parsley

1 tbsp finely chopped gherkin

1 tbsp finely chopped capers

1 tbsp finely chopped onion

2 hard-boiled eggs, chopped

salt and pepper

Worcestershire sauce, to taste

Tabasco, to taste

1   Finely chop the fillet steak. This is best done by slicing it into thin strips, then slicing these strips into small mince-sized cubes. A mincer attachment to your food processor is not a good idea, as it will push and crush the meat rather than cleanly cut through it.

2   Mix the egg yolks, mustard and vinegar together. Crush the anchovy fillets and add these, along with the finely chopped parsley.

3   Mix in the finely chopped meat, then the finely chopped gherkin, capers, onion and boiled eggs.

4   Season with salt and pepper, then with the Tabasco and Worcestershire sauce. The steak tartare can be eaten immediately, but I prefer the flavour after it has been left for 1/2 - 1 hour in the fridge.

### Ingredients

> **You will need less meat proportionately per person** for steak tartare than for a standard steak dish.

> **The dish was usually presented in restaurants as a sort of burger,** with all the component flavourings arranged in a palette around the meat, the egg yolks in half an upturned egg shell and the anchovies criss-crossed over the top. The waiter would then mix the capers, gherkins and the rest into the meat in the sort of proportions the diner asked for. In fact, it is the amount of Tabasco and Worcestershire sauce that are crucial and it is at the moment these are added that careful tasting for spiciness is in order.

> **The perfect accompaniment to steak tartare** is a plate of chips and maybe some lettuce salad. The hot chips will give contrasts of both temperature and texture.

For buying and storing raw meat see **118**    For beef see **126**

# Soy-marinated salmon

**This is a version of the Scandinavian pressed salmon dish, gravad lax.** Gravad lax is made from salmon pressed for three to four days with salt, sugar, brandy and dill. The salt and alcohol are what do the work of preserving, while the sugar and dill flavour the fish. The variations are still based on salt and booze, but the character of the dish can be dramatically altered by changing the dill to some completely different flavouring, in this case ginger and soy. The dish is hardly worth making for four people, as the salmon must marinate as a sort of sandwich, with the flavourings replacing the bone. A small salmon will yield around 10 portions, so if you are feeding fewer than that, the rest may be frozen for use another day.

**Serves 10**

1 x 3kg salmon, filleted

**For the marinade:**

3 tbsp coarse sea salt

3 tbsp chopped fresh ginger

3 tbsp soy sauce

3 tbsp vodka

3 tbsp sugar

1   Combine the salt with the other marinade ingredients.

2   Massage this into the fish and then lay the fillets back together, skin side outermost. Pour a little marinade on to a strip of kitchen foil, then place the salmon sandwich on top. Pour over any remaining marinade, and then fold the foil back across the salmon to make a parcel. Fold the foil along each side to seal in the fish and marinade.

3   Place the foil parcel into a deep-sided container and put a kilo weight along the top. The exact weight is not crucial, and any suitable-shaped container will do the job. Refrigerate.

4   Turn the fish over each day and then, after three days, remove from the fridge, take the fish from the marinade and wipe dry.

5   Slice and serve with salads tossed in teriyaki sauce or a mixture of sesame oil, rice wine vinegar and soy sauce.

**Ingredients**

> **The fillets will contain a line of pin bones along the centre.** These are best removed with a small pair of pliers (see page 81). Grasp the end of each pin bone with the pliers and pull toward the head – that is away from the tail end – of the fish.

For buying and storing fish see **76-7**   For filleting fish see **80-1**

# Pickling

**Usually, pickled fish are actually cooked in hot pickle.** This recipe is an exception, however, as the pickling liquid is cold when the fish is added to it and not heated up afterwards.

# Bismarck herring

**Acid from vinegar, rather than salt, is used to 'cook' the herring fillets in this recipe.** Rollmops, which seem to have disappeared from the national menu, are made in much the same way, but with less spice in the vinegar, and of course were served rolled around small pickled onions.

### Serves 4
8 matjes herring fillets
2 tbsp German mustard
2 dill-pickled cucumbers

### For the marinade:
250ml water
250ml wine vinegar
1 tsp juniper berries, crushed
1 tsp allspice berries, crushed
1 tsp black peppercorns, crushed
1 large onion, sliced

1 Soak the matjes fillets, covered, in the fridge overnight in cold water, then pat dry with kitchen paper.

2 Put all the marinade ingredients in a pan and bring to the boil. Remove from the heat as soon as it comes to the boil, then cool completely.

3 Brush German mustard along one side of each herring fillet, then wrap the fillet around a wedge of pickled cucumber. If you wish, you could pin it together with a cocktail stick.

4 Pour over the cooled marinade – the marinade should cover the fish – cover and refrigerate for three to four days.

5 Serve with rye bread and salad, and possibly even a glass of beer.

### Ingredients

> **Fresh herring can be used, but my preference is for matjes fillets,** a Scandinavian salted herring which needs to be soaked for a few hours before use. If you decide to use fresh herrings you will need to fillet them and then soak the fillets in brine – 600ml water to 60g salt – for 2-3 hours first.

> **Soused herrings are made in a similar way,** using only fresh rather than salted specimens, except that the fish is fried before being marinated.

# Salting and drying

Salting and drying can transform a tough joint – although of course thin slicing helps.

## Bresaola

I was given this recipe by Franco Taruschio, who used to own the Walnut Tree in Abergavenny, and my version of it was in fact published 10 years ago. The problem is that the recipe printed didn't work. Someone at the publishers had read that saltpetre was banned as an ingredient. This turned out to be only true when it was ground into sausage meat to improve its colour. Saltpetre's use in brines was perfectly OK. There were problems also at the time with obtaining saltpetre from neighborhood chemist shops as, combined with flowers of sulphur and sugar, it will make fairly passable gunpowder. Nowadays it transpires that the globe's terrorists have access to smarter weaponry and the good cook is no longer troubled by obtaining the ingredients for salt beef, salami or bresaola.

**Serves 20**

3kg beef topside

**For the brine:**

1 x 750ml bottle red wine

900g salt

15g saltpetre

200g brown sugar

2 tbsp black peppercorns

2 tbsp juniper berries

1 sprig thyme

400g carrots, sliced

6 chillies

1 cinnamon stick

1 litre water

1 Combine all the ingredients for the brine and bring to the boil. Leave to cool.

2 Find a clean, deep tray or plastic bucket. Place the topside in this and pour over the brine. Leave this to marinate, covered, in the fridge for four days. If the meat is not completely covered with marinade, turn it each day so that it marinades evenly.

3 Lift the meat from the marinade and pat it dry. Hang it in a warm, dry spot for two to three weeks. The time taken for the meat to dry depends on the thickness of the joint; it should be firm to the touch when pressed.

4 The outer layer of the bresaola will look awful; cut this away and you will have a far more appetizing deep-purple block of bresaola.

5 This meat will keep for some time in the fridge and can even be frozen to keep longer. It should be thinly sliced and served with shavings of Parmesan and olive oil, or even some cold poached vegetables in vinaigrette.

**Ingredients**

> **Beef topside is a good cut** of meat for this method because it is dry and has very little fat.

**Technique**

> **It's not worth making small quantities of bresaola.** Also, the dried beef keeps well. This will make enough for around 20 servings, even after the shrinkage involved in the drying process.

> **The beef needs to dry somewhere warm but not too humid,** somewhere in the kitchen is usually best. The air has to circulate around the drying joint, so resting it on a shelf rather than hanging it from a hook is not suitable.

> **You can wrap the joints in muslin if the sight of drying meat offends.** The bresaola will never look attractively rustic at this stage though, and the muslin can give the impression of a badly dressed wound. Don't worry, the finished dish looks just fine.

> **The bresaola should be thinly sliced, just like a Parma ham.** This is more easily achieved if the meat is served cold rather than room temperature.

For buying and storing raw meat see **118**   For beef see **126**

# Boiling and steaming

**Steaming and boiling are the most delicate cooking methods.** Two types of protein are particularly well suited to being cooked in these ways: those with delicate-textured flesh, such as fish or poultry, and those that are naturally tough and need to be cooked for a long time, such as silverside of beef or brisket. Vegetables can also be successfully boiled or steamed, as can some some starchy foods – think of pasta and steamed puddings.

When being boiled, food will never reach temperatures above the boiling point of water (100°C). This means that it will cook slowly, never getting hot enough for the browning and caramelization of surface proteins that concentrates the taste and gives all the intensity of flavour that is associated with frying.

In fact, boiling is a misnomer – prolonged hard boiling will break up and dry out meat, and give you an end result that is so tough and dry that it is akin to boiled rags. Equally, vegetables will break up with prolonged hard boiling. You will need to poach rather than boil if you are to have any success with the method, and a gentle simmer in a lidded pan is what's needed for poaching. This way you have some chance of still cooking anything that protrudes from the water – and of not completely steaming up your kitchen.

The main reason to poach rather than steam an ingredient is to obtain the cooking liquor to use when making a stock or sauce. For instance, for fish the poaching liquor is often thickened with cream or butter to make a sauce, while in Hungary they poach chicken in stock flavoured with smoked bacon and paprika and transform the result into chicken paprika by whisking in soured cream and flour. With this in mind, you need to use the minimum amount of water necessary to poach rather than steam the meat or fish, so that you don't have too much water diluting the flavours that leach out of the food.

Steaming can cook food at higher temperatures than poaching, and so it can form a seal on the ingredient. Thanks to this seal, steamed food, unlike poached, loses none of its flavour to the cooking water. Steamed food tends to be served with a stand-alone sauce that contains none of the flavour of the fish or poultry.

# Poaching and steaming poultry

**The main reason why you might poach rather than roast poultry is because you want to make use of the cooking liquor in the meal,** perhaps as the basis for a sauce. Of course, you may also want the texture of a poached bird, which is juicier than that of a roast bird, and you may want the meat to be evenly cooked, something that is not achieved by roasting.

The by-product of poached poultry is a white stock, and it would be a terrible waste if this were not used – but be careful not to spoil it by adding too much salt. There are many ways in which you can make use of this stock. It can form the basis of a sauce or soup to accompany the meat – think of *pot-au-feu*, in which various meats and poultry are poached together with cream, onions and celery, and then the soup is drunk before the meat is eaten. Alternatively, poached meat or poultry served with baby vegetables cooked in the same broth and béarnaise sauce makes a first-rate and comfortably digestible early summer supper, and makes a change from the interminable round of fried, grilled and roast meats. A plainly poached bird will partner any hollandaise-type sauce (see page 226), and is a million miles away from being 'invalid food' – serve it by spooning a little of the cooking liquor around the bird.

Avoid birds labelled 'boiling fowl' unless you intend using them purely as flavouring for a soup or stock. They are older birds, clapped out from intensive laying, and are usually varieties bred for egg production rather than consumption. A standard roasting bird will be fine.

The cooking time for poaching a whole chicken or duck will not be significantly different from that of roasting the same bird, even though the temperature is lower. This is because the meat is completely surrounded by simmering liquid. A standard 1.5kg chicken should cook in 40-50 minutes in a lidded pan. Just as with roast birds, you can tell if the bird is cooked by piercing the thigh and checking that the internal juices are running clear – any sign of blood, and the bird needs more time.

Remember when lifting poultry from the poaching liquor that the central cavity will be full of liquid. Use a long-pronged fork to skewer the bird across the backbone and below the breast meat – this gives you plenty of control and doesn't dig any holes in the valuable meat. Tip the bird slightly as you lift it so that the liquor can run back into the pot.

Poultry can also be steamed, a method employed in the cooking of the famous dish Peking duck. You put roasted salt, pepper, spring onions and ginger over the duck and steam it, and then fry it quickly to get the desired texture.

For paprika chicken see **102**    For poaching and steaming duck see **105**    For poached duck with duck liver sauce see **106**    For storing poultry see **96**

# Steamed chicken breasts with parsley stuffing

**Steaming will produce a delicate chicken dish, but not necessarily a dull one.** The dividing line between subtle and bland, however, is alarmingly narrow, as is the balance between the power of the herbs and chicken liver stuffing and the surrounding chicken. The light texture of a steamed dish will make a change from unending fried and grilled offerings on a good for a summer's day with a bottle of aromatic white wine. Possibly two.

### Serves 4

4 chicken breasts

2 chicken livers

2 tbsp double cream

a little lemon zest

salt and pepper

grated nutmeg, to taste

75g fresh flat-leaf parsley

30g unsalted butter

2 egg yolks

100ml white wine

1 tsp lemon juice

1   There will be a small fillet of meat that tends to detach itself from the underside of each breast – chop up these and the livers. Blend the result with the cream, zest and seasonings, in a liquidizer. Blending small amounts is awkward but unavoidable unless you want to push the mixture through a sieve, which is worse. Be sure to scrape all the mixture out afterwards.

2   Strip the parsley leaves away from the stalk, then wash and dry them with kitchen paper. Finely chop the leaves and stir the result into the chicken mixture. Cut a small pocket in the underside of each chicken breast, from the thicker end downwards, to accommodate the stuffing, then spoon this into the space made. Roll the breast around the cut so that it forms a banana-like shape – think of chicken Kiev – then wrap a piece of oiled or buttered kitchen foil around each breast. This will protect it during cooking and keep the shape intact. Steam the chicken for 20-25 minutes, depending on what size chicken breasts you bought, or until cooked through.

3   Meanwhile, melt the butter. Whisk the egg yolks and white wine together in a bowl over hot water; they will double in volume as they cook. Then whisk in the melted butter. Season with salt, pepper and lemon juice. When the chicken is unwrapped from the foil, whisk any juices that emerge into the sauce, then coat the chicken breasts with it.

### Ingredients

> **The style of chicken breast you want is what used to be called a 'supreme'** in the grandiloquent days of *haute cuisine*. This just means a boneless and skinless chicken breast.

> **The best chicken livers are pale in colour and unfrozen.** Occasionally the gall bladder – the green sac attached to the liver – will be left in. If so, it will have to be carefully cut away along with any pieces of liver that have green patches from it.

### Cooking method

> **The sauce is similar to hollandaise, but with much less butter** so that it is lighter in texture, less over-powering for the chicken.

For hollandaise sauce see **226**   For chicken see **99**

# Poaching meat

**Poached meat has a cleaner, lighter taste than grilled, fried or roast meat.** For those who need to watch their cholesterol and avoid too much fatty food it is ideal, for a poached piece of beef or lamb will not need a buttery or creamy sauce to make it a pleasure to eat in the same way as a fillet of poached fish will. Poaching suits gelatinous cuts of meat, those that will still be interesting to eat after prolonged cooking, for it is generally a slow process. There are exceptions of course. *Boeuf à la ficelle* – poached beef – can mean a slice of rare poached fillet steak or a huge piece of brisket. The word *ficelle'* is French for 'string', as the steak is tied and dropped into boiling stock to cook.

# Knuckle of veal with spinach

**Most great poached meat dishes involve salted and cured joints, such as gammon or salt beef.** A knuckle of veal needs no salt or preservative to be the finest example of the style. It's the equivalent of shin of beef in the younger animal, but is much more tender. The same joint is regularly served cut through into discs as *osso bucco* in northern Italy. As with any veal joint, it produces fine stock to act as accompaniment and is best as a sort of one-meat *pot au feu* with potatoes and vegetable cooked in the same liquor.

Serves 4

1 knuckle of veal
1 calf's foot, split lengthways
500g new potatoes, scrubbed
1kg spinach, washed thoroughly
salt and pepper, to taste
nutmeg, to taste
2 tbsp cream

1   Bring the knuckle and the calve's foot to the boil together in a pan of water, then turn down the heat to a gentle simmer. A lid is a good idea, as the prolonged cooking will steam up the kitchen and leave parts of the meat under-done if the water level drops below that of the meat.

2   After an hour, add the scrubbed new potatoes. After a further 40 minutes, check the progress of both meat and potatoes. They should be almost ready.

3   Decant a ladleful of cooking liquor into a saucepan and boil the spinach. Drain and season with salt, pepper and lots of nutmeg. Blend in a food processer with the cream.

4   Carve the knuckle. Hold it upright with the bone vertical and slice downwards. Serve moistened with some of the cooking liquor in a deep plate with the spinach and potatoes.

Ingredients
> **The calf's foot is not essential** but will make the stock stronger and more gelatinous.

Cooking method
> **Don't salt the water used for cooking the knuckle of veal.** The liquor is an essential part of the dish and may become too salty after prolonged reduction during cooking.

For buying and storing meat see **118**    For veal see **132**

# Boiled leg of lamb with caper and onion sauce

**This is a revelation to those who think of boiled or poached food as something for the elderly or infirm.** It gives the delicacy of lamb with none of the usual fattiness. The dish was originally created for mutton, which is more deeply flavoured than lamb and needs slower cooking in order to be tender. But unlike the other traditional treatments of mutton – serving it with redcurrant jelly and the like – this recipe still suits both the younger animal and the modern palate. The usual accompaniments to boiled leg of lamb are caper or onion sauce. I like both, so I combine the two, but you can leave out the capers if you like.

### Serves 8

2.5kg leg of lamb
1 shallot, halved
a few black peppercorns
1 stick celery, cut into chunks
25g unsalted butter
1 medium onion, chopped
20g plain flour
25ml double cream
a few drops of vinegar
a few drops of Worcestershire sauce
salt and pepper
1 tbsp capers
1 tbsp chopped fresh parsley

1 Place the leg of lamb in a large pot and fill with water. The water should ideally cover the meat, but this is not critical as long as most of the meat is covered and the pan is lidded during cooking. Add the shallot, black peppercorns and celery, then bring this to the boil.

2 Plenty of foam will rise as the water comes to the boil. Skim this off and then lower the heat to a simmer. Cover with a lid and simmer for a further 2 hours. Turn off the heat. The lamb will be OK in the hot cooking liquor for 20-30 minutes, should you need the time to prepare the rest of the meal.

3 Melt the butter, then add the chopped onion and cook without colouring. When the onion has softened, add the flour and stir into a roux. Stir in a ladleful of the cooking liquor from the lamb and beat until smooth. Repeat this twice so that you have a thickish sauce, then add the cream, a few drops of vinegar and Worcestershire sauce. Season with salt and pepper. Should you want a smoother sauce, blend it in a liquidizer at this stage, adding the capers and chopped parsley.

### Ingredients

> **Seam butchery helps if you do not have a pot large enough** to hold a whole leg of lamb – even with the shank bone sawn through – or if you do not have 8 people to feed. If you divide the leg into separate muscles, then each may be boiled as needed.

### Cooking method

> **We are really talking about simmering here,** as with all so-called boiling of anything other than beans and sprouts. If you boil the meat too fast it will have a dry and nasty texture; if you bring it to the boil and simmer it gently, it will have the texture and finesse of smoked salmon when cooked.

> **You can serve the lamb pink if you want** – just reduce the cooking time by about 10 minutes. My preference is for medium- to well-done, so that the full flavour emerges from the meat.

For lamb see **122**

# Poaching and steaming fish

**There are two good reasons to steam or poach a piece of fish rather than grill or fry it.** Firstly, steamed or poached fish can take a buttery sauce or oily dressing – the plainness of the cooking methods shout out for something rich to counterbalance the dish. Secondly, steamed or poached fish can partner powerful spices surprisingly effectively (see the recipe opposite). The most sensible reason to poach rather than steam fish is to make use of the resulting stock in the meal, so that both the fish and its poaching liquor combine in some way to form the finished dish. Otherwise, steaming is a more suitable cooking method as none of the flavour of the fish will leach out into any of the surrounding water.

The poaching cooking liquor and the juices from the cooked fish can be thickened with cream or butter or with a flour roux to make a sauce, or even centrifuged with oil, herbs and aromatics in a liquidizer. Whatever method you employ, the amount of stock needed will be comparatively small or else the sauce will be dilute.

This means that your first consideration when poaching fish must be to make the liquid used for cooking effective in both cooking the fish and flavouring the sauce. It helps if the liquid – which can be wine, water, dry cider or some combination of these – doesn't have to be sufficient to cover the fish. You can achieve this by placing a circle of greaseproof paper, wide enough to cover the saucepan, across the fish to ensure that the parts above water level are also cooked. Also, avoid adding too much salt to the cooking liquor.

Best for poaching and steaming are white-fleshed fish such as sole, plaice and haddock, served warm with a delicate sauce. Escoffier's manual on cookery, for years the chef's bible, lists dozens of possibilities, and Saulnier's *Repertoire de la Cuisine* gives another hundred, mostly with fanciful titles such as '*sole Véronique*' (poached sole fillets with grapes or '*Marie Waleska*' (which came with bits of lobster and a gratinated cheese sauce). All this seems absurdly pompous now, of course, but was a standard restaurant and grand country house offering just 30 years back and shows, if nothing else, that poached fish has possibilities.

When poaching or steaming fish, you can tell if the fish is done by its appearance and texture. With larger fish such as salmon or cod you will sense that the fish can be pressed easily into flakes – you can check it by pressing it with your finger. With small fillets of plaice or sole you will see that the colour has changed completely from opaque to a creamy ceramic white.

Historically, large fish such as whole salmon were traditionally poached in flavoured water called a 'court bouillon'. Peppercorns, salt, a bunch of herbs and vinegar were the usual additions to make the cooking water qualify for this grand name. After its job was done, the liquor was poured away and the fish served with relishes, such as mayonnaise, that had no need of stock. This was a bit of a waste, as the flavour of cold poached fish is muted at best and bland the rest of the time unless the cooking liquid is used in concentrated form as the basis for a sauce or jelly made refreshing with wine, lemon or vinegar as well as whatever herbs and spices fit the bill. Jewish cooking uses cold poached carp as 'gefilte' fish and this appears to go down well in nostalgic areas of Hendon and Golders Green, but it has never appealed to me.

For buying and storing fish see **76-7**

# Steamed sea-bass with Oriental spices

**The chilli and ginger used in Oriental fish cookery will lift the taste of the steamed sea-bass rather than drown it.** The dish has the benefit of low cholesterol for those planning a meal that includes cream or eggs in the pudding. The idea is that the broth in which the cooked fish sits acts as a sauce as well as a soup, so it must be powerful enough to flavour each chunk of fish, even though it has soup's consistency. You will need to offer a soup spoon as well as a fork.

### Serves 4

1 x 1kg sea-bass
4 spring onions, finely chopped
1 tsp Chinese 5-spice mixture
1 tbsp fresh coriander leaves
1 tsp light sesame oil
400ml dashi
1 small knob fresh ginger, peeled and
    cut into strips
1 x ½ inch piece lemon peel
1 small chilli
1 tbsp Japanese soy sauce

1. Fillet and pin-bone the bass – the pin bones are the line of annoying little bones that run along the centre of most round fish; they need to be plucked out with tweezers unless you can persuade your fishmonger to do it for you.

2. Place the fillets on a dish, then scatter the chopped spring onion, Chinese 5-spice and coriander across them. Drizzle the sesame oil across the fish.

3. Steam the fish; the time this takes will depend on the thickness of the fillets. Thin, farmed fish will cook in 2-3 minutes, but thick, wild fish will take 8-9 minutes. Check for doneness by pressing the fish with your finger – if it is cooked it will tend to flake; if it is still raw inside there will be the impression of a hard ball at the centre.

4. Once this fish is cooked, prepare the dashi (don't do this too far in advance as it loses freshness after a while) by bringing it to the boil with the ginger, lemon and chilli and then adding the soy sauce and any fish juices from the bass' steaming plate.

5. Lift the fish fillets on to shallow soup dishes and strain the broth on top. You can decorate the fish with slivers of spring onion, red pepper or leek if you fancy.

## Ingredients

> **Japanese soy sauce is the best** – it is brewed and aged, not just assembled in a large vat. I use the organic brands such as Shoyu and Clearspring. The Japanese company Kikkoman now makes soy sauce in Singapore for the western market, so a Japanese name does not always signify a Japanese product.

> **Dashi is dried bonito (tuna) stock,** with various odds and ends added. It can be bought from Oriental and Japanese delicatessens. When I first worked on this dish I used to make a soy-flavoured fish consommé for the broth/sauce. Sadly I found reconstituted bonito stock tasted better and took a fraction of the time!

## Cooking method

> **There is very little stock produced with this method** – no more than a trickle – but whatever comes can be added to the serving broth.

> **A steamer is handy,** but not essential unless you intend cooking this sort of dish regularly. An upturned ramekin dish placed in a wide saucepan or even a deep roasting tray containing an inch of boiling water will keep a plate of fish fillets in the steamy vapour. You will need a lid to the pan or a tight-fitting cover of kitchen foil for the roasting tray to prevent the steam escaping.

> **The higher the flame, the more pressure that the steam will build up to cook the fish.** Take care that you have a tight-fitting lid though, for if much of the steam escapes rather than condensing back into the pan you will have a burnt pan to clean.

> **Lift the saucepan or boiler lid with caution,** for there will be a gust of searingly hot steam as the lid lifts. This is what cooks the fish of course, so if you lift the lid frequently the cooking time will be longer as the steam has to regain strength.

For filleting fish see **80-1**

# Steamed brill with cider sabayon

**White fish are good steamed, so this dish would work as well with sole,** plaice or turbot. The sabayon is made in a similar way to hollandaise sauce, but is lighter and more fragile because no butter is added.

**Serves 4**

4 x 200g brill fillets
salt and pepper
3 egg yolks
150ml dry cider
Tabasco, to taste
1 tbsp lemon juice

1   Season the fish fillets with salt and pepper, then steam them.

2   Heat a saucepan of water until it is nearly boiling. Whisk together the egg yolks and cider in a bowl – preferably one without too many corners; more rounded is better – then whisk the Tabasco and lemon juice with the yolks and cider mixture over the hot water. Use a lifting action as you whisk so that as much air as possible is incorporated into the sabayon.

3   When the sabayon has risen and thickened, it will be ready to spoon over the cooked fish fillets. This is good served on a bed of spinach.

### Technique

> **Successful sabayon depends on** the absence of egg yolk that has scrambled in corners of the bowl, as this would spoil the texture. Try to find a bowl that is as rounded as possible at the base and preferably one that conducts heat easily – stainless steel is ideal, but a Pyrex dish would also be OK.

> **The volume of sabayon sauce produced is more dependent on the quantity of cider used** than the number of egg yolks used – so to increase the volume, simply add cider, always remembering that there is a point at which the ratio of cider to egg yolk will be too high as you won't have enough egg to thicken the mixture.

### Cooking method

> **Steamed fish is as dull if over-cooked** as fish that has been fried or grilled for too long. The time taken to cook the fish will vary according to its thickness. If in any doubt, separate the fish into sections or cut into the fillet to see how far cooked it is.

For how to make a sabayon see **196**    For hollandaise sauce see **226**

# Boiling and steaming vegetables and fruit

**Most vegetables and fruits follow the same guidelines as fish or poultry when it comes to steaming and boiling:** you need the minimum amount of water and a gently simmering surface to the pan. Root vegetables, artichokes and potatoes will all break up during cooking if roughly handled. Green vegetables are the exception – lots of water or plenty of steam are needed, as is a good rolling boil when the vegetable is added. The reasoning is this: the more boiling water there is in relation to whatever vegetable you are cooking, the faster the water will re-boil, sealing in all the colour and texture that your beans, courgettes or asparagus may have.

For all vegetables and fruit, water should be freshly brought to the boil, as it will lose oxygen during prolonged boiling and darken anything that is cooked in it. It's the same process that works to your advantage when reducing stocks and sauces that need an appetizing brown colour – brown with French beans and broccoli hasn't the same allure. While for greens it's important to add the vegetables to already boiling water, for most other vegetables, such as potatoes, it doesn't matter whether or not the water is boiling before you add the vegetables.

While you poach poultry, meat or fish in order to gain the cooking liquor, which is flavoured by the food being poached, with vegetables you are unlikely to want to use this stock and so the leaching out of flavours from the food is more of a disadvantage. Coarse-textured vegetables, such as root vegetables, are suited to boiling simply because it is the slowest method of cooking.

However, vegetables with a softer texture, such as broccoli, are better suited to steaming. For greens, it is important to build up a good pressure of steam before adding the vegetables.

Fruits suitable for poaching tend to be large specimens, such as pears, plums or peaches, as they will retain their shape after cooking. Poaching fruit tends to be about achieving optimum ripeness. In contrast to vegetables, which are usually poached in tap water, fruits tend to be poached in fruit juice or a syrup, often with spices added to flavour the food. Two exceptions to this principle are gooseberries for gooseberry fool, as you don't need to worry about the texture, and the fruits for summer puddings, as you need the juice for the dish.

For buying and storing vegetables and fruit see **46-7**

# Boiled broad beans with savory

**Boiled vegetables form the traditional side dish that shares the plate with whatever is the star of the meal.** Broad beans are a pain to prepare properly, and deserve to be centre stage for this reason alone. They are seasonal – the cost of air freight from the southern hemisphere is too high for the bulk needed and the price obtained – and, baby specimens aside, broad beans need to be peeled twice, to remove the tannic, leathery casings.

The marriage between broad beans and savory is like strawberries and cream or roast beef and Yorkshire pudding, and well worth buying summer savory to create. If you want to make more of an event of this dish, bake some puff pastry cases to hold the vegetables or place a little boiled fresh pasta tossed in olive oil underneath; even toast would be OK, provided you make it with good bread.

### Serves 4

500g shelled broad beans, 3 times
   that weight unshelled

50g butter

1 small onion, chopped

200ml water

65ml cream

salt and pepper

a pinch of sugar

1 tsp chopped fresh summer savory

1   Drop the beans into boiling water. When the water reboils, drain the beans and wash in cold water. Shell the white casings away.

2   Heat the butter. Fry the onion, then add half the broad beans and the water. Bring to the boil, then add the cream, seasonings and sugar. Purée in a blender or push through a sieve.

3   Reheat, adding the savory and the remaining beans.

### Ingredients

> **Choose unblemished beans from medium-sized pods** for the best return on effort; large pods will give tough beans

> **Savory is powerful, so add it in stages** until the flavour is what you want.

# Steaming dough

Just as you can bake dough into cakes or breads, or boil it into pasta, so you can steam mixtures of fat and flour into dumplings or, more substantially, into puddings. These can be savoury using minced suet, the rich hard fat that surrounds the kidney – think of steak and kidney pudding – or they can be sweet like Christmas pudding.

The pressure of steam achieved will affect the cooking time needed, but this is essentially a slow-cooking process –  a family-sized steak and kidney pudding will need to be steamed for 5-6 hours. So it's essential to keep an eye on the water level at the bottom of the pan or steamer during cooking in case it should boil dry. If this happens the temperature inside the steamer or pan will quickly rise, browning and then burning the top of your pud.

The example below is lighter and, in the same way as savoury dumplings, uses baking powder as a raising agent to produce a lighter, quicker result.

# Steamed orange pudding

**The tradition of steaming hearty puds serves winter nights well.** This particular example will work at any time of year as the absence of suet gives a lighter result. It is also very easy to make and will test your steaming equipment – or lack of it – before you attempt anything more adventurous.

**Serves 4**

100g unsalted butter, softened, plus extra
  for greasing
100g caster sugar
100g self-raising flour
25g fresh breadcrumbs
½ tsp baking powder
2 eggs
2 tbsp milk
juice and zest of 2 oranges, combined
4 tbsp golden syrup
clotted cream, to serve

1   To make the batter, cream the butter and sugar together, then stir in the dry ingredients before beating in the eggs and then adding the milk and combined orange juice and zest.
2   Butter the sides of four ramekins or dariole moulds – these are what you use for crème caramels. Put 1 tbsp of golden syrup in each dish, then pour on the batter. Fasten kitchen foil loosely across the tops to act as lids and tie them on with string or elastic bands.
3   Place the dishes in a steamer or, if you have no such thing, place them in a roasting tray half-filled with boiling water. Either steam on top of the stove or start the cooking off on top of the stove and transfer to an oven preheated to 200°C/Gas mark 6. In either case, steam for 40 minutes.
4   Turn the puddings out into warmed bowls and serve with clotted cream.

Ingredients
> **Baking powder is not everlasting** and loses strength once the packet has been open for any length of time. If in doubt, buy fresh.

Cooking method
> **The pudding batter can be poked and prodded** to check on doneness, as it is reasonably stable.

# Roasting, frying and grilling

**What distinguishes these cooking methods is their high cooking temperature.** Poaching and boiling tenderize sinewy and tough pieces of meat, but the temperature is never high enough to brown the surface of the food. This browning and caramelizing, known as the Maillard reaction, provokes major changes in the flavour of the foods that are roasted, grilled or fried, and is part of the reason why these foods are so attractive to eat: there's always an obvious attraction about things that are sweet.

This chapter explains how to use fat to promote the Maillard reaction to get maximum flavour, while also preventing meat and fish from drying out during cooking. In general, the more tender the ingredient, the more suited it is to being grilled, roasted or fried. You would traditionally boil a leg of mutton, for instance, but roast a leg of lamb. In the same way, you parboil potatoes before roasting them and blanch potato chips in warm oil before crisp-frying them in hot oil. Fish, too, benefits from browning and this chapter looks at how to crisp and brown the outside of fish and shellfish while keeping the inside moist.

# Roasting, frying and grilling meat and poultry

**Most joints have little fat these days.** This is a result of consumer preference, largely caused by worries over cholesterol and suchlike, and reflects the way animals have been bred leaner to meet this demand. All the same, you need some fat to produce a decent roast joint or grilled chop, and if the meat itself is fatless, then some oil, butter or other fat – goose fat, for instance – has to be added. Only naturally fatty meats, such as pork or duck, need no extra help. This doesn't mean that your chop must be awash with butter or oil and that your roast beef gravy will be greasy, provided you use the fat carefully.

For frying or grilling meat, rather than melting fat or putting oil into the pan, I brush the meat itself with oil and then add it to a heated, dry pan. The amount of oil used in these methods is minimal: just enough to paint over those parts that have no natural coating of fat. I tend to use olive oil, in this instance not because of flavour but because its low flash-point means that the meat browns quicker and better than if you used, say, sunflower oil. The extra fat will moisten and protect the meat during cooking and help it to brown, but will otherwise have no effect on the finished dish.

Add the minimum of fat, also, to roasts such as beef and lamb. The quantity depends on the joint's natural lining of fat: plenty for exposed muscle meat and none for rib joints covered in back-fat. The oil's purpose is to keep the meat from drying out under pressure from the heat and will bring little to the final flavour, unless you use an oil infused with an aromatic herb such as rosemary or thyme. I would brush the exposed meat on a rack of lamb with a fine coating of olive oil and add nothing to the rind of a loin of pork or beef.

Before you de-glaze the roasting tray with stock or water, pour off all the fat. It'll seem like a bad idea because you'll lose some of the juices as well, but it is the crusts of cooked-on food that are stuck to the pan and the caramelized juices that really give the flavour to the gravy. If you pour off as much fat as possible before bringing the caramelized juices back to life with some stock or water, the intensity of the natural meat juices will shine through.

Poultry such as chicken, and game birds such as partridge or pheasant, need plenty of oil or butter because they are such dry-fleshed creatures. I would go so far as to add around 200g butter to a small pheasant.

You also need to baste large joints during cooking to help keep the meat moist. Two or three bastings are as much as I have ever felt the need for. In effect, the natural – and added – fats and oils are being re-used to keep the joint from drying out. Turning the meat over during cooking has much the same effect and lets the heat penetrate the meat more evenly – this is what I tend to do with game birds and roast chicken.

Testing the 'doneness' of roast, grilled or fried meat becomes easier with experience, but it is essential to learn, especially if you are cooking for other people. In an emergency, you can always cook meat a little more (though it tends to become grey in the process), but only magic can make meat less cooked once it has been cooked for too long.

For buying and storing raw meat and resting meat see **118**    For carving meat see **120-21**    For lamb see **122**    For beef see **126**    For pork see **128**

When frying or grilling a small piece of meat such as a steak or a chop, press the meat with your thumb or index finger. If it feels like there is a hard rubber ball inside, then the meat is still blue. The more it cooks from this stage, the more it will give in to your touch. From the point at which it is becoming medium to well-done, the whole steak will start to harden. This has a completely different feel to the rubbery internal hardness of the first stage, when it was very under-done.

Leave yourself a little leeway – erring on the side of under-cooking rather than over-cooking – and if there is any doubt, cut the steak in half and look. If it is under-cooked, put it back in the pan. You can always present the cooked steak cut into pieces – your dinner companions may find the *nouvelle cuisine* plate arrangement old-fashioned, but at least you will know how well the damned thing is cooked. In time, and after a lot of steaks, knowing when your meat is done will be as second nature.

When testing to see when roast meat is cooked, you can use a skewer to assess what's happening at the centre of the joint. Pierce the meat right to the core and leave the skewer in place for a few seconds. Pull the skewer out and place the tip against your lips – if it is hot to the touch, the meat is well done; if cold, the meat will be blue. Judging the degrees in-between becomes easier with experience. There will be a trickle of either clear juice or blood from where the joint was pierced, and this also indicates how far the roasting has gone. Clear juices mean well-done; bloody means rare.

Meat thermometers can also be used to test when meat is cooked – if you can bear to have yet another gadget in the kitchen drawer. For beef and lamb, medium is 160°C, well-done 170°C. Using a meat thermometer is OK for big joints, but not really for chops and steaks. I don't use a meat thermometer, but it can be useful, providing you are careful to insert it at the correct point, otherwise the readings will be flawed. You need to put it in the dead centre, but not near a bone, which tends to make the surrounding area cooler than the true temperature of the joint.

White meats, such as chicken and pork, are served cooked right through. This doesn't make life any easier for the conscientious cook; the point at which the meat is cooked through, when the texture of the meat has changed, will still be followed by the drying that goes with meat being over-cooked. Test it in the same way as you would well-done red meat.

Bear in mind that residual heat will continue to cook a piece of meat while it is resting, right up to the time when it is either eaten or has become cold. Rest the meat somewhere warm for 5 minutes so that the heat on the outside reaches the inside, but do not cover the meat or it becomes steamed and the outside less crisp.

For preparing and storing poultry and game birds see **96-7**   For roast turkey see **98**   For chicken see **99**   For duck see **103-04**   For roasting game birds see **113**

# Rack of lamb with persillade

**The rack of lamb is the *à la carte* restaurant's favourite roast.** It cooks in 20 minutes and is susceptible to the chef's art as you can play around with it to advantage. In this recipe, the fat is entirely stripped away, leaving the eye of the meat, and the protection that the fat gave to this delicate meat is replaced by a stuffing called persillade, which takes the ferocity of the surface heat and also absorbs the cooking juices as the meat rests after cooking.

**Serves 4**

4 racks of lamb (6 ribs per rack)
100g unsalted butter
4 shallots, finely chopped
2 tbsp chopped fresh parsley
200g fresh breadcrumbs
salt and pepper
olive oil
2 tbsp Dijon mustard

1   Pre-heat the oven to 200°C/Gas mark 6.

2   Get your butcher to trim the lamb or do it yourself. To do it yourself, cut away the meat from the central bone and pull away one side of the rack. Cut away some of the ribs lengthways, then cut the skin away from the rack. Turn the meat over, then cut and pull the skin away. Entirely strip away the fat to leave the eye of the meat and cut away the membrane that runs the length of the loin (see page 123). Don't cut away the sweet morsels of fatty meat between the ribs, as butchers tend to do.

3   To make the stuffing, melt the butter in a saucepan, then add the shallot. Let this cook gently for few minutes, so that the shallot is not raw but also not coloured. Add the chopped parsley and then the breadcrumbs. Season with salt and pepper.

4   Paint the racks of lamb with olive oil, then season. Heat a dry frying pan and then brown the racks, one by one, on every side. Transfer to a roasting tray, then roast in the oven until pink – this takes around 15 minutes. You can test for doneness by pressing the eye of the meat, just as with a steak (see page 181).

5   Take the racks from the oven and brush with Dijon mustard.

6   Compress the persillade stuffing in the palm of your hand and then press it along the back of each rack, over the part where the skin had been. Let the racks rest for a minute, then either return them to the hottest part of the oven or place them under a grill for a minute, to set and crisp up the stuffing.

7   The racks are simple to carve into cutlets and are good served with new or gratin potatoes and green vegetables or a pulse.

## Ingredients

> **The term 'rack of lamb' may puzzle your butcher** because the joint was traditionally called a 'best end of lamb' and sold in pairs, with both halves of the ribcage still together. There should be six ribs per rack but this varies according to the butcher's whim. If there are eight or nine, cook three racks between four people.

> **The size of the eye of meat** will vary according to the breed of lamb and time of year. An upland breed, or the lamb you get from Shetlands, can be quite tiny, while lambs reaching a year old in February or March will be much bigger than young spring lambs. Adjust your cooking times accordingly – it's just a question of a few more or less minutes either way.

For resting meat see **118**    For carving meat see **120-21**

# Roasting fish

**For home cooks, roasting is the most sensible way to cook fish for a significant number people – for a dinner party, for instance.** Steaming is a nuisance unless you have a double saucepan that is big enough to cope with half-a-dozen portions at once, and deep-frying stinks the house out.

Large fish, such as sea-bass and salmon, are usually cut into steak-like portions for cooking, but this is unnecessary when they are to be cooked in the oven. Large pieces, whether on the bone or not, can be comfortably roasted without the need to buy special fish kettles or suchlike. All you need is a large enough roasting tray.

Fish, especially whole fish, are liable to stick to the roasting tray. You can prevent this by brushing the fish with oil or adding some liquid to the dish. Alternatively, you can raise the fish from the surface of the roasting tray by means of a wire rack or trivet. If you brush the fish with oil, make the exercise part of the flavouring process by choosing an oil that suits the dish, perhaps olive or sesame oil, or clarified butter.

Another advantage of cooking fish in the oven is that the fish juices that gather in the tray during cooking are good in the same way as those from meat, and should be used in whatever sauce you make.

Test whether fish is done by pressing it with your finger. You should be able to sense it breaking into flakes. If it feels resistant and rubbery at the centre, it needs more time.

For buying fish see **76**   For storing and cooking fish see **77**   For filleting fish see **80-1**

# Sea-bass with dill and crème fraîche

**This dish is an example of the routine use of an oven for roasting fish and could have many variations.** Salmon could be used instead of sea-bass, for example, and different herbs substituted –  basil and tomato, for instance, would make a warm, summery sauce.

Serves 4
4 x 150g sea-bass fillets
olive oil, for brushing
salt and pepper

For the sauce:
1 tbsp dry vermouth
1 tbsp chopped fresh dill
50ml crème fraîche
a few drops of lemon juice
salt and pepper
2 tbsp fish stock (see page 210), or pan
    juices, with the quantity made up, if
    necessary, with water
50ml olive oil

1   Preheat the oven to 200°C/Gas mark 6.
2   Brush the sea-bass lightly on both sides with olive oil. Season. Put in a roasting tray with the skin-side up. Bake until done – this should take around 30 minutes, but smaller, thinner fillets, such as 100g fillets from farmed bass, take as little as 15 minutes. Test by touch to see when it is done –  you should be able to sense it breaking into flakes; if it feels resistant and rubbery at the centre, it needs more time.
3   Heat all the sauce ingredients except the olive oil together. Include any cooking liquors that have come from the fish roasting tray. Blend in a liquidizer. With the blender running, pour in the oil to thicken the sauce. You can add the oil all at once, but you can judge the thickness of the sauce more precisely by pouring it in slowly. If you have slightly less cooking liquor than expected you can stop adding oil in time to prevent the sauce over-thickening.
4   Adjust the balance of flavours in the sauce by adding more lemon and salt if needed.
5   Remove the skin and serve the fish with the sauce.

## Ingredients

> **For this dish, I use extra-virgin olive oil,** but not the most expensive, estate-bottled Italian jobs, which are best administered as a finished dressing.

> **Farmed sea-bass are, in theory, a good idea,** although they are rarely grown into the large fish that produce the most magnificent flavour. Smart circles of the grub trade will doubtless turn their noses up at sea-bass. This is largely due to the dull, small bass that are being farmed. My major reservation about farmed fish – bass, halibut or salmon – is that commercial considerations tend to kick in fairly quickly, with poor food and conditions for the fish.

## Technique

> **The skin on fish such as sea-bass,** salmon or red mullet is only good to eat when crisply grilled. But it protects the flesh during cooking, and is best left on and then removed before serving.

> **This is one of the simplest ways of making top-quality sauces.** After emulsifying the sauce in the liquidizer, assess its thickness and flavour by testing a teaspoonful. More oil will thicken it and a little more fish stock or water will thin it down. If necessary, add lemon juice and salt to counter-balance the oil's alkaline blandness.

## Cooking method

> **You can maximize the Maillard reaction by browning the fish before putting it into the oven,** either by grilling it or placing it skin-side-down on to a hot dry pan until it colours; then place it skin-side-up in a small roasting tray and put it in the oven to finish cooking. I like the oiliness in sea-bass, and this is heightened if you brown it first, as the fat below the skin has more chance of melting.

> **Sea-bass takes longer to cook** than the appearance and delicate texture of its cooked flesh might suggest. My experience is that it will take nearly twice as long as an equivalent piece of salmon.

> **Sea-bass rarely come in predictable sizes.** I cut portions from large wild fish and these are quite chunky and firm-fleshed, whereas farmed fish tend to be longer and thinner. Be guided by the thickness of the fish rather than the weight, and test to see if it is done rather than just following the times in the recipe.

For fish stock see **210**

# Shallow-frying, grilling and griddling fish

**The choice of oil or butter is important in shallow-frying fish, as it flavours the fish as well as crisping its outside.** Unsalted butter is my favourite fat for this type of frying; it looks and smells just right as it foams in the pan. Its disadvantage is that it burns at a low temperature and you risk blackening both fish and butter. A mixture of vegetable oil and butter is a reasonable compromise between favour and safety. Alternatively, you can clarify the butter first by heating it slowly so that it separates into butter oil above a puddle of milky salt water; decant the butter oil into a jug or just pour it off carefully as required, avoiding adding any of the residue.

Otherwise, sunflower oil is the neutrally flavoured oil that I tend to use for shallow-frying fish. Olive oil burns almost as easily as butter and can give a bitter, perfumed taste if used in any quantity. Should you want its distinctive flavour on the fish, mix it with groundnut or vegetable oil. Most other highly flavoured oils – walnut, sesame and the like – are totally unsuited to the task of shallow-frying, and will leave quite a nasty taste on the fish. But you can add them at the end to give flavour to the finished dish rather than using them as a cooking medium if you like. Light sesame oil, for example, is a good oil to use with red mullet and scallops, as the nutty flavour works well with the sweetness of the scallops and the faint oiliness of the mullet.

When shallow-frying fish, heat the pan before adding the oil and heat the oil before adding the fish. A cold pan or cold oil will mean that the fish sticks to the base of the pan. Try not to over-crowd the pan as this will reduce the temperature of both pan and oil, with the same result of the fish sticking to the pan. If you are feeding a multitude, it is quicker to cook fish in batches than to try cooking it all at once.

Avoid creamy sauces with fried food. You've got that enhanced and concentrated flavour on the outside of the food and you don't need any more fat or it starts to coat the mouth with grease. Tomato-based accompaniments, or the use of some interesting vegetable or salad, will work better.

Grilling fish can be done either with an overhead grill, known in commercial kitchens as a salamander, a dry frying pan, or a barbecue/charcoal-burning arrangement. This last piece of equipment, which is the grill that most chefs use for meat and fish, represents one of the few real advantages a commercial kitchen can have over a domestic one. It uses under-heat rather than over-head heat, sealing the fish almost instantly and leaving traces of smoke flavour in the finished dish. But I have never lived in a house large enough to warrant a real grill, and doubt whether there are many who do. Still, it is good news for those with gardens and the method is too often wasted on the low-quality sausages and burgers usually cooked at barbecues.

Whatever method of grilling you use, preheat the grill properly until it is really hot. This means the fish should seal fairly swiftly and you don't need to use too much oil to prevent it from sticking.

The skin of white fish doesn't taste very nice, but for other fish leave the skin on. It will protect the fish flesh during cooking and crisp up enough to be quite palatable. The skin will be inclined to shrink during cooking, so make a few cuts right across the fish to stop it being pulled out of shape. Even if you have filleted the fish, try to grill it entirely through the side that still has skin attached, rather than turning it over during cooking. Otherwise, the flesh will dry out under the powerful heat of the grill.

For buying fish see **76**   For storing and cooking fish see **77**   For filleting fish see **80-1**

Griddling or dry-pan-frying is my preferred method of cooking fish and shellfish. Griddling alone will work for fish and shellfish that cook very quickly or that are best left under-done, such as scallops. In conjunction with a moderately hot oven and a separate roasting tray, it will suit almost everything else too.

In this method, you first brush the fish or shellfish with oil, then griddle it on a heated but completely dry frying pan. This means that you can heat the pan – far higher temperature than would be possible if it already contained oil or butter and so you will achieve an immediate, and almost greaseless, sealing of the fish. Don't use a non-stick pan, as the heat may harm the non-stick coating.

You can use almost any of the speciality oils in griddling. They are not heated in the pan and are used because of their low flash-point – they burn quickly to produce a brown, caramelized surface as swiftly and at as low a temperature as possible – as well as to flavour the piece of fish as it cooks. Even so, this is not the moment to use your estate-bottled, extra virgin olive oil; save it for an occasion when it will make more difference.

The advantages of this method are that the crisp seal on the fish will be even and only a fraction deep, so that the inner flesh stays moist; the cooking process will have been given a kick-start, and then you can finish the cooking of the interior quite gently.

To follow the method, preheat the oven to 180°C/Gas mark 4. Brush the fish with olive oil – or sesame, say, if the recipe or flavour dictates. Heat a flat, dry frying pan until it is very hot (to test when the pan is hot enough, put the palm of your hands an inch or two above the dry surface to sense the ferocity of the heat rising). Place the oiled fish on to the hot pan; it will seal almost immediately but, because it has been oiled, it will not stick. Turn the fish over and seal on the other side. Finally, lift the sealed fish on to a roasting tray and transfer to the oven to finish cooking. Test to see if it is done by touch.

For sole fillets in breadcrumbs with tomato béarnaise sauce see **85**    For scallops with lentil and coriander sauce see **188**

# Scallops with lentil and coriander sauce

**This dish, using griddled scallops,** has been a regular item on my menus for the last 15 years and at one point became popular in restaurants across the country – even the great Delia Smith used a more approachable version of the recipe in one of her cookbooks. The secret of its success is its simplicity and the contrast of sweet scallop with the Indian spices.

**Serves 4**

50g brown lentils

16 large scallops

a little groundnut or sunflower oil

$^1/_2$ onion, finely chopped

1 tbsp chopped red pepper

1 tbsp chopped fresh ginger

1 large clove garlic, chopped

$^1/_2$ tsp ground cardamom

$^1/_2$ tsp ground coriander

$^1/_2$ tsp ground cinnamon

$^1/_2$ tsp ground cumin

300ml chicken stock or water

25g unsalted butter

1 tsp crème fraîche

1 tbsp fresh coriander leaves,
    roughly chopped

1 tbsp snipped fresh chives

1 tbsp lemon juice, plus a little extra
    to go on the scallops

salt and pepper

a little light sesame or groundnut oil

1   Put the lentils in tepid water and soak for 2 hours. Simmer for around 10 minutes, or until cooked through.

2   Remove the corals from the scallops.

3   Heat a little sunflower or groundnut oil to a high temperature. Fry the onion, red pepper, ginger and garlic until they start to caramelize, then add the spices and half the cooked lentils.

4   Heat the scallop corals in the stock (this to add a little more flavour to the stock, not to cook the corals, which I do not use), then strain the stock on to the spiced lentils. Bring to the boil and simmer for 5 minutes.

5   Purée the lentil mixture in a liquidizer, then reheat with the butter, crème fraîche, coriander leaves, chives and lemon juice. Season with salt and pepper, then add the remaining cooked lentils. Spoon this sauce on to warmed plates.

6   Slice the scallops into two or three discs depending on their size, and brush lightly with light sesame or groundnut oil. Season with salt and pepper.

7   Heat a dry pan until very hot and then fry the oiled scallop slices quickly on both sides. Squeeze a few drops of lemon on top of the shellfish then place in a heap on top of the sauce.

## Ingredients

> **Only fresh scallops, preferably diver-caught, will do.** Fish dealers tend to keep scallops in water for too long and this is bad news. The mollusc will absorb a fair amount of water, swelling up to look plump and shiny. When the cooking time comes, the water will leak out, shrivelling and toughening the scallops in the process. The best scallops are almost pearl-like to the eye rather than matt white.

> **If you have the time and inclination, you can dry-roast the spices** and grind them yourself. The improvement in flavour is dramatic.

## Technique

> **Take care to have the minimum amount of oil** painted on to the fish surface. If there's too much oil, you'll have smoke everywhere.

> **Season whatever is to be cooked before you start.** There is more time to do this at the beginning than once the frying starts.

> **If the scallops need cleaning,** do it at the last moment and dry them thoroughly afterwards.

> **Put coriander leaves and snipped chives in the sauce** at the last minute. Their function, and that of the lemon juice, is to freshen and lift the sauce. Too long in the heat diminishes this effect.

## Cooking method

> **The pan must be hot and completely dry.** Any trace of water will result in the fish sticking to the surface.

> **The scallops should be cooked a little under-done.** Residual heat will continue cooking the slices as you put them on the sauce and carry the plates to tables. I am not fond of the corals and never use them. If you like their flavour and colour, cook them first and the white meat afterwards, as they take a fraction longer.

For molluscs see **88**    For how to prepare scallops see **89**

# Deep-frying fish

**Fish and chips spring to mind with deep-fried fish.** The traditional grease-up holds real nostalgia value for people who grew up before the burger and pizza chains took hold. But fish and chips is a meal best cooked at home these days, since the take-away version has degenerated into a travesty. Chip shops tend to use commercial batter mix that comes in sacks, and they also use frozen, pre-portioned fish. The only difference between one place and another will be whether the cooking oil is of any quality or not. Usually not, for the long-life oils sold are designed to last for more frying sessions rather than to impart any quality of flavour or taste. Compare a piece of commercial fried fish to a piece of fresh fish passed through a batter made with whisked egg white, self-raising flour, beer and olive oil, and then fried in sunflower oil. It will be a revelation.

Deep-frying fish with any degree of success is dependent on several factors: the use of decent oil at the right temperature, the freshness of the fish and an interesting coating such as batter or possibly breadcrumbs.

For the outside of the fish to be crisp but not blackened, heat the oil to a temperature of 190°C. You can test the temperature by putting a small drop of batter (or bread) into the oil. If it browns almost instantly, the oil is ready; if not, it needs more time. If it blackens straightaway, the oil is too hot. You can cool it down by taking it off the heat or adding more oil, if there's room in the pan.

Bear in mind that the thickness of the piece of fish will have some bearing on the temperature at which it may be fried. You may fry a small piece of fish at a higher temperature than a large one, as the inside will cook quickly before the outside is burnt. I tend to fry one piece of fish at a time and keep them warm and crisp in the oven until they are all cooked.

The batter is there to protect the fish during frying, as well as providing a crunchy contrast to the soft fish when you eat it afterwards. Most batters call for some raising agent in the flour, otherwise they will be heavy and dull, while the ultra-light batter used in tempura relies on whole egg and chilled water to produce a fine coating for the deep-fried vegetables and fish.

Picture captions: For beer batter recipe see **191**; for deep-fried fish in batter see **192**   For John dory with coriander see **84**

# Batters

## Beer batter

**Beer gives a definite character to batter.** This beer batter will taste yeasty but, in fact, relies on the last-minute inclusion of whisked egg white for its lightness and crisp finish.

**Serves 4**
150ml beer
125g plain flour
salt
1 tbsp olive oil
2 egg whites

1  Mix all the ingredients together except the egg whites. Leave for 1 hour.
2  Whisk the egg whites until stiff, folding them into the batter (**1 and 2, opposite**). Folding in requires a combined rotating and cutting motion; it is not essential for every scrap of egg white to be completely incorporated.

## Baking powder batter

**Baking powder works because of the reaction between the tartaric acid and the alkaline bicarbonate of soda.** This produces the gas that aerates a scone dough, soda bread and, in this case, batter. You can produce an even lighter, more delicate batter by adding whisked egg whites as in the beer batter.

**Serves 4**
250g plain flour
1 tsp salt
1 tsp baking powder
300ml water

1  Sieve the flour, salt and baking powder into a bowl.
2  Whisk in the water until the batter is completely smooth. It should have the consistency of cream.

**Technique**
> **Batter has a tendency to fly away from the fish when dropped into hot oil.** If there is any doubt over its sticking power, coat the fish with a fine dusting of plain flour before dipping it into the batter.
> **A piquant tomato sauce** (with chilli-heat, or acid, or both) or tartare sauce works well with fried fish. The difference between home-made tartare sauce and the grey slime in sachets produced at the chippy is similar to that between the home-made and shop-bought battered fish, with the bonus that the egg yolks used to make tartare sauce will leave the right amount of egg white to make perfect batter.

**Cooking method**
> **The batter will absorb cooking oil and become greasy if fried in oil that is not sufficiently hot.** Test the temperature by frying a drop of batter in advance.

# Deep-fried fish in breadcrumbs or batter

**Deep-frying fish is the same process whether it is coated in batter or breadcrumbs.**
The finest deep-fried fish comes from the Jewish kitchen, where it is customary to eat the fish cold – not something to be recommended for the local chippy's offering. Prime fish such as Dover sole and halibut can be used with this method.

### Serves 4

sunflower oil, for deep-frying

fish, such as 4 fillets of cod, each
    roughly 150g

plain flour, for coating

salt and pepper

1 egg (if using breadcrumbs)

breadcrumbs or batter (see page 191),
    to coat

1   Heat a large, heavy-based saucepan – preferably one kept solely for the purpose – filled with sunflower oil.

2   Coat the fish with the seasoned plain flour.

3   If using breadcrumbs, pass the fish through beaten egg then coat with the crumbs. If using batter, place the bowl next to the saucepan and dip the fish first into the batter then straight into the hot oil (**see pics 3-6**, page 190). I tend to cook one piece of fish at a time and keep the cooked fish warm in an oven while I cook the rest.

4   The fish will tend to rise to the surface as it cooks. The thicker the fillet, the longer it will take to cook. If your pieces of fish are of different thicknesses, cook the thickest piece first, in the hottest oil, and the thinnest piece last.

5   Drain on kitchen paper and serve.

### Ingredients

> **Fresh crumbs can be quickly made from stale bread.** Cut the bread into cubes, then either process in a machine or, if being made in quantity, in a food mixer with a paddle attachment. If you are bereft of such gadgets, or in the midst of a power cut, or are just plain lazy, you can use matzo crumbs, which are the best of the commercial products on offer and are available in Jewish shops. Never use the ready-prepared commercial breadcrumbs that come in strange tartrazine colours.

> **Vegetable oil, groundnut oil or, indeed, any commercially prepared concoction, will be fine.** What's more important is that the oil hasn't been used too often, or at too high a temperature. Olive oil is not suitable for deep-frying, as it burns at too low a temperature, imparts too distinctive a flavour, and in any case costs too much money to be economical when used in quantity.

### Technique

> **Place a tray lined with kitchen paper near the pan you are using,** ready for each piece of fish to drain. If its nicely fried, there should be next to no fat coming from it.

### Cooking method

> **Do not attempt to deep-fry too much at the same time.** A whole batch of fish will cause a swift reduction in the oil temperature. By the time this has recovered, the fish will have absorbed plenty of grease. What you are looking for is a crisp, thin seal on the fish, which then cooks without absorbing any more fat.

> **Never leave a pan of oil unattended,** as they are a major cause of accidents. Should the pan catch fire, quickly place a cloth across the top to smother the flame, with no gaps for oxygen to enter and switch off the heat. If you throw water at the pan you will have no house in which to cook.

> **If you intend to deep-fry on a very regular basis,** it may be wise to invest in some air-extraction unit, as the kitchen walls will otherwise begin to smell of stale oil.

For batter recipes see **191**

# Frying, grilling and roasting vegetables

The late Elizabeth David once berated an illustrious chef, Raymond Blanc, for referring to a cooking method as pan-frying. 'Frying, my dear M. Blanc', she declared, 'frying.' Well, for once the great lady was wrong. The word may be clumsy, but it is not our fault that in English one word has to do duty for two distinct methods of cooking. In French you can choose between '*frire*' for deep-frying and '*sauter*' for shallow or pan-frying.

There are one or two important points about pan-frying. Only those vegetables in contact with the surface of the pan get any direct heat, so it is important not to overload the pan. Similarly the pan must be preheated to have any chance of sealing and cooking the cold vegetables. Use only small quantities of butter or oil; the idea is that the fat should flavour the vegetables and finely coat them on the outside so that they crisp on the surface. Pan-frying is a slow method that only suits delicate-fleshed vegetables such as courgettes; harder vegetables, such as cauliflower or potato, need to be parboiled or blanched before frying, and are in fact being flavoured and crisped by the butter or oil rather than completely cooked.

Stir-frying vegetables in a wok requires intense heat. Small amounts of oil swirling round a wok base will quickly seal whatever vegetables are used. Often the process is completed by the addition of a spoonful of liquid, such as soy sauce, at the end of cooking. This sends a shock of steam through the vegetables, de-greasing them as well as finishing the cooking. I regularly stir-fry veg – particularly those such as sugar-snap peas, mushrooms and most members of the cabbage-leek-onion family – and use a wok even if I boil the vegetables first. The extended rim and shape of the pan means that it's easy to toss the hot, drained vegetables with a few drops of oil or butter, making a type of seasoned emulsion with the residual steam and water, and leaving the vegetables glistening and fresh rather than greasy.

It is important to cut and cook vegetables for stir-frying in such a way as to ensure that they will all be cooked through together at the end of the proceedings. There is no point in adding whole cauliflower florets, for example. Similarly, in mixed vegetable stir-fries, it is sensible to add hard vegetables such as carrots ahead of tender ones such as bean sprouts, or else cut them into smaller pieces.

Vegetables suitable for deep-frying need to have either a texture that cooks through quickly, such as courgettes and onion rings, or else be some fritter-like concoction made with pre-cooked vegetables, such as cauliflower florets dipped in a protective coating of batter. This gives scope for quite a few interesting mixtures if you toss the cold vegetables – cauliflower, broccoli or whatever – in a herb, cheese or spiced sauce beforehand.

Grilling suits small, young or tender vegetables, such as sweetcorn, peppers, courgettes, aubergines and asparagus, which can be cooked through before the outside becomes burnt. The flavours will become more concentrated, and crunchy vegetables such as asparagus and sea kale will lose none of their original texture. Grilled vegetables go well with grilled meat and fish, or else as warm components of a salad.

The best vegetables for roasting are root vegetables such as parsnips and swedes. The slow caramelizing during cooking helps highlight their natural sweetness and they start to acquire a certain grandeur cooked this way.

For buying and storing vegetables and fruit see **46-7**   For spiced root veg see **50-1**   For stir-fried spinach see **52**   For spiced aubergine fritters see **54-5**

# Garlic and lemon courgettes with girolle mushrooms and crème fraîche

**Courgettes are available year-round, but they aren't good year-round.** If recently harvested, they are delicately-flavoured and crunchy. If chilled and stored for air-freighting, they turn dry and coarse. During the summer, when courgettes should be cheap and plentiful, they are worthy of extra effort and make an interesting starter. Their usual accompaniment is tomato, as in ratatouille, but later in the season, when the first wild mushrooms appear, they can be given this treatment. My introduction to mushroom-gathering came during my first job as head chef, from my Italian *sous* chef, Luigi, who showed me places in London parks where mushrooms could be found. Now those who gather wild mushrooms have one thing in common – secrecy – for the mushrooms tend to reappear in the same spots each season, and to tell another is to find an empty space where once there has been a kilo of girolles, hedgehog mushrooms or ceps. It's 25 years since Luigi and I worked together and he is long since retired, but I receive a card each Christmas from him, still with a detailed report on the mushroom season and even occasionally a few new places to find them.

**Serves 4**

8 small courgettes

a little olive oil, for grilling

salt and pepper

1 tbsp chopped parsley

1 small clove garlic, crushed

a little grated lemon zest

1 tbsp finely shredded basil

50g unsalted butter, softened

**For the mushrooms:**

10g unsalted butter

100g girolle mushrooms

1 shallot, finely chopped

salt and pepper

25ml white wine

50ml crème fraîche

1   Split each courgettes lengthways, brush with olive oil, season with salt and pepper, then grill for 3-4 minutes on each side.

2   Work the parsley, garlic, lemon zest and basil into the soft butter until they are well mixed. Brush the cooked courgettes with around half the herb butter.

3   For the mushrooms, heat a little butter. Halve each girolle, then cook in the butter with the shallot. Season with salt and pepper, then add the white wine and crème fraîche. Bring to the boil. Whisk in the remaining herb butter.

4   Serve the grilled courgettes on a small pool of girolle sauce.

## Ingredients

> **The names by which wild mushrooms are known has only recently begun to settle.** The boletus mushrooms, previously called penny buns, became ceps and then porcini as first French and then Italian recipes called for them in their own language. Girolles used to be known as chanterelles (their Latin name) but now this name has been affixed to an inferior, unrelated mushroom.

> **There is an old wives' tale that you should never wash mushrooms.** Those who like gritty food will be OK, but for the rest of us it is good to give them a quick dunk in cold water. Provided they are dried swiftly afterwards there will be no harm done.

## Technique

> **The butter in this recipe is used in two stages,** firstly to flavour the grilled courgette, then to thicken the sauce. It should be soft but not melted.

> **This recipe would particularly suit a barbecue,** for the searing would be ideal as a cooking method and the black markings from a charcoal grill quite attractive on the vegetables.

# Grilled asparagus with saffron and almond hollandaise

**This is a variation of the classic asparagus treatment,** steamed asparagus with hollandaise sauce. The additional spicing works well with the pronounced flavour of the grilled asparagus.

## Serves 4
20 large stems of asparagus
a little olive oil for grilling
salt and pepper

### For the sauce:
100g butter
a pinch of saffron threads
1 tbsp nibbed almonds
25ml white wine
2 egg yolks
1 tsp orange juice
1 tsp lemon juice
a dash of Tabasco
a few fresh dill leaves

1  Melt and clarify the butter. To do this, heat the butter slowly so that it separates into butter oil above a puddle of milky salt water. Pour off the butter oil into another jug or saucepan without adding any of the residue.

2  Heat the saffron and almonds in the white wine, then pour into a heatproof bowl. Whisk in the egg yolks.

3  Heat a pan of water until hot but not boiling. Place the bowl containing the white wine and yolk mixture over this and whisk until the mixture starts to thicken. Try to whisk as if whisking egg whites; that is, trying to incorporate as much air as possible. This action and the heat will make the egg yolk and wine mixture expand into a thick sabayon.

4  Take the bowl from the heat and slowly whisk in the melted butter oil. Finish the sauce by adding the orange and lemon juices, salt, pepper, a dash of Tabasco and a few dill leaves.

5  Brush the asparagus with oil and season with salt and pepper. Grill on both sides until done. Asparagus can be eaten at any stage from raw to mush, so the timing depends on how crunchy you want the texture to be. I like it crunchy. 5 minutes on each side would be plenty for extra-thick stems.

## Ingredients
> **Asparagus is at its best when most recently cut.** As with so many things in life, hard and firm is good and limp not so clever. Any sign of wetness in the buds will be a disaster and any sign of browning on the stems will mean a tannic dark result after cooking.

## Cooking method
> **If you have a grill with heated bars,** like a barbecue or a ridged griddle pan, you will make the trademark dark lines across the asparagus. In fact, you are not particularly looking for it to brown at all: it will probably be over-cooked by the time there is significant colouring. You are after a crunchy texture as much as flavour.

> **The hollandaise sauce can be made an hour in advance,** if this helps, as it is quite stable. Keep it somewhere warm and don't allow it to become cold in case it splits when used with the hot asparagus and warm plate. If need to reheat the sauce, add a few drops of boiling water and whisk it. All the watch-points for hollandaise sauce apply here (see page 226).

For hollandaise sauce see **226**    For steamed brill with cider sabayon see **172**

**Braising and stewing are slow methods of cooking, done to soften the texture of tough joints.** Until recently, when the fashion for quick frying and grilling shifted the tenderizing aspects of meat cookery towards mincing chewy cuts so that they would cook more easily, these were the most common and practical cooking methods for the majority of meat joints.

The differences between the two methods are small. Braising involves browning the meat or vegetable before any liquid is added and stewing does not. Both rely on liquid released by whatever is being cooked – the stock and juices from any other ingredients – to moisten the final result.

Most great flavour combinations have come to us through braised dishes, and a lot of the world's best-known dishes have arrived in this way. Every *gulyas*, *cassoulet* and curry originates in cheap cuts of meat being braised, partly because this was what most people could afford – if indeed they could afford any meat at all – and partly because most farm animals were multi-purpose, providing milk or carting heavy loads as well as eventually being dinner. The eating quality of the meat would have been only one factor of several in the development of breeds.

The advantages of braising and stewing are two-fold: the meat is cooked out completely, yielding a deeper flavour, and any other ingredients used will have been able to amalgamate properly over time. In Indian cookery, aromatics such as ginger and garlic will be added at the start of cooking for this reason, while others such as the spice mix garam masala are added shortly before serving the finished dish so that they give a subtle fragrance to it.

Forget the idea of braising anything if you have no lidded pots. The liquids will evaporate and the meat burn if the combination of steam pressure and condensation going back into the pot doesn't happen. Some meats will produce plenty of liquid – veal for instance – but others render little and will need the assistance of water or wine. If wine adds something then so much the better; otherwise water will be as good as anything. You should not need stock, as whatever meat you are using should have enough intrinsic flavour without further help.

The smart trick that Escoffier and his disciples conceived was to merge the advantages of these great braised dishes with the demands of a restaurant kitchen and the need to make best use of the textures of prime cuts of meat. The slow-cooked flavours were replaced by stocks cooked over long periods and then combined with whatever major spice and herb combinations had been used to make a sauce for some piece of beef, chicken or veal that could be fried or grilled in minutes when ordered. You may follow the same practice at home of course. On the other hand, you may find it just as rewarding to explore the dishes that inspired the restaurant versions originally.

# Braising vegetables

**There are plenty of mixed stewed or braised vegetable dishes.** Most are vehicles for some herb or spice mixture – for instance, ratatouille for garlic and tomato or the Sicilian dish *caponata* for capers and parsley.

Swedes, carrots and parsnips will stew and braise well, and are often used to make up weight in meat stews. Mushrooms can also be successfully braised, and leak out a lot of juice to help moisten the finished dish – mushrooms *à la grecque* being one of the most popular braised mushroom dishes.

The texture of most green vegetables will be destroyed rather than enhanced by prolonged cooking. Exceptions are celery and fennel, which need careful peeling away of the stringy fibre that runs along each stem before cooking. Either of these will nicely partner boiled gammon or beef and can stand alone as a vegetable course if helped by a little sauce, either a white butter-based sauce or a brown stock-based sauce, mixed in with the cooking liquors, and some chopped herbs or ground spices.

The Eastern method of stir-frying (see also page 194) extends to braising vegetables. The frying element is enough alone for spinach and sugar snap peas, but a sort of speed-braising is needed to cook anything that has a denser texture.

The method works like this: firm-textured vegetables such as asparagus or broccoli are initially flash-fried. Both wok and oil have to be very hot for this – the hotter the pan the less oil needed to coat the wok and cook the vegetables. However, this sealing of the vegetables may not be enough to cook every type of vegetable to the stage you want.

Don't add more oil as this will just make the vegetables greasy. The answer is to add 1 tbsp of some liquid, soy sauce or stock if that helps the dish along, otherwise tap water. This will send a shock of steam through whatever is being cooked, hastening the cooking process but, once evaporated, still leaving a stir-fried feel to the dish. Hard vegetables, carrots maybe, may need even more cooking – a lid over the wok will send the steam back into the vegetables to build and retain pressure quickly.

As with all stir-frying, the sequence in which the vegetables are added is important. For instance, if the mange tout go into the pan at the same time as the carrots, one or other will suffer. The essence of the method is high-heat pressure and speed. If too much liquid is added the temperature in the wok will drop and the benefits of the method be lost. If in any doubt, cook the vegetables in batches, combining them only at the end for a final visit to the wok before serving.

For buying and storing vegetables and fruit see **46-7**    For ratatouille see **56-7**

# Braised chicory with caramelized orange

**There is confusion between chicory and endive.** In France, and consequently for all who train and work in French-style kitchens, chicory is a curly-leafed winter salad ingredient also called batavia. That which in Britain we call chicory is known as endive. Botanical Latin is no help, designating the whole family *Cichorium endivia*.

The type of chicory – or *endive belge* as the French would have it – we need for this dish is the tight white blanched chicons of the family, also called *witloof* by the Belgians, who developed the blanching of the plants in the mid 19th century. Don't trouble to remember all this, for it makes little sense – enough to buy the white spear-shaped jobs and not the frizzy lettuce for this dish.

**Serves 4**

25g butter
4 heads of chicory (witloof, endive)
juice of 1 orange
25g granulated sugar
1 orange, segmented

1   Heat the butter until it foams, then briefly fry the chicory.

2   Place the fried chicory in a deep ovenproof dish or roasting tray. Heat the orange juice and pour it over the vegetables. Cover tightly with kitchen foil and braise in a moderately hot oven – 190°C/Gas mark 5 – for an hour.

3   Put the sugar in a small saucepan with 1 tsp of water. Bring this to the boil and cook until the sugar caramelizes into a light brown colour. Turn off the heat and let it develop into a darker, richer colour. Add the orange segments and the cooking liquor from the vegetables. Boil and pour back over the chicory.

## Technique

> **The chicory needs little washing** and will discolour if left in water for any length of time. Cut away a thin layer of the base and the outermost layer of the leaves if they look tired or have patches of damp.

> **Caramel, like any sugar, will combine with water to form a syrup.** This is handy for the washing up, so don't attempt to scrape the pan clean immediately. Leave it filled with water for an hour.

> **The dish is best served alone,** but could partner some fatty meat such as duck or pork – perhaps even dark game such as mallard.

## Cooking method

> **The transformation of sugar into caramel** is straightforward, but needs care as the caramelizing sugar is both sticky and extremely hot. Once the sugar turns a light brown, take the saucepan from the direct heat and let it colour more slowly. Sugar becomes progressively less sweet as it colours, and will turn bitter beyond the stage at which it is dark brown. Caramel splatters when in contact with the smallest drop of water. Let the caramel cool for a few moments before adding liquid.

# Braising fish

**Fish doesn't entirely suit braising.** This doesn't mean that it hasn't a long and reasonably honourable history of being cooked in this way; just that the process destroys the delicacy and immediacy of the flesh. The two best-known examples of fish stew are *bourride* and *bouillabaisse*. Each comprises a selection of fish cooked out until all flavour has been yielded up. This comes at a real cost to texture – the broth of *bouillabaisse* is wonderful but the fish contained therein is rubbish, its texture and subtlety completely surrendered to the greater good.

My attempt at a solution – see page 214 – follows the principles of Escoffier in trying to retain the character of the original dish by slow-cooking most of its component ingredients while adding the fish later on so that it may serve as something more than flavouring and become part of the pleasure of eating the dish.

Squid braises very nicely, and is often cooked in this way in eastern Mediterranean countries. Squid can be cooked very quickly, but the obvious benefit of cooking it slowly is that the sauce is infused with the flavour of the squid.

For buying fish see **76**    For storing and cooking fish see **77**    For fish stock see **210**    For fish soup see **214**

# Braised turbot with shallots

**Fish over-cooks easily, so braising does not suit many fish – really only thick-fleshed or large specimens.** The definition of 'long, slow cooking' is of course relative to the ingredient being cooked and, since fish cooks quickly, this recipe falls within the braising definition. The advantages are that you have the juices of the fish to make a sauce and, for those fish suited to the process, a more moist texture.

**Serves 4**

30ml olive oil

4 shallots, chopped

4 x 200g turbot fillet from a large (3kg) turbot

salt and pepper

100ml white wine

50ml water

1 tbsp crème fraîche

1 egg yolk

1 tsp lemon juice

1 Heat the olive oil. Fry the chopped shallots in the oil until they start to colour. Transfer the shallots to a heavy, lidded pan. Return the pan containing the oil to the heat.

2 Season each fish fillet with salt and pepper, then fry these in the heated oil, one at a time, quickly on each side. Transfer them to the pan containing the shallots.

3 De-glaze the frying pan by pouring in the wine, letting it boil and, as with any gravy, dissolve and incorporate any residues. Add the water to make up for any reduction.

4 Pour this over the fish and chopped shallots. Fit the lid and transfer to a hot – 200°C/Gas mark 6 – oven for 10 minutes. The time needed to cook the fish will vary with the thickness of the fillets, but not by much.

5 When the fish is cooked, remove it from the cooking liquor. Whisk together the crème fraîche and egg yolk, then add the cooking liquor to this. Whisk, then pour back over the fish. Check the seasoning and add lemon juice, salt and pepper as needed.

**Ingredients**

> **The size of fish is important,** as fillets from a small fish (less than 2kg) will be thinner and better suited for grilling or frying.

**Technique**

> **The slight thickening that an egg yolk and cream liaison produces is quite fragile,** so try not to boil the sauce after it has been added.

> **If you want to alter the flavour by adding, say, chopped parsley or chervil,** whisk these into the sauce at the same time as the egg yolk and cream so that they receive a burst of heat to release their flavour but aren't cooked long enough to lose freshness.

For filleting fish see **80-1**

# Braising poultry and game

**Braising works well with poultry provided care is taken with the cooking time.** White meat such as chicken or guinea fowl will dry out if braised for too long, but it will be dangerous, not just unpalatable, if under-done. Luckily there is a fairly comfortable zone between these two extremes. A lot of game is naturally dry and suits braising. Pheasants and old grouse are two birds that particularly suit this method. You can also braise the legs of any game bird that you intend roasting. But game birds, and for that matter all poultry, do have an optimum cooking time beyond which the meat dries out and forms shreds.

## Tarragon and mustard chicken

**Chicken meat isn't tough, so it doesn't need to be braised in order to make it more palatable.** It does, however, benefit from the opportunity to slowly incorporate other spices and flavours. The process should ensure that the meat is cooked right through, so there are no problems with the meat and cooking liquor souring if it is to be kept for reheating another time.

### Serves 4

15g unsalted butter

1 x 1.5kg chicken, divided into breasts
    and legs

8 small onions, diced

2 small leeks, washed and cut into
    5cm lengths

1 tbsp plain flour

350ml Riesling

1 tbsp Dijon mustard

1 tbsp chopped fresh tarragon

50ml double cream

salt and pepper

1   Heat the butter in a heavy-lidded pan, then seal the chicken pieces on each side. You don't need the chicken to colour.

2   Add the onions and leeks and fry these gently too.

3   Sprinkle on the flour and stir it until it has combined with whatever liquids are in the pan.

4   Add about a third of the wine and stir until thickened by the flour roux you have made, then pour on the rest of the wine. Stir in the mustard, then cover and cook in a moderate oven – 190°C/Gas mark 5 – or on a low heat on top of the stove for about 30 minutes. Check the chicken is completely cooked.

5   Lift out the chicken pieces, onions and leeks and put them into a serving dish or, if you are ready to eat straightaway, on to warmed plates. Scatter the chopped tarragon on top.

6   Add a little cream to the cooking liquor and check for consistency – too thick and it will need to be let down with hot water; too thin and it will need to be boiled – and seasoning – it may need a few drops of lemon juice or vinegar. Strain over the chicken.

### Ingredients

> It's preferable to cut the chicken legs into two joints – thigh and drumstick – while leaving the breasts intact, so they will be cooked simultaneously.

### Cooking method

> **Don't let the chicken cook until it is dry.** If the simmering liquid reduces too quickly or the lid doesn't exactly fit the pot, moisten the dish with water as it cooks. Too little liquid will alter the ratio of fat to broth and leave the resulting dish looking separated; again a little water will put things right.

> **Chicken will dry out if severely over-cooked.** There is some leeway once the meat is done before this stage is reached, so err on the side of well-cooked and use a joint from the leg rather than breast to check on progress, as this takes longer to cook. Any sign of blood when pierced with a knife and the meat is not ready.

For preparing, storing, serving and cooking poultry and game see **96-7**

# Braised hare with celariac and horseradish

**It's unlucky to kill a hare, I'm told.** But nobody says it's tempting fate to eat one, and this is just as well for the meat is singularly fine, like venison only more so, and completely unlike its furry doppelganger the rabbit. The traditional braising method is called 'jugged hare'; I believe that this refers to the blood that was kept in a jug and used to thicken the sauce. I never do this and find that the extra blood gives the memories and taste of a visit to the dentist on a hot day. Not something I need for dinner. It is a shame to braise the saddle, so I would roast that and let the legs provide the deep flavour and cooking juices needed to make the dish.

**Serves 4**

1 hare, skinned and divided into saddle
    and legs
salt and pepper
25g lard or goose fat
2 shallots, roughly chopped
1 small stick celery, chopped
20g plain flour
375ml (half bottle) of red wine
50ml double cream
salt and black pepper, to taste

**For the celariac mash:**

1 small celeriac, peeled and cut into cubes
1 tbsp grated horseradish
1 tbsp double cream
salt and pepper, to taste

4 rashers smoked streaky bacon, cut
    into strips

1  Preheat the oven to 150°C/Gas mark 2.
2  Divide the hare's back legs into two, season them with salt and pepper, then fry them in the some of the lard or goose fat until they are brown.
3  Add the shallots and celery, then the flour. Let this cook gently for a couple of minutes.
4  Add the red wine, bring to the boil, then fit a lid to the pot and transfer the dish to the oven to cook for 2½ hours. The meat should be very tender.
5  30 minutes before serving, boil the celeriac cubes until tender, drain them, then blend with the horseradish, cream, salt and pepper in a food processor.
6  20 minutes before serving, cut the fillets from the saddle. Heat some of the lard or goose fat in a hot pan and fry the fillets, then transfer to the moderate oven to finish. They should be quite pink.
7  Towards the end of the cooking time, heat the remaining lard or goose fat and fry the bacon. When it's cooked and crispy, break into small pieces.
8  Serve a piece of braised hare leg on each plate and strain the cooking liquor on top. Slice the two fillets of pink roast saddle into four lengthways and lay two slices on top. Serve with the horseradish-flavoured celeriac mash, with the crispy bacon scattered over the top, and whatever treatment of potato or pasta takes your fancy.

**Technique**

> **Hare is not gelatinous and will make thin stock.** The flour will give enough thickness to the finished sauce, but this can be supplemented by adding a chopped calf's foot to the braising meat or by adding some veal demi-glace should you have some.

**Cooking method**

> **The leg meat needs long, slow cooking** – don't be tempted to speed things up by increasing the oven temperature.

For veal demi-glace see **219**

# Braising meat

**When being braised, the meat needs to be sealed – caramelized on the surface – right at the beginning of the cooking, or else it will stew.** To do this properly, heat the pan before adding any oil or butter. Then heat the oil. Then, and not before, add whatever chopped onions and meat is to be braised.

You will come across the term 'pot roast' occasionally. This means the same as 'braise', but has implications of size, conjuring up the idea of a large piece of meat cooked whole rather than diced up and therefore more imposing when presented at table. Joints such as topside of beef, which are fatless and tend to be chewy, suit this sort of process more than roasting.

## Braised pork with cider, lemon and parsley

**Pork is not the usual contender for braising, as most joints can just as well be roasted.** This combination of lentils and pork will cook comparatively swiftly for a braised dish and the flavourings work well together.

**Serves 4**

2 tbsp olive oil

1kg diced pork (shoulder or leg meat), cubed

1 tbsp capers

zest of half a lemon

30g chickpeas, soaked overnight then boiled for 30 minutes

250ml dry cider

salt and pepper

1 tsp cinnamon

2 tbsp chopped parsley

25ml crème fraîche

1   Heat the olive oil in a heavy pot. Fry the cubes of pork until brown, then add the capers, lemon zest, chickpeas and cider. Fit on the lid, then lower the heat. Season with salt, pepper and cinnamon.

2   Let the meat simmer gently until completely done – about 40 minutes – then stir in the chopped parsley and crème fraiche.

### Ingredients

> **If you have forgotten to soak the chickpeas,** buy tinned, for the dried variety is unforgiving and will need to be cooked for ages if unsoaked

> **Any joint of pork may be used.** Most butchers who offer diced pork will tend to make use of the neck or shoulder end, which has less uses otherwise. Cubes cut from the loin or leg will cook a little faster.

### Technique

> **The lid is essential to the cooking process,** as the stock will otherwise dry out during cooking.

For buying and storing meat see **118**    For pork see **128**

# Gulyas

**This Hungarian beef dish can variously be spelt as 'goulash' or 'gulyas'.** It makes little difference to the Hungarians, who know it as 'porkolt', a word that signifies the meat has been seared before the lid goes in the pot. It is a traditional cowboy dish – there are great plains called the *puzstas* in Hungary where they raise and drive cattle – just like the Wild West but without Red Indians, rawhide or John Wayne. 'Gulyas' means 'cowboy'.

*Gulyas* is often made with beef and can be made with pork. In the region around Debrecen they make a pork *gulyas* and add soured cream and *sauerkraut* to the pot, but this is a little rich for beginners to Hungarian cuisine. The best *gulyas* is made with veal.

Luckily, this is an occasion where good taste and good farming practice coincide, for the white milk-fed veal is markedly inferior in this dish to the darker veal reared in this country. Veal is the best

meat for braising generally – better even than beef – for it has all the gelatinous quality of the older animal with the advantage of producing much more liquor as it cooks. Its milder flavour is also more amenable to subtlety in spicing.

This dish is not subtle however; more robust and assertive. It is served with *galuska* – a small egg dumpling similar to the *spaetzli* of Alsace – but rice or a crusty French bread will do just as well.

### Serves 4

2 tbsp lard
3 large onions, finely chopped
1 small chilli, deseeded and chopped
1 heaped tbsp paprika
900g veal (any forequarter cut will be fine if you have choice), cut into large dice
2 tbsp tomato passata
1 tbsp plain flour
1 large red pepper, deseeded and cut into dice
1 tsp ground cumin
1 tsp chopped fresh marjoram
2 tsp salt

### For the cucumber salad:

1 cucumber, peeled and thinly sliced
salt and pepper
1 tbsp white wine vinegar
1 tbsp sugar
a little soured cream (optional)

1  To make the cucumber salad, sprinkle salt over the cucumber slices then place them in a container. Use a small plate that will fit inside the container to cover the cucumber and then weight it with something heavy. You want to press out the juices from the cucumber. Leave this to press for an hour, then mix together the vinegar, sugar and some pepper in a small bowl. Squeeze out as much juice and liquid from the cucumber as possible and toss it in the dressing. This salad is served separately, but at the same time as the *gulyas*. A dollop of soured cream is optional.

2  Heat a heavy-based pan. Add the lard and heat this also. Then – and only then – add the onions and chilli. Fry these until the onions start to colour.

3  Take the pan away from direct heat, then add the paprika. Stir this for a few moments, then return the pan to the heat and add the veal. Let this cook for a few minutes before adding the passata, then cover with a lid and simmer slowly over a low heat.

4  About 40 minutes later, lift off the lid and dust the *gulyas* with a little plain flour. Stir it in and replace the lid. When the *gulyas* is almost cooked – about another 30 minutes, but this will depend on the size of the veal cubes and can be tested by tasting a piece – add the red pepper, cumin and marjoram. Cook for another 10 minutes, then serve with the cucumber salad.

### Ingredients

> **The key to *gulyas* is paprika.** In Hungary it comes in differing strengths. Most paprika you get here is Spanish *pimentón*. Paprika that has been lying around for ages is known as 'brick dust'; buy a fresh packet. How hot you have *gulyas* is a matter of taste. As we don't have access to hotter paprika, chilli is needed for bite.

### Technique

> **You will need to fry paprika for a few seconds before any liquid is added.** This transforms the spice and is pivotal to the success of the dish.

> **The Hungarians are happy to scatter plain flour over the braising meat** halfway through cooking so the sauce thickens slightly.

For spring lamb stew see **124**   For sauerbraten see **127**

# Stocks, sauces and soups

**Sauce-making is the chef's favourite aspect of cookery.** It offers an opportunity to create a vehicle for flavours that either derives from or builds on the integral flavour of the fish or meat that is central to the meal or acts as a contrast to it. Most aspects of a meal are really down to astute shopping and careful adherence to cooking technique (not buggering up the food with careless handling), but sauce-making offers a genuine opportunity for personal taste and ingenuity to come to the fore.

Plenty of factors come into play. The thickness of the sauce will determine how much of it sticks to the meat or fish and whether or not you will need a spoon to negotiate it. The strength of the sauce will determine how much or little of it is needed. And the aromatic ingredients used will either mask the meat or fish, getting in the way of its natural flavour, or enhance it, giving focus to the entire dish. Importantly, the soft, liquid texture of the sauce will make the whole meal easier to eat, joining the diverse elements of protein, vegetable and starch.

Sauces fall into two main categories: those that derive from whatever is being cooked (basically gravy) with spices or wine added; and those that give contrast, with acidic and tangy notes from perhaps tomatoes or some reduction of white wine with lemon and herbs. The first kind will use cooking juices from the meat or fish and possibly some stock to form an extension of the meat or fish's natural flavour while acting as a vehicle for some sympathetic additional flavours, such as wild mushrooms or red wine. The second kind will act as a relish in much the same way as a spoonful of mustard or ketchup. The hollandaise/béarnaise family of emulsified sauces falls into this category, as do salsa-type confections of chilli, pepper and tomato. Their task is to liven up the meal and give an extra dimension of contrast.

These relish sauces are best suited to grilled and fried food. The acidity they bring cuts through any greasiness left by the combination of high temperature and cooking oil. In general they are an easier proposition for the home cook, with no laborious stock-making and reduction needed.

Stock-based sauces are more versatile; the variations are endless. But they will not bring anything extra to the meal unless they are carefully made. This needn't always involve time-consuming stocks and reductions, but it does involve some extra work. It is daft, for instance, to roast a joint of meat and then put the roasting tray into washing-up liquid without first de-glazing it to get the rich caramelized stock it will yield. Still dafter if some bland, chemical-filled gravy mix is then poured over the meat as a substitute.

Time and care spent on stock will repay you with a clear, well-flavoured sauce or soup. Conversely, carelessness at this point will produce a greasy stock not dissimilar to dishwater. And all stocks freeze well, so you can do this well in advance of cooking a meal.

Commercial stock cubes are available, but not yet to be recommended. They are salty and artificial and, if reduced for added concentration, will give a taste like pot noodles. Tap water, even chlorinated tap water, is preferable, for while it adds nothing, it does no damage either.

Thickness can be achieved by reduction (slow evaporation), by the use of flour or cornflour, or by the incorporation in a liquidizer of some solid ingredient such as leeks or potatoes, or by the emulsion of butter or oil. In the traditional French kitchen this last method was known as '*monter au beurre*', 'lifting with butter', and entailed the whisking in of knobs of unsalted butter until the sauce was thick and shiny. In fact, both fish- and meat-based sauces are usually made using some combination of these methods. Once the basics have been mastered, it really is a question of taste and preference.

# Fish stock and soup

Both fish stock and fish soup require the lightness of touch needed in cooking fish. The stock cooks for only 30 minutes and the soup can be made in the same time. They are also both rare examples of boiling as a cooking method for fish. There is no point in either poaching or boiling fish unless you intend to make use of the cooking liquor. Boiled fish itself is dull, but the stock produced is wonderful, much in the same way as a well-done steak tastes boring but produces excellent pan juices for gravy. It would be a pity to waste them.

## Fish stock

**Fish bones for stock are usually free.** Turbot and Dover sole are the best, but also good are halibut, monkfish, cod, haddock, hake and whiting bones; mediocre are plaice, salmon, bass and mullet bones; poor are herring, mackerel and any other oily fish's bones.

### Makes 1 litre

1kg fish bones

30g butter

1 medium-sized leek, washed
     and coarsely chopped

3 shallots or 1 onion, coarsely chopped

250ml dry white wine or cider

1.5 litres water

a few peppercorns

1 bay leaf

1   Wash the bones in cold water. Remove any traces of blood.
2   Cut the bones into manageable lengths, depending on the size of your saucepan. Melt the butter and gently fry the vegetables.
3   Add the bones. Turn them over as they cook. When they start to smell cooked, after a minute or two, pour on the wine or cider.
4   Add the water and seasonings. Do not add salt, as stock is an ingredient, not a finished dish, and you may wish to use it with salty ingredients such as soy sauce or anchovy essence; possibly you may need to reduce it for a fish glaze. In any case you will add whatever salt is needed at some other stage.
5   Bring to a gentle boil, then simmer for 30 minutes. Remove from the direct heat and allow it to settle for a further 10 minutes.
6   Decant the stock through a strainer, ready for freezing or using.

### Variations

> **The main variant is shellfish stock.** This calls for shellfish bones as well as those listed above. Generally some strong flavourings, such as tomato or even a chilli, are added. A serviceable shellfish stock can be made using the above recipe, but adding 100g whole shell-on prawns, 1 tbsp of tomato passata and 1 tsp of brandy.

> **The basic recipe can be tailored to suit a particular dish.** Saffron or any strong herb can be added, as can mussels or cockles. The resulting stock will obviously not be so versatile.

### Ingredients

> **Avoid powerful aromatics** such as celery, or use them sparingly. The flavour of fish bones can't compete with them in the way roast veal bones might and the stock could taste like a fishy celery broth.

> **Stock is ideal for making the best use of trimmings.** But it is not a substitute for the dustbin and should not have to withstand the addition of irrelevant leftovers. A compost heap takes care of onion and carrot peelings and a dog will normally eat anything else.

### Technique

> **The bones should cook gently in a little butter or oil before water is added.** This develops the flavour of the stock in the same way as the roasting of veal or chicken bones for meat stocks.

> **To achieve a greater concentration of flavour,** either increase the ratio of bones to water or, once the stock has been cooked and strained, reduce the volume through boiling. Do not to cook it for longer than the recommended time, or it will deteriorate into a cloudy, heavy tasting liquid.

> **After you have strained the stock,** let any debris cool before wrapping and consigning it to the bin. The combination of heat and spiky bones is lethal to bin liners.

For poaching and steaming fish see **170**

# Saffron, leek and scallop soup

**This is basically a leek and potato soup, spiced with saffron and used as a foil for the sweetness of the seared scallop.** The secret is to be sparing with most of the ingredients: small amounts of potato will thicken quite a lot of liquid and too much saffron will over-power everything else involved. Try not to look for a deep-yellow colour, for instance, as some sign of success – a custard-coloured soup will be too strong.

### Serves 8
1 chicken leg, divided into thigh
    and drumstick
500g leeks, washed and chopped
1 medium onion, chopped
200g maincrop potatoes, peeled and diced
1.5 litres water
5g saffron threads
1 tsp cumin
100ml crème fraîche
50ml white wine
salt and pepper
1 tsp lemon juice

### For the scallops:
4 scallops, sliced into quarters
a little olive oil for frying

1   Preheat the oven to 200°C/Gas mark 6. Roast the chicken until it is almost cooked – about 30 minutes, Put this in the soup pot along with the leeks, onion, potato and water. Add the saffron and cumin, then fit with a lid.

2   Bring to the boil, then simmer until the potatoes are done. The timing will depend on the thickness of the potatoes, but 30 minutes should do the trick.

3   Lift out the chicken and strip away the meat from the bones. Return the meat to the pot and discard the bones. Blend in a liquidizer. Do this in several batches, as hot liquids will tend to rise up while being blended and a scalded arm is on the cards. Add some crème fraîche, wine, salt, pepper and lemon juice to each batch. This gives you scope for altering the level of lemon or cream in the soup. Remember when tasting that this is a soup rather than a sauce and that a bowlful will be eaten by each diner.

4   Brush the scallop pieces with oil, then heat a dry frying pan ready to cook them. When the pan is very hot, sear the scallops quickly on each side. Dry the cooked scallops on kitchen paper, then add to the soup. The scallop should be barely cooked.

### Technique

> **The chicken has two functions in the recipe.** First, it is a neat substitute for a chicken bouillon cube, with none of its industrial flavour and saltiness. Second, it will help to thicken the soup. It is essential, however, that the chicken is completely cooked before it is blended into the soup. If you have any doubts once the bones are removed, return the meat to the broth for a few minutes more.

> **Potato as a thickening agent works well, but needs care.** If it becomes over-cooked it will be glutinous and the resulting soup will be diminished. Cut the peeled potatoes into even cubes and test these as if you were making mash to tell you when the soup is done.

For preparing scallops see **89**

# Fish soup with garlic, saffron and orange

**This version of *bourride* is thickened with garlic mayonnaise.** While the main flavours are the same as in traditional *bourride*, I'm loath to apply the traditional name lest some smart-arse pipes up to let me know that it should have some arcane ingredient added or left out to truly qualify for the title. This tastes just fine and will make four large main-course meals.

## Serves 4

1 tbsp sunflower oil

2 shallots, chopped

½ average-sized red pepper

1 tbsp chopped celery, deseeded and diced

1 clove garlic, finely chopped

a large pinch of saffron threads

1 birdseye chilli, deseeded
   and chopped

2 slices orange

1 litre chicken stock (see opposite)

100g brill fillet

100g red mullet fillet

100g white scallop meat

### For the garlic mayonnaise:

1 tbsp lemon juice

1 tbsp Dijon mustard

2 egg yolks

1 clove garlic, crushed

salt and pepper

50ml olive oil

50ml sunflower oil

1   First, make the garlic mayonnaise by whisking together the lemon, mustard, egg yolks, garlic and seasoning and then slowly whisking in the oils.

2   For the soup, heat the sunflower oil and then sweat the shallots, pepper, celery and garlic. Add the saffron, chilli and orange, then add the stock. Bring this to the boil, then simmer for a few moments.

3   Add the fish in the order in which they take to cook – in this case the brill first, followed by the mullet and then at the last moment the scallops. When the fish are cooked, remove from the liquid using a slotted spoon.

4   Take the pan from direct heat and pour all the liquid into a blender along with the bits and pieces of orange and vegetables. Liquidize, adding the mayonnaise a tablespoonful at a time, stopping when the soup begins to thicken.

5   Pour the soup back over the fish and serve with croûtons.

## Ingredients

> **You can put whatever fish you want into this soup,** and those suggested are merely a guideline. It will make a more interesting dish if there are two or more types, hopefully with differing textures.

## Cooking method

> **The soup will be fairly stable once the mayonnaise is added,** but shouldn't be subject to any prolonged boiling or it will split back into oil and stock. Should this happen, blend the soup again.

> **Over-cooked fish will spoil the dish,** so drop the fish into the cooking liquor only when you're sure the soup is to be served.

For buying, storing and cooking fish see **76-7**    For poaching and steaming fish see **170**

# Chicken stock, consommé and gravy

**Make good chicken stock and you have an almost unlimited range of soups available.** It is truly versatile, able to stand on its own – with a little cream or thickening – as chicken soup, or to partner some herb such as tarragon. It can also lend body and background to ingredients that are inadequate by themselves in soups or sauces, such as watercress or almonds.

In each case, the success of the finished dish will depend on the quality of the chicken stock used. The substitution of commercial bouillon cubes will give results that taste 'bought-in' rather than 'home-made' because the additives and high concentration of MSG in those products will predominate. Should time or ingredients for stock-making be a problem, use these substitutes with caution. Make the stock up separately rather than crumbling the cube into the other ingredients, so you may judge the strength.

## Chicken stock

**There are two styles of chicken stock: white and brown.** The white stock involves boiling chicken carcasses with water and aromatic vegetables for half an hour, then straining off the liquid. I have opted to concentrate on a darker stock, which involves roasting or frying the bones, but the tips will be the same for both. Brown chicken stock has a more pronounced flavour than white.

### Makes 1.5 litres

2 whole chicken carcases or 750g winglets
   necks and gizzards
2 litres water
1 onion, coarsely chopped
1 leek, washed and coarsely chopped
1 small carrot, peeled and coarsely chopped

1 The giblets come in a plastic pouch. The liver and heart aren't needed for stock. Wash the necks and gizzards.

2 Preheat the oven to 200°C/Gas mark 6. Roast the carcasses and giblets until they acquire some colour – this should take about half an hour. Lift them from the roasting tin into a big saucepan.

3 De-glaze the roasting tin by emptying any grease, then adding 285ml of the water. The idea is to convert any residues stuck to the base of the roasting tin into liquid. Bring this to the boil, then pour into the saucepan with the chicken and remaining water.

4 Bring the stock to the boil. Skim off any foam, then add the veg. Re-boil and simmer for 40 minutes. Should the water level recede below the level of the chicken, top it up. Skim periodically.

5 Strain the stock and leave it to cool, preferably overnight. Refrigerate as soon as, but not before, it is cool. The fat will then rise to the surface and solidify, albeit softly. It will skim off easily.

### Technique

> **Carcasses can be bought cheaply from butchers or fishmongers** who sell chicken legs and breasts as separate items, especially if you ask in advance. They are too bulky to be on display at your supermarket, however, so chicken winglets can substitute.

> **A golden brown,** not black, is the objective for roast carcasses.

> **For a more concentrated flavour,** add more chicken carcasses or giblets rather than cooking the stock for ages. The chicken will deliver up all its flavour within an hour.

> **Clear clean stock will have no grease or fat.** Most grease will rise to the top as the stock cools, and can be skimmed off then. But if the stock boils too hard and for too long, some fat will emulsify into it. Aim for a simmer, or at most a gentle boil.

> **When simmering,** have the pot squarely on the heat, creating warmer and cooler areas of the surface. Fat accumulates in cooler areas.

> **Chicken stock sours quite quickly,** so use it within a couple of days. It's much safer to freeze the stock if it's not needed.

For chicken consommé see **216** For chicken gravy see **217**

# Chicken consommé

**Consommé is a clear soup,** which is also sometimes used as the base for a variety of soups. It's essential that the stock is good – there's no hiding place if it isn't.

The method for chicken consommé is the same as that for beef or fish consommé, so once you have mastered this you will find no problem in making the other two using veal and fish stocks respectively. The aim, in all cases, is to remove every imperfection and every spot of grease from well-flavoured stock. The following recipe gives the standard method for achieving this.

Chicken consommé calls for the addition of chicken meat, just as a beef consommé calls for the addition of chopped beef. The addition of meat is done because the stock will need strengthening after it has been bared of imperfections.

### Makes 1 litre

1 onion
1 leek, washed and trimmed
10cm stick celery
1 small carrot, peeled
2 egg whites
2 tbsp tomato passata or 1 tsp
    tomato purée
1 clove garlic, chopped
2 chicken legs, meat cut away and
    chopped into cubes the consistency of
    minced meat
1.5 litres cold chicken stock (see page 215)
salt

1   Chop or food process the vegetables to roughly the same size as the chicken. Size is not crucial. Smaller pieces will, however, cook more quickly, adding their flavour to the broth by the time it has clarified as well as incorporating more easily among the egg-white crust which forms on top of the clarifying stock.
2   Put the egg whites into a clean bowl and whisk lightly for a few seconds; just enough to give a foam and increase the volume slightly. Whisk the tomato passata into the whisked egg whites.
3   Stir the vegetables, garlic and chicken into the egg white mixture. Mix in a cup of cold stock and allow this to rest for 20-30 minutes.
4   Pour in the remaining cold stock and mix thoroughly.
5   Bring to the boil, stirring often to avoid fragments of the clarification mixture and its egg-white coating catching.
6   As soon as the stock starts to bubble up to the boil, lower the heat to a simmer. The clarification ingredients and any other tiny bits will rise to the surface in a white foam. The idea is to let this cook out a little so it solidifies enough to enable the consommé underneath to be easily decanted; half an hour should do the job.
7   Ladle out the consommé and pass it through a fine strainer. When it is cool enough to taste, add salt. If you want stronger consommé, boil it down to reduce it and add the salt afterwards.

### Technique

> **Everything you add will affect the flavour.** For instance, if you put extra celery, perhaps to tidy away left-overs, it will change the flavour emphasis. The same applies to carrots, herbs and garlic.
> **Temperatures are important.** The mixture of stock, egg white and veg should start off cold – some people advocate ice cubes – rest for 20 minutes, then be brought slowly to the boil.
> **The egg white forms a crust above the simmering stock.** This catches and binds all the imperfections as they rise. If the consommé boils too hard the crust will break up and the whole process will need to be started again; a gentle simmer is the aim.

> **Stir the mixture** of stock and clarifying ingredients as they heat, as the egg white makes it susceptible to catching and burning.
> **The finished consommé is customarily strained** through fine muslin. If you have none, a coffee filter will substitute.
> **If you have a disaster,** say the egg whites were too weak to bind and clarify the other ingredients, you will have to do the whole process again with more egg whites. Lesser catastrophes can usually be rectified – let the consommé cool completely, then decant the clear broth from the top; most imperfections, strands of egg white and the like, will be at the bottom of the pot.

# Chicken gravy

**The word 'gravy' has strange overtones.** It has, on the one hand, the feel of something homely and honest, that will taste familiar and have none of the surprises indicated by a word like 'sauce'. On the other hand, there is the implication of a crude concoction that requires neither skill nor care. The trick is to get the homely, good taste while taking care with the choice of ingredients and preparation.

For a start, all packet confections of brown colouring, thickening and chemical additive should be jettisoned. These are nasty and over-powering. Worse, they provide no individual taste of the meat just cooked. Real gravy makes use of the residues cooked on to the pan or roasting tray in which the meat has been cooked and any juices that escape from the meat after cooking, while it rests. A little water is the only other absolute requirement to give you chicken-flavoured gravy.

Optional extras for chicken gravy will move you ever so slightly towards sauce-making. If you sprinkle the bird with herbs or garlic and a little butter before roasting, these will affect the result. In the same way, some people like to add a little liquid, such as white wine or water, to the roasting tray before cooking the bird. This produces softer meat and, once again, alters the gravy produced.

**Makes 300ml**

the roasting tray in which the bird
   has cooked
1 tsp tomato passata
500ml water
salt and pepper

**Optional**

50ml white wine
1 tbsp fresh herbs
1 clove garlic, crushed
25g mushrooms

**For thickening**

1 tsp plain flour, cornflour or potato starch

1 When the chicken is cooked, lift it on to a large dish to rest while you make the gravy and finish any other parts of the meal.

2 Pour any fat in the roasting tray into a dish.

3 If you are making an unthickened gravy, place the roasting tray on to a low heat and add the passata and then the wine (if you are using any) and water. Boil hard for a couple of minutes.
If you are thickening the gravy with plain flour, add 1 tsp of the reserved fat and 1 tsp of flour to make a roux; let this cook for a few minutes, stirring, then add the passata and water a little at a time, stirring to incorporate and thicken the gravy. If you are thickening with cornflour or potato starch, proceed as for a thin gravy: moisten the starch with an equal quantity of water or wine and stir into the gravy. Let it come to the boil.

4 Add any juices that have drained from the roast bird. The fat poured from the roasting tray in point 2 will have separated into a top layer of fat and a dark concentrated liquid which you can also add. Spoon off the fat until you are left with this residue.

5 Add anything else that you feel will contribute: garlic, herbs and the like, and strain into a jug.

## Variations

> **All gravy is made using the same method.** For beef, lamb, pork or game gravy, substitute the fat from the roasting pan the meat was cooked in for the chicken fat. You can mix in whatever herb you like: marjorum goes well with lamb, while pork can take fractionally stronger flavoured herbs such as thyme.

## Technique

> **Beware of tomato purée:** a little will give body and a deeper colour; too much will over-power the poultry. If you use 1 tsp, remember it needs to cook for a while. Add it to the roasting tray while it's hot and let it 'fry' for a minute before adding the liquid.

> **Gravy from poultry will never be as dark** as that made from roast beef. It doesn't matter if the gravy is quite light in colour.

> **Chicken gravy is generally left unthickened,** and this is how I prefer it. The plain flour method of thickening will produce a very light-coloured gravy that needs passing through a sieve.

# Veal stock and demi-glace

**Veal stock is expensive to make.** Butchers will give chicken carcasses free of charge, but not veal bones, which are in demand for this staple of *haute cuisine* disproportionately to the need for any other part of the calf. Look upon the cost as an aid to concentration while you are doing all the roasting and skimming.

## Veal stock

**Veal stock can be used for veal demi-glace or** as the base for either a soup or a lamb or game sauce.

### Makes 3 litres
3kg veal bones, cut into 10cm lengths
1kg mixed onion, carrot and celery,
    roughly chopped

1   Roast the veal bones until lightly browned. Lift into a clean pot and add enough water – 5 litres approximately – to cover.
2   Pour off any fat from the roasting tray and then add a little water to de-glaze the base of the hot tray. Add this to the pot, then bring to the boil. Skim off the foam that rises to the surface.
3   Add the chopped mixed vegetables and simmer for about 8 hours, occasionally skimming away any foam or fat. If the water level drops below the bones, top it up.
4   Strain into a clean pot ready for the demi-glace method or to be made into soup or for freezing.

### Cooking method
> **The bones should be golden brown rather than charred,** and have as much of the fat cut off as possible. Any fat left on will render down during cooking and need to be skimmed away.
> **Simmering is what's needed.** Hard-boiling will not speed things up; rather it will emulsify any fat and leave you with cloudy stock.

For veal see **132**

# Veal demi-glace

**Veal demi-glace is the cornerstone of the classic kitchen and on its quality depends the success or otherwise of most restaurant-type meat sauces.** The gelatinous aspect of the finished sauce is impossible without veal bones, so most sauces for meats such as lamb or venison will use this as a base flavouring and then the sauce will be customized with lamb or venison trimmings as needed. There are no short-cuts, so if you don't fancy the work don't make these sorts of sauces.

**Makes 3 litres**

3 tbsp olive oil

1kg mixed onions, garlic, carrot and leek, chopped

1kg shin of beef, cut into cubes

3 tbsp plain flour

3 litres veal stock (see opposite)

3 tbsp sieved tomato passata

375ml (half a bottle) decent but not expensive red wine

1  Heat some of the olive oil in a pan. Fry a third of the vegetables and beef; when they start to colour add 1 tbsp of plain flour and let this cook for a few seconds before scraping them into a dish and putting to one side while you repeat the process with the second and third batches of meat and vegetables. The idea is that they should caramelize and colour, and if you over-load your frying pan they will bubble and boil instead.

2  When the final batch is ready, put the lot into the hot veal stock. With the final batch, also add the tomato passata and red wine.

3  Let all this come to the boil, then skim. Simmer for 4 hours, skimming off the fat regularly. When the level drops too far, add a little cold water. This will draw out the fat and impurities from the demi-glace, and these can be skimmed away. I do this eight or ten times during cooking.

4  Strain the result into another clean pot, then bring this to the boil. Simmer for another hour or two, skimming away the foam and adding more water to keep the final quantity at around 3 litres.

## Variations

> **This sauce base calls for a lot of time.** The reward is that little further needs to be done to produce a myriad of differing, but still excellent, sauces, and the base will freeze perfectly. The addition of 1 tbsp of Meaux mustard and knob of butter will make a first-rate sauce for beef or veal; a few reconstituted dried morel mushrooms or a splash of Madeira will produce similarly good results, and the addition of de-glazed pan juices from a joint of lamb will give a superb lamb-flavoured sauce, especially with the addition of some diced bacon and lentils or haricot beans.

## Technique

> **Demi-glace keeps in the fridge for a week or two** – it's more stable than chicken stock. It also freezes perfectly, and is best frozen in small user-friendly batches.

# Vegetable stock and soup

**Vegetable soups can be stock-based, with pieces of vegetable suspended in the liquid,** or they can be thickened through blending in a liquidizer or food processor – the vegetable itself used as thickening. Both types can be adorned with cream or egg yolks, or with a combination of the two (do this with the soup off the heat) if need be, but are rarely improved by such attentions.

The principles of soup-making are no different from those of sauce-making: the liquid is a vehicle for whatever flavours and ingredients you choose. Soups thickened with potato handle slightly differently – once potato is over-cooked it becomes glutinous, so you should blend the soup as soon as the potato is cooked through.

There is no reason why stock for use in vegetable dishes such s soup should taste of fish, veal or chicken unless you want that flavour. The essence of making a vegetable stock is no different from making any other type of stock, but unfortunately vegetable stock can be better in theory than practice, and can resemble murky water if you don't take care in the preparation. Even a good vegetable stock will lack the gelatinous quality that bones add to a stock, but it is fresh and light if that is what you are looking for.

Some vegetables will give depth, others flavour. Some, such as turnips, are totally unsuited to the task. In all cases, there is an optimum amount of time they should spend boiling, after which they become lifeless, greasy and dull – qualities they will impart to your stock if left there too long.

Stock for vegetarian dishes rather than vegetable dishes may need a little extra help, as delicate vegetable stocks will not cope with strong pulse dishes or the likes of fermented beancurd. Yeast – the sort from which Bovril is made – can 'beef' up the liquid and provide a healthy dose of vitamin B. For carnivores, though, who are looking for flavour rather than purity of diet, there is little point in this, as nothing beefs up a stock quite so well as veal or beef bones.

The Swiss commercial vegetable stock in granulated form isn't great, but comes nearer to home-made than those for fish or chicken stock.

For buying and storing vegetables see **46-47**

# Vegetable stock

**Stock, whether from vegetables, fish or meat,** is a primary building block of good cooking. Poor stock will devalue everything in which it is subsequently used. A complex or ornately decorated dish, perhaps a soup with fanciful garnishes and great swirls of cream, for instance, which turns out to be bland and under-flavoured, will feel preposterous and ridiculous, like wearing a starched collar and dirty underwear.

**Makes 750ml**

1 medium-sized onion, sliced

2 cloves garlic

2 leeks, sliced

25ml olive oil

2 medium-sized carrots, peeled and diced

3 sticks of celery, sliced

1 aubergine, diced

25g brown lentils

1 lite water

2 tbsp fresh herbs (basil, parsley, thyme, marjoram)

1 Wash the leeks, carrots and celery. Gently stew the onion, garlic and leeks in olive oil.

2 Add the rest of the vegetables, the lentils and cold water.

3 Bring to the boil and simmer for half an hour.

4 Add the herbs then, 5 minutes later, strain the stock.

5 The stock can be frozen if not for immediate use, or it would be fine, topped up with a little water, in the soup that follows.

## Ingredients

> **Don't use the stockpot as a swill bin** – your conscience may feel better if kitchen scraps are recycled, but not necessarily your stock.

> **Scrub any vegetables** whose peelings and trimmings are to be used, as there may be residual dirt, soil, chemical preservatives or worse.

> **Salt is unnecessary** as stock is a component, not a finished dish. If you want to gauge the stock's suitability as a soup or sauce base, you can sprinkle salt over a sample tablespoon and taste it.

> **There are seasonal fluctuations in the ingredients** most suitable for stock. Runner beans would be fine in early summer, or wild mushrooms in autumn. As a guideline to quantity, use equal volumes of water to chopped vegetables. The yield will be around two-thirds the quantity of water used, the rest having evaporated during cooking.

> **Some vegetables are more central than others** to good stock. Leave out the onion family and the stock will suffer. However, ingredients such as aubergine or lentils are optional, improving the quality of the stock rather than being a vital part of the proceedings.

For summer vegetable soup see **222**

# Summer vegetable soup

**This soup is blended in a liquidizer.** If you have the vegetable stock to make this soup with, so much the better; if not, water will substitute. Puréed soups are easy providing you own a liquidizer or food processor – these are genuine labour-saving devices, an improvement on pushing hot, cooked vegetables through a sieve. Soup-making is a good exercise in achieving balance in both seasoning and texture (thickness and smoothness). What seems fine by the teaspoonful, when tasting, may not work so well by the bowlful.

**Serves 4**

1 small onion, finely chopped

2 tbsp olive oil

1 litre vegetable stock or water

1 small potato, peeled and cut into
   small cubes

2 asparagus spears, cut into 1cm lengths

2 tbsp shelled broad beans

2 tbsp shelled peas

1 tbsp crème fraiche

1 tbsp basil leaves

salt and pepper

a dash of Worcestershire sauce

1   Gently fry the onion in half the olive oil. Add the stock or water and the potato, asparagus, broad beans and peas.

2   Cook until the vegetables are tender, then remove the pan from the heat and blend the soup in a liquidizer. You may need to do this in more than one batch, as the initial spurt from a liquidizer can coat surrounding walls with soup if over-filled.

3   As the soup blends, add the crème fraîche, basil and the remaining olive oil.

4   Season with salt, pepper and Worcestershire sauce.

## Ingredients

> **If there seem to be a lot of ingredients** in small quantities and this poses an awkward shopping trip, there is scope for the judicious substitution of fresh vegetables already in the fridge. Remember not to use the soup purely as a vehicle for recycling scraps, however. The soup is a platform for your judgement of what mixes well from the season's crop, not a makeshift waste disposal unit.

> **The crème fraîche and Worcestershire sauce** should lift the soup, which could easily be dull or bland, no more than a thin vegetable purée. If you are using ordinary cream or do not like the flavour of Worcestershire sauce, add a few drops of lemon juice or wine vinegar instead. The objective is a soup that is fresh tasting and summery, and the touch of sharpness is important in achieving this.

> **The same method can be used concentrating on one vegetable only,** leeks for instance, or just asparagus, rather than the combination of asparagus, peas and beans.

## Cooking method

> **Take as much care in cooking the vegetables** as you would if you intended to eat them whole. They need to be cooked through, but not cooked to a sludge or that is how the soup will taste. Either cut up the vegetables so you have some chance of them all being cooked at the same time or add them in a sequence that reflects their cooking time – onion, then potatoes, then asparagus etc.

For vegetable stock see **221**

# Starch-based sauces

**The principal thickeners in starch-based sauces are plain flour and cornflour.** The following are also sometimes useful:

*Fécule de pommes de terre (potato flour)*: this handles just like cornflour and gives a similar texture. We used 4 tbsp of this in each gallon bucket of veal stock to thicken the demi-glace rather than flour at the Capital Hotel.

**Rice flour:** used to be a kitchen standby for thickening certain soups. Needs more cooking than cornflour, but has a similar slightly gooey effect on the texture.

**Arrowroot:** acts like warm gelatine, giving body to a sauce but without any flour-like properties. The effect wears off if the sauce is kept hot for any length of time.

**Cornflour:** pastry cooks use this in custards for the smooth, almost silky texture it lends. It is easy to use – it is simply mixed with a little cold water and then whisked into the sauce – but it can give a nasty snot-like texture if used in excess. Whatever commercial companies use to thicken ready-made dishes is similar.

**Plain flour:** usually mixed with butter or oil to ensure it is effectively incorporated into a sauce. It is most commonly used as a cooked roux – an equal mixture of flour and oil or butter is cooked slightly before any liquid is added. There are other methods though. *Beurre mani* is an equal mix of butter and flour beaten until smooth and then whisked into a sauce for thickening. This does have pitfalls: if the sauce is on direct heat or still boiling when the *beurre mani* is added, for instance, you will have small dumplings rather than a thickened sauce. In Hungary they have the most eccentric method of adding flour to thicken stews such as *gulyas*. It's known as 'dusting' and involves nothing more than sprinkling flour on to the stew as it cooks and then stirring. Presumably it mixes with fat that has risen to the top of the pot during cooking. Whatever the reason, it always seemed to work.

# Basic white sauce

**The basic white sauce is known as béchamel sauce in the classic French kitchen.** Large kitchens will almost always keep just this and demi-glace to use as starting point for a range of sauces. It is simple to make, but once made properly is capable of a thousand variations to suit whatever meat, fish or vegetable it is to partner. There are two stages. First you make a butter and flour roux, then you incorporate warm milk. The thickness needed will determine the exact ratio of milk to roux, but what follows will give the most usual sauce. If you are making this in advance, note that the sauce thickens in the fridge when cold and will need extra milk added when reheating.

100g butter
90g plain flour
1 litre milk, warmed
salt and pepper

1 Melt the butter but do not let it colour.
2 Stir in the flour and beat the mixture into a smooth ball – this is the roux. Let this cook gently on a low heat for a couple of minutes, stirring. Again, you don't want it to colour
3 Warm the milk and add a third of the warmed milk to the roux. Stir the milk and roux until they come to the boil. This is the most important stage of the sauce and you should stir harder as it nears boiling point, for it is here that it will thicken into a smooth, if very thick, sauce.
4 Add the remaining milk in two batches, each time stirring while you bring the sauce to the boil, then season with salt and pepper.
5 You shouldn't need to sieve the sauce if you have stirred it properly during cooking.

### Variations

The base sauce is quite dull, but these variations can be excellent:

> **Cheese sauce (for cauliflower or broccoli):** add 50g grated mature Cheddar, a 1 tbsp mustard and a few drops of Worcestershire sauce
> **Parsley sauce (for ham):** add a good bunch of chopped parsley and 1 tbsp of dry sherry.
> *Fish velouté* **(for poached fish dishes):** substitute fish stock for some or all of the milk and finish the sauce with any cooking juices and some herb such as tarragon or chervil.

### Cooking method

> **The flour in the roux has to cook but not colour.** A low heat and patience are all that's needed. Once cooked together, the flour and butter will come away cleanly from the saucepan's base.
> **The traditional recipe calls for equal quantities of flour and butter,** but the roux is easier to handle if the ratio of butter to flour is increased slightly. The weight of flour is more crucial to the finished sauce, for it is this that does most of the thickening.

The classic recipe also calls for an onion studded with cloves to be infused in the warm milk. I have never done this, for it adds nothing I want to the proceedings.

> **The milk is added in three or four stages,** and the sauce is stirred until it is cooked after each addition. Just as with the initial roux, you can tell when the embryonic sauce is ready for the next batch of milk because it will come away cleanly from the saucepan's base.
> **It's easier to blend the sauce if the milk is warm** when it is added, but it is not essential.
> **If you are making the sauce to keep for use some other time,** cover the surface with melted butter or clingfilm or else a thick skin will form.

# Butter-based sauces

**The difficulty with butter-based sauces is preventing them from curdling.** This happens as soon as the balance of oil to non-oil liquid is out of kilter. You don't need to do anything to make it happen, as non-oil liquid will start to evaporate quickly and cause the sauce to curdle. Thankfully it's quite an easy problem to solve – a tablespoonful of boiling water will normally do the job.

## Hollandaise sauce

**The final distinct sauce base is hollandaise.** This is a warm emulsion of egg yolks with wine or a wine and vinegar reduction and clarified butter. It takes a strong wrist and a little patience but is otherwise reasonably straightforward.

**Serves 4**

200g unsalted butter

3 egg yolks

50ml white wine

1 tbsp lemon juice

salt and pepper

a dash of Tabasco

1  Clarify the butter by heating it and then allowing the butter oil to separate leaving a milky residue underneath – it's the butter oil you want.

2  Warm a pan of water. Whisk together the yolks and wine in a stainless-steel bowl and then suspend the bowl over the warm-to-hot water. Whisk until the yolks are cooked and thick

3  Take the bowl from the heat and whisk in the warm butter. Do this at a trickle initially, and then faster as the sauce holds the butter more confidently.

4  Add lemon juice, salt, pepper and Tabasco.

### Variations

Here are some variations:

> **Nibbed almonds and saffron** added at the end.

> **Purée of fresh parsley** whisked in at the end.

> **Béarnaise sauce:** a reduction of wine vinegar, chopped shallot and tarragon at the beginning instead of the plain white wine.

### Technique

> **The sauce must never get too hot or the yolks will curdle.** This is avoided by whisking over warm-to-hot water. The hotter the water, the quicker your sauce cooks and the pain in your wrist eases from the whisking. Don't be tempted to try to do this too quickly. If in doubt, have a bowl of cold iced water handy to instantly stop the cooking process.

> **The ratio of wine or other non-oil liquid to butter** will determine the amount of sauce you end up with and the relative density or otherwise of the sauce. I prefer a lightish sauce and use plenty of white wine. Similarly, the amount of butter the sauce is able to absorb will be dependent on this wine – too much butter to not enough liquid will result in a curdled sauce; too little and the sauce will be thin. The point you choose between these two extremes is a matter of taste.

> **The sauce has to be kept warm until it is used.** This generally involves being left on a high shelf near the stove for the hour or so that it will stay in good condition. If it starts to separate for any reason, you have two courses of action you can take. First, you can try to whisk in a tablespoonful of hot water to restore the equilibrium between butter and liquid that may have altered due to evaporation. Second, you may take another yolk and some more wine and make a fresh batch, slowly incorporating the curdled sauce into the new one.

# Beurre blanc

**This is the simplest butter sauce, but has little keeping quality,** so make it just before serving. You need cold butter cut into small cubes and a reduction of white wine. The wine needs to reduce in order to become viscous enough to hold the butter. Perversely, this sauce shouldn't taste particularly buttery, rather silky smooth, with the lemon or vinegar coming to the fore. It's really like a hot salad dressing, just as hollandaise is a warm mayonnaise.

**Serves 4**
50ml white wine
1 shallot, finely chopped
200g cold unsalted butter
1 tbsp lemon juice
salt and pepper
a dash of Tabasco

1   Heat the wine and shallot together and let this reduce gently by half.
2   While this is still hot, and still over a gentle heat, whisk in a few cubes of butter.
3   When this has been completely incorporated, whisk in some more butter – and so on until the sauce is thick and warm.
4   Season with lemon juice, salt, pepper and Tabasco.

## Variations
> **Almost any herb or spice can be added,** as can capers or chopped olives and tomato, to make a sauce for vegetables or steamed fish.

## Cooking method
> **If the wine has reduced too much,** it can be let down with a few drops more to no ill effect.
> **The sauce will not keep stable for too long,** but any that is left over can be refrigerated and then used again provided it is whisked into a freshly made and warm wine reduction.

# Relish sauces

The acidity and strength of flavour of relish sauces brings freshness to fried foods. Most liquidizers recommend you don't pour in boiling hot liquid to blend. You can blend a warm sauce or soup, but you must be careful not to over-fill the jug – it should be no more than a third full – and have the lid securely in place.

## Sweet pepper and orange sauce

This sauce is good with muscular fish such as monk or turbot rather than oily specimens such as mackerel or herring. The principle is that the main ingredients make up much of the thickening as well as the flavouring, with the texture being supplied by olive oil.

Serves 4

1 tbsp olive oil, for frying

2 shallots, finely chopped

2 medium red peppers, deseeded and
    finely chopped

1 small chilli, deseeded, and finely chopped

zest of ½ orange

1 clove garlic, finely chopped

35ml white wine

75ml fish stock (see page 210) or water

25ml olive oil

1 tbsp lemon juice

salt and pepper

1   Heat the oil in a pan, then gently simmer the shallots, peppers, chilli, zest and garlic until they are hot but not brown.

2   Add the wine and stock, then bring to the boil. Turn the heat down to a simmer and cook for 20 minutes.

3   Liquidize. As the sauce centrifuges, pour in the olive oil then balance the seasoning with lemon juice, salt and pepper.

Ingredients
> **Check that you have discarded any seeds** or innards from the peppers and chilli.

Cooking method
> **The peppers should be gently fried** so that there is no colouring.
> **The amount of liquid in the sauce will vary** by the time you come to blending it, depending on how hard it boiled and by how much it reduced. You can vary the quantity of olive oil to compensate for this – the more oil the thicker the sauce – or add a little stock or water if needed.

For fish stock see **210**

# Blender dressings and sauces

**Just as soups can be thickened in a liquidizer, so can sauces and dressings.** The solid elements will help thicken the sauce, and olive oil, butter or cream can be poured in as well, not just for thickening but also to give a silky sauce-like texture. Puréed sauces made without any oil or butter will give the impression of soup poured over fish or meat. Here's an example of how the method works.

## Caesar dressing

**This dressing is better than its cliché status suggests.** The story behind it claims that it was invented by a restaurateur in Tijuana, Mexico. This is the border town with California and did a roaring trade with Hollywood stars during America's prohibition era – in much the same way as pubs on the English side of the Welsh border used to fill on Sundays when there were 'dry' areas of the country. Anyway, the story goes that Caesar Cardini was short of ingredients when one such party pitched up, and so he concocted a Caesar salad  and its dressing with whatever was to hand. In the event, he bottled and marketed the resulting dressing very successfully thereafter. The dressing is, however, spectacularly good when made fresh. This needn't be done as cabaret in front of those dining, as Mr Cardini did, and a liquidizer makes short work of it.

1 egg
25g Parmesan, grated
1 clove garlic, crushed
50ml olive oil
1 tbsp lemon juice
2 anchovy fillets
black pepper
a few drops of Tabasco

1    Boil the egg for 1 minute. It should be starting to coagulate, but not far off raw. Spoon the egg from its shell into the blender.
2    Add the other ingredients and whiz until you have a thick creamy dressing.

### Technique
> **If the dressing is too thick,** let it down with a few drops of hot water.
> **The original salad that goes with the dressing is made with very few ingredients,** mostly cos lettuce and a few croûtons rubbed with garlic.

For salads see **58**    For dressings see **63**

# Pecorino, garlic and olive oil sauce

**This basic sauce for pasta is creamy textured but has little or no cream.** The predominant flavour comes from the olive oil, which forms around a third of its volume.

Warmed olive oil in any quantity would normally separate from the pasta and form an unappetising puddle at the bottom of the plate. The texture given by blending it into an emulsion with cheese and stock overcomes this.

There are countless variations to this sauce for vegetarians and others. Wild mushrooms can be fried and scattered across the pasta and residual juices blended into the sauce; strips of smoked salmon can be added and any trimmings blended into the sauce; fresh sage can be blended into the sauce and the pasta garnished with deep-fried sage leaves and Parma ham; fried chicken livers can be added and extra lemon and garlic added to the sauce.

**Serves 4**

200ml vegetable (or chicken) stock (see pages 215 and 221)

1 clove garlic, crushed

50g pecorino cheese, grated

200ml olive oil

1 tsp crème fraîche

black pepper

a few drops of lemon juice

1. Warm the stock with the crushed garlic.
2. When it comes to the boil, add the cheese, oil and crème fraîche.
3. Pour into a liquidizer and blend.
4. Finish the sauce with black pepper and lemon juice.
5. Toss with the pasta.

## Ingredients

> **Why not use cream to achieve a creamy sauce?** It would seem the reasonable course to take. Unfortunately, when used alone as the base for a sauce or even in any quantity as part of a sauce, cream will be cloying and heavy: too much for anything as uncomplicated as pasta, and too much for most meat or fish, also.

## Cooking method

> **This type of sauce is not as stable as one based on stock** thickened with flour or cream. If kept for any length of time, or cooled then reheated it will tend to separate slightly. It is easily restored to peak texture, however, by a short return visit to the liquidizer.

> **The most likely problem with any emulsified sauce,** hollandaise and mayonnaise included, will be that the ratio of oil to other liquid gets out of kilter. More oil will make a thicker sauce but if the sauce over-thickens – and this can happen by evaporation if it is kept warm for any length of time – it will split into an oily mess. Do not despair, for a little hot water and a whisk will put things right. The water redresses the imbalance and the whisk incorporates it and emulsifies the sauce once more.

For fresh pasta see **30-31** For chicken stock see **215** For vegetable stock see **221**

# Conversion charts and index

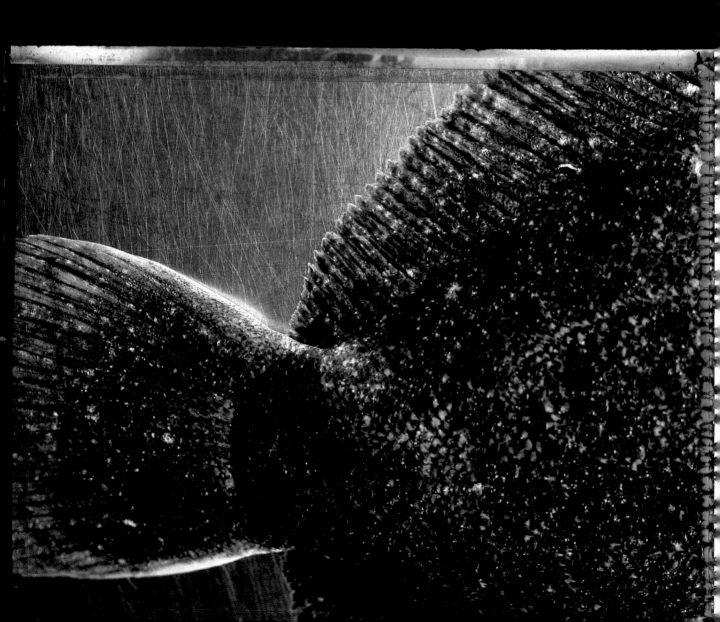

# Conversion charts

## Weight

| Metric | Imperial | | | | |
|--------|----------|--------|--------|--------|--------|
| 5g | $^1\!/_8$ oz | 375g | 13oz | | |
| 10g | $^1\!/_4$ oz | 400g | 14oz | | |
| 15g | $^1\!/_2$ oz | 425g | 15oz | | |
| 25-30g | 1oz | 450g | 1lb | | |
| 35g | $1^1\!/_4$ oz | 500g | 1lb 2oz | | |
| 40g | $1^1\!/_2$ oz | 550g | 1lb 4oz | | |
| 50g | $1^3\!/_4$ oz | 600g | 1lb 5oz | | |
| 55g | 2oz | 650g | 1lb 7oz | | |
| 60g | $2^1\!/_4$ oz | 700g | 1lb 9oz | | |
| 70g | $2^1\!/_2$ oz | 750g | 1lb 10oz | | |
| 85g | 3oz | 800g | 1lb 12oz | | |
| 90g | $3^1\!/_4$ oz | 850g | 1lb 14oz | | |
| 100g | $3^1\!/_2$ oz | 900g | 2lb | | |
| 115g | 4oz | 950g | 2lb 2oz | | |
| 125g | $4^1\!/_2$ oz | 1kg | 2lb 4oz | | |
| 140g | 5oz | 1.25kg | 2lb 12oz | | |
| 150g | $5^1\!/_2$ oz | 1.3kg | 3lb | | |
| 175g | 6oz | 1.5kg | 3lb 5oz | | |
| 200g | 7oz | 1.6kg | 3lb 8oz | | |
| 225g | 8oz | 1.8kg | 4lb | | |
| 250g | 9oz | 2kg | 4lb 8oz | | |
| 275g | $9^3\!/_4$ oz | 2.25kg | 5lb | | |
| 280g | 10oz | 2.5kg | 5lb 8oz | | |
| 300g | $10^1\!/_2$ oz | 2.7kg | 6lb | | |
| 325g | $11^1\!/_2$ oz | 3kg | 6lb 8oz | | |
| 350g | 12oz | | | | |

## Volume

| Metric | Imperial |
|--------|----------|
| 15ml | $^1\!/_2$ fl oz |
| 30ml | 1fl oz |
| 50ml | 2fl oz |
| 75ml | $2^1\!/_2$ fl oz |
| 100ml | $3^1\!/_2$ fl oz |
| 125ml | 4fl oz |
| 150ml | 5fl oz/ $^1\!/_4$ pint |
| 175ml | 6fl oz |
| 200ml | 7fl oz/ $^1\!/_3$ pint |
| 225ml | 8fl oz |
| 250ml | 9fl oz |
| 300ml | 10fl oz/ $^1\!/_2$ pint |
| 350ml | 12fl oz |
| 400ml | 14fl oz |
| 425ml | 15fl oz/ $^3\!/_4$ pint |
| 450ml | 16fl oz |
| 500ml | 18fl oz |
| 600ml | 20fl oz/1 pint |
| 700ml | $1^1\!/_4$ pints |
| 850ml | $1^1\!/_2$ pints |
| 1 litre | $1^3\!/_4$ pints |
| 1.2 litres | 2 pints |
| 1.3 litres | $2^1\!/_4$ pints |
| 1.4 litres | $2^1\!/_2$ pints |
| 1.5 litres | $2^3\!/_4$ pints |
| 1.7 litres | 3 pints |
| 2 litres | $3^1\!/_2$ pints |
| 2.5 litres | $4^1\!/_2$ pints |
| 2.8 litres | 5 pints |
| 3 litres | $5^1\!/_4$ pints |
| | |
| 1.25ml | $^1\!/_4$ tsp |
| 2.5ml | $^1\!/_2$ tsp |
| 5ml | 1 tsp |
| 10ml | 2 tsp |
| 15ml | 1 tbsp/3 tsp |
| 30ml | 2 tbsp |
| 45ml | 3 tbsp |
| 60ml | 4 tbsp |
| 75ml | 5 tbsp |
| 90ml | 6 tbsp |

These charts are reproduced with the kind permission of The Guild of Food Writers.

# Index

# Acknowledgements

Very few recipes are original to anyone. Mine, like most, are reworkings of combinations that have appealed to me over the years. These have been collected from books, magazines and restaurants in which I have worked, and chefs I have worked alongside. I have credited those I remember in the text, but am grateful to all.

My thanks also to Rebecca Spry and Hattie Ellis for their patience and great help with the book, and of course to my wife Anja who does half the work here at the Merchant House and generally keeps me in order. No harm can be done, either, by reminding Jason Lowe what an exceptional talent he has and by thanking Pete at Grade Design Consultants for making the book look just right.